TRADING
PLACES
SOURCEBOOK

TRADING
PLACES
SOURCEBOOK

READINGS
IN THE INTERSECTING
HISTORIES
OF JUDAISM
AND CHRISTIANITY

BRUCE CHILTON
AND JACOB NEUSNER

THE PILGRIM PRESS
CLEVELAND, OHIO

The Pilgrim Press, Cleveland, Ohio 44115
© 1997 by Bruce Chilton and Jacob Neusner

All rights reserved. Published 1997

Printed in the United States of America on acid-free paper

02 01   00   99   98   97   5   4   3   2   1

Library of Congress Cataloging-in-Publication Data

Chilton, Bruce.
    Trading places : the intersecting histories of Judaism and
Christianity / Bruce Chilton and Jacob Neusner.
        p. cm.
    Accompanied by: Trading places sourcebook.
    Includes bibliographical references and index.
    ISBN 0-8298-1141-9 (alk. paper)
    1. Judaism—History—Talmudic period, 10–425.   2. Church history—
Primitive and early church, ca. 30–600.   3. Judaism and politics—
Comparative studies.   4. Christianity and politics—Comparative
studies.   5. Judaism—History—Talmudic period, 10–425—Sources.
6. Church history—Primitive and early church, ca. 30–600—Sources.
I. Neusner, Jacob, 1932- . II. Title. III. Title: Trading places sourcebook.
BM177.C45 1996
261.2'6'09015—DC20   96-44694
                                                               CIP
                                                               r96

CONTENTS

PREFACE

This sourcebook is a companion and complement to *Trading Places: The Intersecting Histories of Judaism and Christianity.* It amplifies the presentation of topics set forth in that book, and also introduces new topics to deepen readers' understanding of the two religions at a critical time in their histories. To place the matter in its proper context, we wish to explore the exchange of indicative characteristics that left Judaism in the fourth century remarkably like Christianity in the first, and vice versa. In each case a nascent religious system responded to political change by completely reconsidering initial policies and doctrines, and both religions emerged from the formative age with a remarkable capacity to solve problems and deal with the challenge of change. During the centuries examined in *Trading Places,* the primary religions of Western civilization, Christianity and Judaism, reached the structures that would prevail from then to the present day.

This book, then, serves as a supplement to our systematic statement of matters. It represents a rich selection of primary sources, in English translation, so that readers, and especially students, can examine for themselves the documents on the strength of which we have constructed the account set forth here.

The two volumes of *Trading Places* took shape in the classrooms of Bard College from 1994 to 1996, where the two of us taught a course (1994) on Judeo-Christian relations through history, as well as another (1995 and 1996) bearing the same title as this book. There in the classroom we pursued discussions of comparisons and contrasts, allowing us to solidify our thoughts in amiable argument with one another. Our students, indeed, accused us of never holding conflicting opinions on anything. But that judgment pertains to other than intellectual matters—after all, an Episcopal priest and a rabbi of Judaism cannot concur on absolutely everything and remain true to their deepest convictions. We share not only collegiality and friendship but learning and, if we concur on many things, it is because of a shared reason that unites. We take this occasion also to express our shared respect for Bard College, which made our work together possible. In that context we thank the president of Bard, Leon Botstein, for bring about the visiting professor appointment that led to this collaborative venture that has proved so stimulating for us both. This book in only one of the contemplated projects in consequence.

We also express our thanks to Pilgrim Press for serving us so well as a publisher, and our high esteem for Richard Brown, our editor. If he has referred to us as an editor's dream authors, we reciprocate and conceive him to be the ideal editor for an academic religious book such as this one.

It was at the University of Göttingen in the summer semester of 1995 that Jacob Neusner wrote the first draft of his half of the book, as Von Humboldt Research Professor in the Faculty of Theology. He thanks his principal host, Professor Gerd Lüdemann, as well as other colleagues in the Faculty of Theology for their hospitality and friendly interest in his work. He further expresses his thanks to the University of South Florida for the research chair that he occupies there. No one in the academic world enjoys more favorable circumstances for scholarship than does one with the advantage of a Distinguished Research Professorship in the Florida state university system. He expresses further thanks for a substantial research expense fund, ample research time, and stimulating, straightforward and cordial colleagues, many of whom also are cherished friends. As noted, in the time in which this work was done, he also served as Visiting Professor of Religion at Bard College, which awarded a further research grant. These visits to Bard proved intellectually stimulating and rewarding, and he expresses thanks for the college's supererogatory support of his work.

Bruce Chilton acknowledges the continuing incentive within the Episcopal Diocese of New York to appreciate the role of patristic sources in articulating the faith. From its bishop, the Rt. Rev. Richard Grein, through theologians such as the Rev. Dr. Richard Norris, and on to parochial priests such as the Rev. Dr. Paul Clayton, the place of the Fathers is remembered. As a scholar of the New Testament, Professor Chilton has been challenged to explain how the grounding concerns of early Christianity are brought to conscious expression in the patristic theologies of the classical period.

The Fathers are more easily dated than the sources of Rabbinic literature. But there is a tendency to see each father too much in isolation, when their themes must be related to one another in order to be understood. When the reader comes to the Christian sources, cross-referencing among subjects will become especially appropriate. Eusebius is listed under "Politics," but he is crucial as an antecedent of Augustine's under "History." Clement of Alexandria makes his appearance under "Values," but one cannot understand Origen's contribution to "Teleology" without him.

So we may end our preface on a note of paradox. Rabbinic literature is synthetic, and must be analyzed in order to be atomized historically. Christian literature of that same period is atomistic in its authorship, and must be synthesized in order to be understood philosophically. There we have one more reason to insist that Judaism and Christianity in late antiquity are to be comprehended together, or not at all.

Bruce Chilton
Bard College

Jacob Neusner
University of South Florida

PART 1

JUDAISM

1

SAGES' EMPOWERED ISRAEL

SYMBOLIC CHANGE AND SOCIAL CHANGE IN DOCUMENTARY FORM

How do the sages of the Talmud of the Land of Israel, in the fourth century, respond to the theory of Israel's politics set forth in the Mishnah? That question draws our attention to the way in which, in the documents at hand, we follow the unfolding of important propositions, the amplification of principles of politics from age to age. Given its character as a commentary to the Mishnah, we anticipate that the Yerushalmi will spell out the Mishnah's points entirely within the framework of the Mishnah's structure and system. It is when the authorship of the Yerushalmi speaks not about the Mishnah but about other matters that it will make its own statement, and there, we see, that statement attests to a system quite different from the Mishnah's politics. Let us take only one example of how when the Yerushalmi's exegetes read the Mishnah's rules of politics, they paraphrase and amplify what the Mishnah says, while when they take initiatives on their own, they make an altogether different statement. That will suffice to show us once again the familiar fact that, when they read the Mishnah, the successor authorships amplify and clarify, but do not innovate.

It is only when they move on to their own program that they make a statement particular to themselves, and, when they do, it is not the statement of the Mishnah at all, but a different one, signified by categories for which the Mishnah makes no place.

Here is a single instance of the Yerushalmi's reading of the Mishnah on politics. We give the Mishnah passage in boldface type, then the Talmud's treatment of the passage in regular type.

MISHNAH-TRACTATE SANHEDRIN 2.1

A. **A high priest judges, and [others] judge him;**

B. **gives testimony, and [others] give testimony about him;**

C. **performs the rite of removing the shoe [Deut. 25:7-9], and [others] perform the rite of removing the shoe with his wife.**

D. **[Others] enter levirate marriage with his wife, but he does not enter into levirate marriage,**

E. **because he is prohibited to marry a widow.**

F. **[If] he suffers a death [in his family], he does not follow the bier.**

G. **"But when [the bearers of the bier] are not visible, he is visible; when they are visible, he is not.**

H. **"And he goes with them to the city gate," the words of R. Meir.**

I. **R. Judah says, "He never leaves the sanctuary,**

J. **"since it says, 'Nor shall he go out of the sanctuary' (Lev. 21:12)."**

I.   A. It is understandable that **he judges others.**

B. But as to others judging him, [is it appropriate to his station?]

C. Let him appoint a mandatory.

D. Now take note: What if he has to take an oath?

E. Can the mandatory take an oath for his client?

F. Property cases involving [a high priest]—in how large a court is the trial conducted?

G. With a court of twenty-three judges.

H. Let us demonstrate that fact from the following:

I. **A king does not sit in the Sanhedrin, nor do a king and a high priest join in the court session for intercalation [T. San. 2:15].**

J. [In this regard,] R. Haninah and R. Mana—one of them said, "The king does not take a seat on the Sanhedrin, on account of suspicion [of influencing the other judges].

K. "Nor does he take a seat in a session for intercalation, because of suspicion [that it is in the government's interest to intercalate the year].

L. "And a king and a high priest do not take a seat for intercalation, for it is not appropriate to the station of the king [or the high priest] to take a seat with seven judges."

M. Now look here:

N. If it is not appropriate to his station to take a seat with seven judges, is it not an argument *a fortiori* that he should not [be judged] by three?

O. That is why one must say, Property cases involving him are tried in a court of twenty-three.

✡
—
5
⳨

II. A. [What follows is verbatim at M. Hor. 3:1] Said R. Eleazar, "A high priest who sinned—they administer lashes to him, but they do not remove him from his high office."

B. Said R. Mana, "It is written, 'For the consecration of the anointing oil of his God is upon him: I am the Lord' (Lev. 21:12).

C. [Here omitted:] ("That is as if to say: 'Just as we [stand firm] in my high office, so Aaron [stands firm] in his high office,'")

D. [Here omitted:] (Said R. Abun, "'He shall be holy to you [for I the Lord who sanctify you am holy]' (Lev. 21:8).)

E. "That is as if to say, 'Just as we [stand firm] in my consecration, so Aaron [stands firm] in his consecration.'"

F. R. Haninah Ketobah, R. Aha in the name of R. Simeon b. Laqish: "An anointed priest who sinned—they administer lashes to him [by the judgment of a court of three judges].

G. "If you rule that it is by the decision of a court of twenty-three judges [that the lashes are administered], it turns out that his ascension [to high office] is descent [to public humiliation, since if he sins he is publicly humiliated by a sizable court]."

The discussion remains wholly within the framework of the Mishnah's interests. Now in the following we leave that matter and move on to other questions. We also leave behind the politics of the king and the high priest and enter a new realm altogether. We have not the king but the *nasi,* the patriarch. And at stake in what follows is the very stark question, Whose acts of violence are legitimate and whose illegitimate? It goes without saying that the sages' acts of violence are legitimate, and the patriarch's not, even though sages have to concede that greater power inheres in the patriarchal government than in theirs. The claim that "they"—sages—possess authority to administer sanctions to the patriarch now is at issue. The theoretical clarity of the Mishnah is lost in the practical politics of real power, and so we leave the Mishnah's politics far behind. But that understates the shift. We cannot point to a single passage in the Mishnah or the Tosefta in which the several components of the political structure are represented as competing, let alone in which the sages' component in *political* terms and contexts of the legitimation of violence (as distinct from mere status) is set above that of the king or the high priest. The following therefore not only digresses from Mishnah exegesis. It makes a point that is entirely beyond the framework of the Mishnah's politics.

III A. R. Simeon b. Laqish said, "A ruler who sinned—they administer lashes to him by the decision of a court of three judges."

   B. What is the law as to restoring him to office?

   C. Said R. Haggai, "By Moses! If we put him back into office, he will kill us!"

   D. R. Judah the Patriarch heard this ruling [of R. Simeon b. Laqish's] and was outraged. He sent a troop of Goths to arrest R. Simeon b. Laqish. [R. Simeon b. Laqish] fled to the Tower, and, some say, it was to Kefar Hittayya.

   E. The next day R. Yohanan went up to the meetinghouse, and R. Judah the Patriarch went up to the meetinghouse. He said to him, "Why does my master not state a teaching of Torah?"

   F. [Yohanan] began to clap with one hand [only].

G. [Judah the Patriarch] said to him, "Now do people clap with only one hand?"

H. He said to him, "No, nor is Ben Laqish here [and just as one cannot clap with one hand only, so we cannot teach Torah if my colleague, Simeon b. Laqish, is absent]."

I. [Judah] said to him, "Then where is he hidden?"

J. He said to him, "In a certain tower."

K. He said to him, "You and we shall go out to greet him tomorrow."

L. R. Yohanan sent word to R. Simeon b. Laqish, "Get a teaching of Torah ready, because the patriarch is coming over to see you."

M. [Simeon b. Laqish] came forth to receive them and said, "The example which you [Judah] set is to be compared to the paradigm of your Creator. For when the All-Merciful came forth to redeem Israel [from Egypt], he did not send a messenger or an angel, but the Holy One, blessed be He, himself came forth, as it is said, *'For we will pass through the Land of Egypt that night'* (Exod. 12:12)—and not only so, but he and his entire retinue.

N. [Here omitted:] ([*"'What other people on earth is like thy people Israel, whom God went to redeem to be his people'* (2 Sam. 7:23).] 'Whom God went' (sing.) is not written here, but 'Whom God went' (plural) [—meaning, he and all his retinue].")

O. [Judah the Patriarch] said to him, "Now why in the world did you see fit to teach this particular statement [that a ruler who sinned is subject to lashes]?"

P. He said to him, "Now did you really think that because we were afraid of you, we would hold back the teaching of the All-Merciful? [And lo, citing 1 Sam. 2:23 f.] R. Samuel b. R. Isaac said, '[*Why do you do such things? For we hear of your evil dealings from all the people.] No, my sons, it is no good report [that we hear the people of the Lord spreading abroad]. [Here omitted:] (If a man sins against a man, God will mediate for him; but if a man sins against the Lord, who can intercede for him? But they would not listen to the voice of their father, for it was the will of the Lord to slay them'* (1 Sam. 2:23–25). [When] the people of the Lord spread about [an evil report about a man], they remove him [even though he is the patriarch].")

This brief abstract suffices to make the simple point that the politics of the Mishnah, treated by the Yerushalmi, is carried forward without noticeable change as to basic structure and system. But when—as at III—the Yerushalmi then portrays power relationships not in the context of Mishnah exegesis, it provides a quite different picture.

Now we have not the king but the patriarch, not the sages' court with clearly differentiated power to administer sanction, but with a generalized power to do what the sages want—if they can. And while the Mishnah's king exercises violence legitimately, the Yerushalmi's patriarch uses foreign troops and enjoys no more legitimacy than does the foreign government that has supplied those troops.

ISRAEL AS AN EXTENDED FAMILY

We have noted that in the post-Constantinian documents sages' Israel is portrayed as a family, rather than as a hierarchized social structure. A single example of the consequence of representing Israel as an extended family emerges from Genesis Rabbah. Here "Israel" as family also understood itself to form a nation or people. That nation-people held a land—a rather peculiar, enchanted or holy, land at that—one that, in its imputed traits, was as *sui generis* as (presently we shall see) in the metaphorical thought of the system at hand, Israel also was. Competing for the same territory, Israel's claim to what it called the Land of Israel—thus, *of Israel* in particular—now rested on right of inheritance such as a family enjoyed, and this was made explicit. The passage shows how high the stakes were in the claim to constitute the genealogical descendant of the ancestors.

GENESIS RABBAH LXI:VII.1

A. "But to the sons of his concubines, Abraham gave gifts, and while he was still living, he sent them away from his son Isaac, eastward to the east country" (Gen. 25:6):

B. In the time of Alexander of Macedonia the sons of Ishmael
came to dispute with Israel about the birthright, and with them
came two wicked families, the Canaanites and the Egyptians.

C. They said, "Who will go and engage in a disputation with
them."

D. Gebiah b. Qosem [the enchanter] said, "we shall go and engage in a disputation with them."

E. They said to him, "Be careful not to let the Land of Israel fall
into their possession."

F. He said to them, "we shall go and engage in a disputation with
them. If we win over them, well and good. And if not, you may
say, 'Who is this hunchback to represent us?'"

G. He went and engaged in a disputation with them. Said to them
Alexander of Macedonia, "Who lays claim against whom?"

H. The Ishmaelites said, "We lay claim, and we bring our evidence from their own Torah: 'But he shall acknowledge the
firstborn, the son of the hated' (Deut. 21:17). Now Ishmael
was the firstborn. [We therefore claim the land as heirs of the
firstborn of Abraham.]"

I. Said to him Gebiah b. Qosem, "My royal lord, does a man not
do whatever he likes with his sons?"

J. He said to him, "Indeed so."

K. "And lo, it is written, 'Abraham gave all that he had to Isaac'
(Gen. 25:2)."

L. [Alexander asked,] "Then where is the deed of gift to the other
sons?"

M. He said to him, "'But to the sons of his concubines, Abraham
gave gifts, [and while he was still living, he sent them away
from his son Isaac, eastward to the east country]' (Gen. 25:6)."

N. [The Ishmaelites had no claim on the land.] They abandoned
the field in shame.

The metaphor now shifts, with the notion of Israel today as the
family of Abraham, as against the Ishmaelites, also of the same
family, gives way. But the theme of family records persists. Canaan
has no claim, for Canaan was also a family, comparable to Israel—

but descended from a slave. The power of the metaphor of family is that it can explain not only the social entity formed by Jews, but the social entities confronted by them. All fell into the same genus, making up diverse species. The theory of society before us—that is, the theory of "Israel"—thus accounts for the existence, also, of all societies, and, as we shall see when we deal with Rome, the theory of "Israel" does so with extraordinary force.

> O. The Canaanites said, "We lay claim, and we bring our evidence from their own Torah. Throughout their Torah it is written, 'the land of Canaan.' So let them give us back our land."
>
> P. Said to him Gebiah b. Qosem, "My royal lord, does a man not do whatever he likes with his slave?"
>
> Q. He said to him, "Indeed so."
>
> R. He said to him, "And lo, it is written, 'A slave of slaves shall Canaan be to his brothers' (Gen. 9:25). So they are really our slaves."
>
> S. [The Canaanites had no claim to the land and in fact should be serving Israel.] They abandoned the field in shame.

The same metaphor serves both "Israel" and "Canaan." Each formed the latter-day heir of the earliest family, and both lived out the original paradigm. The mode of thought at hand assigns to the same genus both social entities, then makes it possible to distinguish among the two species at hand. The final claim in the passage before us moves away from the metaphor of family. But the notion of a continuous, physical descent is implicit here as well. "Israel" has inherited the wealth of Egypt. Since the notion of inheritance forms a component of the metaphor of family (a conception critical, as we shall see in the next section, in the supernatural patrimony of the "children of Israel" in the merit of the ancestors), we survey the conclusion of the passage.

> T. The Egyptians said, "We lay claim, and we bring our evidence from their own Torah. Six hundred thousand of them left us,

taking away our silver and gold utensils: 'They despoiled the Egyptians' (Ex. 12:36). Let them give them back to us."

U. Gebiah b. Qosem said, "My royal lord, six hundred thousand men worked for them for two hundred and ten years, some as silversmiths and some as goldsmiths. Let them pay us our salary at the rate of a *denar* a day."

V. The mathematicians went and added up what was owing, and they had not reached the sum covering a century before the Egyptians had to forfeit what they had claimed. They abandoned the field in shame.

V. [Alexander] wanted to go up to Jerusalem. The Samaritans said to him, "Be careful. They will not permit you to enter their most holy sanctuary."

W. When Gebiah b. Qosem found out about this, he went and made for himself two felt shoes, with two precious stones worth twenty-thousand pieces of silver set in them. When he got to the mountain of the house [of the Temple], he said to him, "My royal lord, take off your shoes and put on these two felt slippers, for the floor is slippery, and you should not slip and fall."

X. When they came to the most holy sanctuary, he said to him, "Up to this point, we have the right to enter. From this point onward, we do not have the right to enter."

Y. He said to him, "When we get out of here, I'm going to even out your hump."

Z. He said to him, "You will be called a great surgeon and get a big fee."

The Ishmaelites, Abraham's children, deprived as they were of their inheritance, fall into the same genus as does Israel. So too, as we said, did Canaan. As to the Egyptians, that is a different matter. Now "Israel" is that same "Israel" of which Scripture spoke. The social metaphor shifts within the story, though, of course, the story is not affected.

METAPHORICAL THINKING ABOUT ISRAEL

Metaphorical thinking in context moves beyond the metaphor of genealogy. All of this required the invention of a new metaphor, and the one that was chosen—borrowed of course from Daniel—bears a not-very-subtle polemic, comparing as it did various nations with various animals. Only Israel is spared an assignment in the political bestiary. The main point, of course, is Esau. Esau is compared not only to Israel—unambiguous Israel—but also to a pig—the most ambiguous of beasts within the levitical taxonomy. The analogy is apt, for the pig exhibits public traits expected of a suitable beast, in that it shows a cloven hoof, such as the levitical laws of acceptable beasts require. But the pig does not exhibit the inner traits of a suitable beast, in that it does not chew the cud. Accordingly, the pig confuses and deceives.[1] Here is how the matter is expressed, in a passage that rings the changes on all of the themes before us: legitimate as against illegitimate power, the complex genealogy of Israel and Rome, the victim and the victor now and in the end of history:

LEVITICUS RABBAH XIII:V.9

    A. Moses foresaw what the evil kingdoms would do [to Israel].

    B. "The camel, rock badger, and hare" (Deut. 14:7). [Compare: "Nevertheless, among those that chew the cud or part the hoof, you shall not eat these: the camel, because it chews the cud but does not part the hoof, is unclean to you. The rock badger, because it chews the cud but does not part the hoof, is unclean to you. And the hare, because it chews the cud but does not part the hoof, is unclean to you, and the pig, because it parts the hoof and is cloven-footed, but does not chew the cud, is unclean to you" (Lev. 11:4–8)].

    C. The camel (GML) refers to Babylonia, [in line with the following verse of Scripture: "O daughter of Babylonia, you who are to be devastated!] Happy will be he who requites (GML) you, with what you have done to us" (Ps. 147:8).

    D. "The rock badger" (Deut. 14:7)—this refers to Media.

    E. Rabbis and R. Judah b. R. Simon.

    F. Rabbis say, "Just as the rock badger exhibits traits of uncleanness and traits of cleanness, so the kingdom of Media produced both a righteous man and a wicked one."

G. Said R. Judah b. R. Simon, "The last Darius was Esther's son. He was clean on his mother's side and unclean on his father's side."

H. "The hare" (Deut. 14:7)—this refers to Greece. The mother of King Ptolemy was named "Hare" [in Greek, *lagos*].

I. "The pig" (Deut. 14:7)—this refers to Edom [Rome].

J. Moses made mention of the first three in a single verse and the final one in a verse by itself [(Deut. 14:7, 8)]. Why so?

K. R. Yohanan and R. Simeon b. Laqish.

L. R. Yohanan said, "It is because [the pig] is equivalent to the other three."

M. And R. Simeon b. Laqish said, "It is because it outweighs them."

N. R. Yohanan objected to R. Simeon b. Laqish, "'Prophesy, therefore, son of man, clap your hands [and let the sword come down twice, yea thrice]' (Ezra 21:14)."

O. And how does R. Simeon b. Laqish interpret the same passage? He notes that [the threefold sword] is doubled (Ezra 21:14).

In the apocalypticizing of the animals of Lev. 11:4–8/Deut. 14:7—the camel, rock badger, hare, and pig—the pig, standing for Rome, again emerges as different from the others and more threatening than the rest. Just as the pig pretends to be a clean beast by showing the cloven hoof, but in fact is an unclean one, so Rome pretends to be just but in fact governs by thuggery. Edom does not pretend to praise God but only blasphemes. It does not exalt the righteous but kills them. We cannot imagine a more expressive anti-politics than the composition before us.[2] Of greatest importance, while all the other beasts bring further ones in their wake, the pig does not: "It does not bring another kingdom after it." It will restore the crown to the one who will truly deserve it, Israel. Esau will be judged by Zion, so Obadiah 1:21. Beyond Rome, standing in a straight line with the others, lies the true shift in politics, which is a caesura in history, the rule of Israel and the cessation of the dominion of the nations.

This static tableau tells us the structure of the politics. What of its system: its account of how things actually work from day to day? Leviticus Rabbah also presents recurrent lists of events in Israel's (unique) history, meaning Israel's history solely in scriptural times, down through the return to Zion. The lists, all of them concerning the exercise of power, sometimes legitimately, sometimes not, again and again ring the changes on the one-time events of the generation of the flood, Sodom and Gomorrah, the patriarchs and the sojourn in Egypt, the Exodus, the revelation of the Torah at Sinai, the golden calf, the Davidic monarchy and the building of the Temple, Sennacherib, Hezekiah, and the destruction of northern Israel, Nebuchadnezzar and the destruction of the Temple in 586, the life of Israel in Babylonian captivity, Daniel and his associates, Mordecai and Haman. These events occur over and over again. They turn out to serve as paradigms.

We find, in fact, a fairly standard repertoire of scriptural heroes or villains, on the one side, and conventional lists of Israel's enemies and their actions and downfall, on the other. The boastful, for instance, include the generation of the flood, Sodom and Gomorrah, Pharaoh, Sisera, Sennacherib, Nebuchadnezzar, the wicked empire (Rome)—contrasted to Israel, "despised and humble in this world." The four kingdoms recur again and again, always ending, of course, with Rome, with the repeated message that after Rome will come Israel. But Israel has to make this happen through its faith and submission to God's will. Cain, the Sodomites, Pharaoh, Sennacherib, Nebuchadnezzar, Haman—all exemplify the illegitimate uses of power, which expresses arrogance. So the political virtue is its opposite: to be politically correct, one must eschew power; to be politically illegitimate, one exercises power. we cannot think of a finer example of what it means to compose a counterpart-category, an anti-politics in place of a politics.

LEGITIMATE POLITICS: THE SAGE-MESSIAH

Then who rules legitimately? It can only be the sage, who defines the political class and the political institution of Israel, rightly construed. Israel is *sui generis* in that it exhibits the traits of the sages, and sages' group's traits, for their part, have no counterpart, in sages' view, in this world, but only in heaven. In God's image, after

God's likeness, Moses "our rabbi" forms the model for sages, and sages, for "Israel." Conformity to sages' rule, which is the sole legitimate power within Israel, defines the condition for the Messiah's coming, that is, the establishment, in place of the illegitimate government, of a legitimate politics. That conviction comes to expression in repeated calls for "repentance," meaning, of course, conformity to the Torah as sages represented it.

For a concrete portrait of legitimate power we turn to David, ideal king in the past, model of the coming Messiah in the future. What mattered of course is that David then adhered to the model of the sage now. If David, King of Israel, was like a rabbi today, then a rabbi today would be the figure of the son of David who was to come as king of Israel. He was the sage of the Torah, the avatar and model for the sages of their own time. David and Moses are represented as students of Torah, just like the disciples and sages of the current time. An important presentation shows us how David is represented as a rabbi, and how, specifically, what made David exemplary was his devotion to study of the Torah:

Y. Berakhot 1:1.XII

> O. "We will awake the dawn" (Ps. 5:7, 8)—we will awaken the dawn; the dawn will not awaken me.
>
> P. David's [evil] impulse tried to seduce him [to sin]. And it would say to him, "David. It is the custom of kings that awakens them. And you say, we will awake the dawn. It is the custom of kings that they sleep until the third hour [of the day]. And you say, At midnight we rise." And [David] used to say [in reply], "[I rise early] because of thy righteous ordinances (Ps. 119:62)."
>
> Q. And what would David do? R. Phineas in the name of R. Eleazar b. R. Menahem [said], "[He used to take a harp and lyre and set them at his bedside. And he would rise at midnight and play them so that the associates of Torah should hear. And what would the associates of Torah say? 'If David involves himself with Torah, how much more so should we.' We find that all of Israel was involved in Torah [study] on account of David."[3]

This extract has shown us how the Talmud's authorities readily saw their concerns in biblical statements attributed to David. "Water" meant "a teaching of Torah." "Three mighty men" were of course judges. At issue was whether or not the decision was to be stated in David's own name—and so removed from the authoritative consensus of sages.

Since systems set forth their messages through their selection of opposites, we turn to ask how legitimate power finds its exact match in the illegitimate kind. Sages, in the model of David, educated in the Torah of our rabbi, Moses, weigh in the balance against pagan kings, in the model of every malefactor in scriptural times. At stake in the outcome is God's rule and presence on earth: once more, the sole legitimate power. That the stakes in politics have been revised upward—infinitely upward—is shown in the following statement that illegitimate power aims at destroying knowledge of God in the world, and legitimate power, nurturing that knowledge and consequence submission to God's will:

Genesis Rabbah XLII:III.2

A. "And it came to pass in the days of Ahaz" (Isa. 7:1):

B. "The Aramaeans on the east and the Philistines on the west devour Israel with open mouth" (Isa. 9:12):

C. The matter [of Israel's position] may be compared to the case of a king who handed over his son to a tutor, who hated the son. The tutor thought, "If we kill him now, we shall turn out to be liable to the death penalty before the king. So what I'll do is take away his wet-nurse, and he will die on his own."

D. So thought Ahaz, "If there are no kids, there will be no he-goats. If there are no he-goats, there will be no flock. If there is no flock, there will be no Shepherd, if there is no Shepherd, there will be no world."

E. So did Ahaz plan, "If there are no children, there will be no adults. If there are no adults, there will be no disciples. If there are no disciples, there will be no sages. If there are no sages, there will be no prophets. If there are no prophets, the Holy One, blessed be he, will not allow his presence to come to rest in the world." [Lev. R.: . . . Torah. If there is no Torah, there will be no synagogues and schools. If there are no synagogues and schools, then the Holy One, blessed be he, will not allow his presence to come to rest in the world.]

F. That is in line with the following verse of Scripture: "Bind up the testimony, seal the Torah among my disciples" (Isa. 8:16).

G. R. Huna in the name of R. Eleazar: "Why was he called Ahaz? Because he seized (*ahaz*) synagogues and schools."

The vision of an "Israel" as a political entity defined by the absence of power and the presence of humility and submission, an entity that takes shape around synagogues and schools, which none can possibly (then or now) have identified with a political structure and system.

That judgment requires qualification, however, since the master in the setting of the school also served as clerk in the context of the administration and court. Not only so, but the sage as clerk exercised power that was not that of abnegation or denial, but of material sanctions. So the political theory of humility and power-lessness contrasted with the representation of a political reality of sages' forceful intervention into the social order. Sages' political authority was practical and involved empowerment; sages formed a political class in the this-worldly sense indeed. The first and most important sort of power a rabbi under some circumstances and in some cases maintained he could exercise was to sort out and adjudicate rights to property and personal status affecting property. The rabbi is described as able to take chattels or real estate from one party and to give them into the rightful ownership of some other.

The second sort of power rabbis are supposed to have wielded was to tell people what to do, or not to do, in matters not involving property rights. Sages moreover are represented as defining the status of persons in such ways as to affect property and marital rights and standing. Rabbis declare a woman married or free to marry; permitted as wife of a priest to eat food in the status of leave-offering or prohibited from doing so; enjoying the support of a husband's estate or left without that support; having the right to collect a previously contracted marriage settlement or lacking that right. In all of these ways, as much as in their control of real estate, commercial, and other material and property transactions among Jews, the rabbis held they governed the Jewish community as effective political authorities.[4]

The sage, moreover, is represented as mediating between Jews and the outside world. The legitimacy of that mediation derived solely from his mastery of the Law. That is, he could permit actions normally prohibited in the Law. He is represented not as negotiating, but only as accommodating. The unstated supposition is that Israel stands in a subordinated relationship, able to resist only with difficulty, and then at a very high cost. The alternative to submission is assumed to be death. The rabbi's authority as representative of the Jewish nation and mediator between that nation and the gentile world in general, and the government in particular, bore heavy symbolic weight. The rabbi as a public official was expected to perform certain supernatural deeds, to exercise power in its legitimate form. He stood at the border between heaven and earth, as much as he stood at the frontier between Israel and the nations: wholly liminal, entirely exemplary, at one and the same time.

SUPERNATURAL POWER AND POLITICS

What is important here is the representation of the rabbi as public authority deemed to exercise supernatural power. His task was to use his supernatural power in pretty much the same context and for the same purpose as he used his political-judicial and legal power and learning, on the one side, and his local influence and moral authority on the other. What is striking is that sages exercised their responsibility equally through this-worldly and otherworldly means. One example of legitimate power suffices to make the point:

Y. TAANIT 3:4.I

A. There was a pestilence in Sepphoris, but it did not come into the neighborhood in which R. Haninah was living. And the Sepphoreans said, "How is it possible that that elder lives among you, he and his entire neighborhood, in peace, while the town goes to ruin?"

B. [Haninah] went in and said before them, "There was only a single Zimri in his generation, but on his account, twenty-four thousand people died. And in our time, how many Zimris are there in our generation? And yet you are raising a clamor!"

C. One time they had to call a fast, but it did not rain. R. Joshua carried out a fast in the South, and it rained. The Sepphoreans said, "R. Joshua b. Levi brings down rain for the people in the South, but R. Haninah holds back rain for us in Sepphoris."

D. They found it necessary to declare a second time of fasting, and sent and summoned R. Joshua b. Levi. [Haninah] said to him, "Let my lord go forth with us to fast." The two of them went out to fast, but it did not rain.

E. He went in and preached to them as follows: "It was not R. Joshua b. Levi who brought down rain for the people of the South, nor was it R. Haninah who held back rain from the people of Sepphoris. But as to the Southerners, their hearts are open, and when they listen to a teaching of Light [Torah] they submit [to accept it], while as to the Sepphoreans, their hearts are hard, and when they hear a teaching of Light, they do not submit [or accept it]."

F. When he went in, he looked up and saw that the [cloudless] air was pure. He said, "Is this how it still is? [Is there no change in the weather?]" Forthwith, it rained. He took a vow for himself that he would never do the same thing again. He said, "How shall we say to the creditor [God] not to collect what is owing to him."

✡
19
☦

True, God could do miracles. But if the people caused their own disasters by not listening to rabbis' Torah-teachings, they could hardly expect God always to forgo imposing the sanction for disobedience, which was holding back rain. Accordingly, there were reliable laws by which one could deal with the supernatural world, which kept those laws too. The particular power of the rabbi was in knowing the law. The storyteller took for granted, to be sure, that in the end the clerk could bring rain in a pinch.

If the sage stood for the legitimate exercise of power, who represented, even within Israel, illegitimate power? It was not only the patriarch, but—much more to the point—the illegitimate Messiah. And what makes a Messiah a false Messiah is not his claim to save Israel, but his claim to save Israel without the help of God. The meaning of the true Messiah is Israel's total submission, through the Messiah's gentle rule, to God's yoke and service. Israel does not save itself. The antipolitics before us never permits to control its own destiny, either on earth or in heaven. The only choice is whether to cast one's fate into the hands of cruel, deceitful men, or to trust in the living God of mercy and love. We shall now see how this critical position is spelled out in the setting of discourse about the Messiah in the Talmud of the Land of Israel.

Bar Kokhba, above all, exemplifies arrogance against God. He lost the war because of that arrogance. In particular, he ignored the authority of sages, as we saw at Yerushalmi Taanit 4:5, cited in *Trading Places,* chapter 3. There we notice two complementary themes. First, Bar Kokhba treats Heaven with arrogance, asking God merely to keep out of the way. Second, he treats an especially revered sage with a parallel arrogance. The sage had the power to preserve Israel. Bar Kokhba destroyed Israel's one protection. The result was inevitable.

Bar Kokhba, an Israelite, stands for illegitimate power; the sage, in the form of Eleazar of Modin, legitimate and also true power (both).[5] The one shows us how the reality of power is misunderstood, the other, the transvaluation of values that, in politics, serves as the counterpart to the same rereading of real value accomplished in the formation of the counterpart category to economics. The upshot is that the successor system has reconsidered not merely the contents of the received structure, but the composition of the structure itself. In place of its philosophy, we have now a new medium for the formulation of a worldview; in place of a way of life formulated as an economics, a new valuation of value, in place of an account of the social entity framed as a politics, a new conception of legitimate violence. So much for the formation of counterpart categories. Our task is now to portray the results of this categorical reformation in the new structure, seen whole and on its own.

POLITICAL ISRAEL IN THEORY AND IN PRACTICE

If we want to know how people reached and carried out decisions in the villages, we shall be disappointed by the premise of the following:

MISHNAH-TRACTATE MEGILLAH 3:1

> Townsfolk who sold a street of a town buy with its proceeds a synagogue. If they sold a synagogue, they buy an ark. If they sold an ark, they buy wrappings . . .

In the following case as well, we find no local authority, rather a "they" that is supposed to conduct public life in accord with acknowledged requirements.

MISHNAH-TRACTATE TAANIT 2:1

> A. How was fasting carried out?
> B. They bring the ark into the street of the town and put wood ashes on the ark, the head of the patriarch, and the head of the court.
> C. And each person puts ashes on his head. The eldest among them makes a speech of admonition.

The premise is that people obey the rule at hand. But what happens if they fail to do so? And how do they reach their decisions and carry them out, in conformity to law? The townsfolk have reached a consensus, but have they then effected the decision in conformity to law, and to whom are they answerable if not? The passage at hand invites a variety of inquiries, none of which finds suitable response in the document. Yet it is clearly a political case, for it is assumed that the townsfolk form a political entity and own public property and can dispose of it as they like, within the framework of rules set forth by sages for that purpose. On that basis we should anticipate the representation, in the political writing at hand, of the institutional forms of power as these are realized in the village. But there is no picture at all of other than an inchoate consensus which is, more or less, identical with "the law."

Local government is, unsurprisingly, portrayed as the work of sages, who operate through the medium of ad hoc decrees rather than through day-to-day administration, which is essentially beyond imagining. The assumption, then, is that the decrees will be followed rather than enforced, and that all parties will conform. We have no notion of how the system imagines those who do not concur can be coerced. In the following, by contrast, the source of the "decree" clearly is sages, and this tells us that on the local scene, sages were supposed to exercise authority:

> A. They do not decree a fast for the community to take place on the new moon, Hanukkah, or Purim.
>
> M. Ta. 2:10
>
> D. They decreed a fast in Lud. It rained before noon.
> E. R. Tarfon said to them, "Go, eat, and drink, and celebrate a festival day." So they went and ate and drank and celebrated a festival day. Then they assembled at twilight and proclaimed the Great Hallel.
>
> M. Ta. 3:9
>
> A. As to bakers:
> B. sages required them to separate from their produce only an amount sufficient for priestly ration taken for tithe and dough-offering. Shopkeepers are not permitted to sell doubtfully tithed produce.
>
> M. Dem. 2:4

These items leave no doubt that sages were represented as local authorities. But the Mishnah's items also suggest that the government of village affairs is not routinely part of sages' duties. Local government is, rather, an ongoing institution that is not described at all. And yet while those who determined to continue the fast can have done so privately, what about the bakers? To them sages' decree represented a cost, and, as we shall see in due course, when sages made rulings about the administration of prices, then someone lost, and it was invariably the merchant or capitalist. Such a person could not have given up profits willingly and voluntarily and, since the consumer or purchaser surely would not have paid more than required, coercion in some form and by some medium would have found a prominent place in the system. But there is simply no hint as to how that coercion, even by means of public opinion, could have been brought to bear. So the everyday administration of law and local affairs (economic as much as judicial), attributed to sages as bureaucrats and representatives of a government that could make decisions, is scarcely explained, and no organized domination through continuous administration is represented. Here is a case in which power is assumed but not explained.

We turn now from our discussion of sages' power over village government to their ability to enforce decisions of their court. As a party made up of educated males, sages rule.[6] And properly trained for their task, with the right attitudes, sages staff the earthly court and make the decisions of life and death, property and wealth that that court is imagined to make. To show that such a court forms the institutional centerpiece of the politics, we turn, as is our way, to the matter of sanctions (in the present instance, these involve not life and death but—as we already recognize—everyday matters of prices, personal status, and the disposition of property). Any picture of the earthly court, which is to say, of the exercise of power in the here and now, must commence with evidence that, within the system, an administration plays a critical role. Here are representative decisions, among a fair number covered by the Mishnah, supposedly made by a court or its agency, governing such concrete and therefore critical issues as prices and markets and personal status:

> A. R. Tarfon gave instructions in Lud: "Fraud is an overcharge of eight pieces of silver to a sela, one third of the purchase pride."
>
> B. So the merchants of Lud rejoiced.
>
> C. He said to them, "All day long it is permitted to retract."
>
> D. They said to him, "Let R. Tarfon leave us where we were."
>
> E. And they reverted to conduct themselves in accord with the ruling of sages.

M. B. M. 4:3

Power to control prices, by decree imputed to sages, derives from their standing as officers of the court, not from their personal charisma. This is not only explicit in the law, but also a reasonable supposition, since the power to deprive persons of their property—for example, of their right to get as high a price as they can for their goods and services—cannot derive solely from broad-based voluntary compliance to the law.

The power to determine the still more critical matter of personal status, moreover, is explicitly assigned to the court, even though, in parallel cases, individual sages are represented as reaching such decisions:

> A. If the court instructed a woman to remarry, then the marriage is deliberately carried out on her part and the remarriage is not an inadvertent transgression and null.
>
> M. Yeb. 10:1

> A. A certain man performed *halisah* [the rite of removing the shoe, Deut. 25:1 ff.] with his deceased childless brother's widow when the couple were by themselves in prison, and when the case came before R. Aqiba, he validated the rite.
>
> M. Yeb. 12:5

> A. A certain man in Asya was let down by a rope into the sea and they drew back up only his leg.
> B. Sages said, "If the recovered part included from the knee and above, his wife may remarry, and if only from the knee and below, she may not."
>
> M. Yeb. 16:4

What is important in these three entries is the parallel among the decisions of the court, Aqiba, and "sages." That trait shows that the system treats as equivalent the rulings of a court in general, a named sage, and a collectivity of sages. It follows that the court system falls wholly within the framework of sages and their decisions. These sages are empowered by the Torah, we know, and, in particular, by their knowledge of the Law of the Torah, as it has come down to them from prior courts ("administrations"). So the institutional forms of power take shape wholly within the framework of sages, and, on an everyday basis, the administration of legitimate power is assumed to lie in their hands.

That prevailing assumption nonetheless competes with other equally well-founded assumptions. The first is that other authorities, besides sages, applied the law and made decisions.[7] The document's framers include evidence that sages were not the only, or necessarily the main, agencies of the administration of the social entity. But when they concede the existence of competing agencies, they include evidence that sages formed opinions concerning the work and rulings of those agencies, and when the politics of this Judaism turns to the description of the institutions of power, agencies other than the approved ones never play a role. So the representation of competing authorities makes the paramount point that sages really disposed of what others proposed.

Let us take note of part of an account of how a competing administration is described:

MISHNAH-TRACTATE KETUBOT 13:1–9

A. Two judges of civil law were in Jerusalem. Admon and Hanan b. Abishalom.

B. Hanan lays down two rulings.

C. Admon lays down seven.

I   D. He who went overseas, and his wife [left at home] claims maintenance—

E. Hanan says, "Let her take an oath at the end, but let her not take an oath at the outset [that is, she takes an oath when she claims her marriage contract after her husband's death, or after he returns, that she has not held back any property of her husband]."

F. Sons of high priests disputed with him and ruled, "Let her take an oath at the outset and at the end."

G. Ruled R. Dosa b. Harkinas in accord with their opinion.

H. Said R. Yohanan b. Zakkai, "Well did Hanan rule. She should take an oath only at the end."

This account of the two civil law judges and their rulings treats the entire case as a matter of fact. Each case report introduces opinions concerning the civil law judges' rulings of "sons of high priests," Dosa b. Harkinas, and Yohanan b. Zakkai giving a judgment of the whole. And that, of course, is the institutional judgment: whatever other courts made decisions, sages had the power to approve, or disapprove, of what they did.

Accordingly, according to the Mishnah's portrait, at least three institutions of administration operate: the civil law judges, "sons of high priests," and a sage (Dosa, and then Yohanan b. Zakkai). The sage settles matters, concurring with Hanan against sons of high priests. This somewhat complex jurisdiction, with three courts addressing the same issues, covers matters wholly in the charge of sages' courts, at least, so far as sages in the Mishnah represent their own courts. The courts govern the disposition of the property of an absent husband, support for a wife in the case of an absent husband, dividing an estate, claims in cases of bailment, contract violations, real estate cases, and deeds, bonds, and other commercial paper. Not a single area of law over which jurisdiction was conceded to the judges in Jerusalem and, as a matter of implicit fact, to the "sons of high priests" (presumably some sort of Temple court), falls outside the jurisdiction of "the court," which is to say, the sages' court system. Accordingly, we deal with an account of a politics in which power is shared among competing authorities or administrative bodies.

But even that picture of an administration of Israel's affairs, involving not only sages' courts but also civil priestly courts, vastly overstates how much the politics of this Judaism finds itself willing to concede to competing authorities and their institutions. As a matter of fact, when it comes to describing the institutional forms of power as distinct from conceding the adventitious facts of how power presently is shared, only a single institution of administration is fully and normatively set on display. That is, once more, "the court."[8] The court comprised sages and disciples, the more experienced of whom made the decisions.

Consider this fantastic account of the principal institution of decision making:

MISHNAH-TRACTATE SANHEDRIN 4:3–4

A. The sanhedrin was [arranged] in the shape of a half of a round threshing-floor [that is, as an amphitheater],

B. so that [the judges] should see one another,

C. and two judges' clerks stand before them, one at the right and one at the left.

D. And they write down the arguments of those who vote to acquit and of those who vote to convict.

E. R. Judah says, "Three: one writes the opinion of those who vote to acquit, one writes the opinion of those who vote to convict, and the third writes the opinions both of those who vote to acquit and of those who vote to convict."

On the surface we deal with a court of judges. But when we review the things this court did, we realize that that is not so. The "court" in fact is a theoretical model for the institutions that actually govern. A given number of members of the court is required for decisions of one kind (e.g., judicial ones); another number is needed for decisions of a different kind (e.g., political and administrative ones).

The members and procedures prove interchangeable, hence we have a unicameral institution based on sages, many or few. But the distinctive tasks assigned to the court made up of one number of sages as against another has also to be taken into account in our consideration of the institutionalization of power. The interchangeability of sages in the several distinct political functions is clear in the following, which tells how men are qualified for political tasks:

A. And three rows of disciples of sages sit before them.

B. Each and every one known his place.

C. [If] they found need to ordain [a disciple to serve on the court],

D. they ordained one who was sitting in the first row.

E. [Then] one who was sitting in the second row joins the first row, and one who was sitting in the third row moves up to the second row.

F. And they select for themselves someone else from the crowd and set him in the third row.

G. [The new disciple] did not take a seat in the place of the first party [who had now joined in the court] but in the place that was appropriate for him [at the end of the third row].

M. 4:4

One enters the administration through discipleship. Everyone who was qualified could serve in any of the several courts, each with its own task and role. So the sages are undifferentiated, while the institutions, distinguished by the number of members required for each, were very carefully differentiated from one another. Each one in his place, the disciples work their way up to the status of serving on the court, and the court, we see, is a combination of legislature, judiciary, and executive.

How about a legislature? Since God makes the laws and reveals them in the Torah, the only basis for amplifying the law rests on the exegesis of the revealed laws and extension of their principles to new cases. That produces a significant consequences for the portrait of institutional structures. Specifically, in the Mishnah I can identify no law-making agency. The nearest counterpart is the council of state or great Sanhedrin, because to it are entrusted the decisions assigned to the legislative arm in governments familiar to us. But the system scarcely concedes that legislation *de novo* is plausible, since its fundamental insistence is that everything comes from Sinai, that is, from Heaven. Law is not made but discovered in the Torah. So while occasional concessions to pressing need encompass the changing of established custom, the general picture excludes substantial legislative activity.9 The appeal to tradition—people do not know the answer to a question so they go to Jerusalem and ask whether anybody has a tradition on the subject—forms the counterpart to that political agency. But there was a council of state, with its seventy-one members, the large ("great") Sanhedrin. The political task of policy making—social and political, at home and abroad—fell into the hands, of course, of sages. The difference between the council of state and the local court, then, was simply that the former required the largest number of sages, seventy-one in all.

Let us consider first of all how the court functions as administration and council of state. At stake here are, first, the maintenance of social order against sedition and revolution; second, the use of the army and other instrumentalities of state; third, the government of the capital; fourth, the relationships between the central government and the provinces or outlying constituencies of the state ("tribes"):

MISHNAH-TRACTATE SANHEDRIN 1:5

A. (1) They judge a tribe, a false prophet [Deut. 18:20], and a high priest, only on the instructions of a court of seventy-one members.

B. (2) They call [the army] to wage a war fought by choice only on the instructions of a court of seventy-one.

C. (3) They make additions to the city [of Jerusalem] and to the courtyards [of the Temple] only on the instructions of a court of seventy-one.

D. (4) They set up *sanhedrins* for the tribes only on the instructions of a court of seventy-one.

E. (5) They declare a city to be "an apostate city" [Deut. 13:12 ff.] only on the instructions of a court of seventy-one.

F. And they do not declare a city to be "an apostate city" on the frontier,

G. [nor do they declare] three [in one locale] to be [apostate cities],

H. but they do so in the case of one or two.

The executive—the court of seventy-one members—takes charge of the maintenance of civil order. It disposes of sedition ("apostate city"), decides the administration of important offices of state ("a high priest"), and reaches decisions concerning foreign policy ("they call the army to wage a war "). As supreme authority, it also calls to judgment the activities of entire administrative districts or units of state ("tribes").

Judicial functions, we realize, are carried out by the same personnel, that is to say, members of "the court," though the number of personnel required varies for the function. In general, when "the court" is portrayed as a judiciary, from three to twenty-three judges are involved—three for settling property cases, twenty-three for capital cases. Here is the account of "the court" now seen as judiciary:

MISHNAH-TRACTATE SANHEDRIN 1:1–2

    A. (1) Property cases [are decided] by three [judges];

    B. (2) those concerning theft and damages, before three;

    C. (3) [cases involving] compensation for full-damages, half-damages [Exod. 21:35], twofold restitution [Exod. 22:3], fourfold and fivefold restitution [Exod. 21:37], by three;

    D. (4) "cases involving him who rapes [Deut. 32:28–29], him who seduces [Exod. 22:15–16], and *him who brings forth an evil name* (Deut. 22:19), by three," the words of R. Meir.

    E. And sages say, "He that brings forth an evil name is [tried] before twenty-three,

    F. "for there may be a capital case."

M. 1:1

    A. (5) [Cases involving the penalty of] flogging [Deut. 25:2–3] are before three.

    B. In the name of R. Ishmael they said, "Before twenty-three."

M. 1:2

MISHNAH-TRACTATE SANHEDRIN 1:4

    A. (1) Cases involving the death penalty are judged before twenty-three judges.

    B. (2) The beast who commits or is subjected to an act of sexual relations with a human being is judged by twenty-three,

    C. since it is said, *And you will kill the woman and the beast* (Lev. 20:16).

    D. And it says, *And the beast you will slay* (Lev. 20:15).

    E. (3) An ox which is to be stoned is judged by twenty-three,

F. since it is said, *And the ox will be stoned, and also its master will be put to death* (Exod. 21:29).

G. Just as [the case of the master], leading to the death penalty, [is adjudged], so is the [case of] the ox, [leading to] the death penalty.

H. The wolf, lion, bear, panther, leopard, and snake—a capital case affecting them is judged by twenty-three.

I. R. Eliezer says, "Whoever kills them first acquires merit."

J. R. Aqiba says, "Their capital case is judged by twenty-three."

M. 1:4

Here we see how the court system as a judiciary is imagined to organize its jurisdiction. The important part is what is left scarcely stated: all courts are made up of sages. So all of the variations and diverse modes of organization rest on the fundamental uniformity of the system, which finds its coherence in the mode by which personnel are educated, qualified, and selected for service. The details are essentially beside the point. Courts of diverse sizes are impaneled to deal with various kinds of cases. M. 1:4H–J dispute whether E applies to all other beasts or only to the ox. That is why I am not inclined to see H–J as a fourth, independent item on the list. The main point then is at B–D, E–G, as is clearly expressed by G. The same "court" that administers criminal cases deals with issues of public policy that we should identify with an administration or executive. So the court works out the calendar, atones for civil crimes that cannot be imputed to any specific person, makes decisions on matters of personal status (such as we noted above), assesses the value of property donated to the Temple and in that way asserts its rights over Temple affairs, and in other ways carries out tasks not ordinarily assigned to the judiciary.

The upshot is precisely what I signaled earlier. The institutional distinctions make no difference in the actual management or manipulation of power. The tripartite plan of institutions—court, Temple, monarchy—proves a mere formality. Whatever the organizational structure, the system appealed to a uniform mode of domination. Sages, bearers of legitimate power, required obedience by reason of their preparation and, in a broad and very specific sense, particular knowledge, rather than because of their institutional affiliation. Physical violence and moral authority joined together in the person of the sage.

Indeed, having come this far, we must wonder what difference administrative arrangements among competing foci of power—heavenly, earthly, and intermediary—can have made. For the simple fact is that the institutional forms of power draw upon a single type of person who is empowered to carry out diverse tasks. That is to say, whether large or small, whether administrative and executive, judicial, or legislative (in the making of law), the "court" was always one and the same, namely, a formation of sages.

In the following we find an identification of "member of the court" with "the congregation," which in the context of Scripture meant "any male Israelite." But the definition of "any Israelite" in this context can mean only "sage," that is to say, a disciple who works his way up the rows of the half-circle to the front rank:

M. Sanhedrin 1:6

A. The great sanhedrin was [made up of] seventy-one members,

B. and the small one was twenty-three.

C. and how do we know that the great sanhedrin was to have seventy-one members?

D. Since it is said, *Gather to me seventy men of the elders of Israel* (Num. 11:16)

E. Since Moses was in addition to them, lo, there were seventy-one.

F. R. Judah says, "It is seventy."

G. And how do we know that a small one is twenty-three?

H. Since it is said, *The congregation shall judge,* and *The congregation shall deliver* (Num. 35:24, 25)—

I. one congregation judges, and one congregation saves—thus there are twenty.

J. And how do we know that a congregation is ten? Since it is said, *How long shall I bear with this evil congregation* [of the ten spies] (Num. 14:27)—excluding Joshua and Caleb.

K. And how do we know that we should add three more?

L. From the implication of that which is said, *You shall not follow after the many to do evil* (Exod. 23:20), I derive the inference that I should be with them to do good.

M. If so, why is it said, *After the many to do evil?*

N. Your verdict of acquittal is not equivalent to your verdict of guilt.

O. Your verdict of acquittal may be on the vote of a majority of one, but your vote for guilt must be by a majority of two.

P. Since there cannot be a court of an even number of members [twenty-two], they add yet another—thus twenty-three.

Evidently, the unit behind the system of institutionalization of power—executive, legislative, and judicial—derives from the type of person who serves in all three units and the foundation for that person's qualifications: it is a male Israelite who has come up through the processes of discipleship to join in the government of the community.

Yet—to return to our initial observation—the system of sanctions reveals that beside the sages there existed a civil authority, an earthly court. The account of the institutions of power clearly envisions a king and a high priest. Not only so, but the Mishnah is explicit in comparing the king to the high priest and in setting forth the charismatic privileges and standing imputed to each. It effects its comparisons in wholly personal terms, as we should anticipate, abstract conceptions being inaccessible to the system builders, but nonetheless, king and priest clearly were deemed institutions of enormous consequence.

The king and the high priest are set forth in such a way that the rights and immunities of each are compared to those assigned to the other. By consequence, the high priest is shown to be a subordinate figure, the king an autocephalous authority. If we work through the comparison's terms, it introduces us to the power and authority of both the king and the high priest. So let us consider the entire passage here. The comparison runs as follows:

M. Sanhedrin 2:1–3

A. A high priest (1) judges, and [others] judge him;

B. (2) gives testimony, and [others] give testimony about him;

C. (3) performs the rite of removing the shoe with his wife.

D. (4) [Others] enter levirate marriage with his wife, but he does not enter into levirate marriage,

E. because he is prohibited to marry a widow.

F. (5) [If] he suffers a death [in his family], he does not follow the bier.

G. "But when [the bearers of the bier] are not visible, he is visible; when they are visible, he is not.

H. "And he goes with them to the city gate," the words of R. Meir.

I. R. Judah says, "He never leaves the sanctuary,

J. "since it says, *Nor shall he go out of the sanctuary* (Lev. 21:12)."

K. And when he gives comfort to others

L. the accepted practice is for all the people to pass on after another, and the appointed [prefect of the priests] stands between him and the people.

M. And when he receives consolation from others,

N. all the people say to him, "Let us be your atonement."

O. And he says to them, "May you be blessed by Heaven."

P. (6) And when they provide him with the funeral meal,

Q. all the people sit on the ground, while he sits on a stool.

M. 2:1

A. (1) The king does not judge, and [others] do not judge him;

B. (2) does not give testimony, and [others] do not give testimony about him;

C. (3) does not perform the rite of removing the shoe, and others do not perform the rite of removing the shoe with his wife;

D. (4) does not enter into levirate marriage, not [do his brothers] enter levirate marriage with his wife.

E. R. Judah says, "If he wanted to perform the rite of removing the shoe or to enter into levirate marriage, his memory is a blessing."

F. They said to him, "They pay no attention to him [if he expressed the wish to do so]."

G. [Others] do not marry his widow.

H. R. Judah says, "A king may marry the widow of a king.

I. "For so we find in the case of David, that he marries the widow of Saul.

J. "For it is said, *And I gave you your master's house and your master's wives into you embrace* (II Sam. 12:8)."

M. 2:2

A. (5) [If] he suffers a death in his family, he does not leave the gate of his palace.

B. R. Judah says, "If he wants to go out after the bier, he goes out,

C. "for thus we find in the case of David, that he went out after the bier of Abner,

D. "since it is said, *And King David followed the bier* (II Sam. 3:31)."

E. They said to him, "This action was only to appease the people."

F. (6) And when they provide him with the funeral meal, all the people sit on the ground, while he sits on a couch.

M. 2:3

The passage's contrast stands clear:[10] by reason of his genealogy, the high priest enjoys certain immunities in his person; the king, who exercises power above the community, stands immune from all rules that apply to the community. The two heads of state therefore are alike, but different—and the king is the superior figure. The high priest and the king form a single genus, but two distinct species, and the variations between the species form a single set of taxonomic indicators. The one is like the other in these ways, unlike the other in those ways. The comparison of the two yields, therefore, the amazing judgment that a figure who is scarcely acknowledged, to whom is assigned no substantial bureaucracy or administration as counterpart to the temple's and the courts', is deemed utterly autocephalous: the state, above the law. That assessment can scarcely be squared with the inconsequential role assigned to the monarchy, but it does accord with the representation of the king and queen as humbly seeking sages' approval (a picture Josephus draws for historic time as well). Within the larger politics, therefore, the king serves to deliver the systemic message: the state, embodied by the king, enjoys full sovereignty, and the sages run the state. Citing verses of Scripture and underlining that the king is superior to the high priest but inferior to the Torah, which he must obey, reveals this important fact even while it is not made articulate: the king obeys the sages, who are the masters of the Torah.

The key to the monarchy lies in the rule that "the king does not judge, and [others] do not judge him, does not give testimony, and [others] do not give testimony about him." What then does the king do?

M. Sanhedrin 2:4–5

A. [The king] calls out [the army to wage] a war fought by choice on the instructions of a court of seventy-one.

B. He [may exercise the right to] open a road for himself, and [others] may not stop him.

C. The royal road has no required measure.

D. All the people plunder and lay before him [what they have grabbed], and he takes the first portion.

E. *He should not multiply wives to himself* (Deut. 17:17)—only eighteen.

F. R. Judah says, "He may have as many as he wants, so long as thy do not entice him [to abandon the Lord (Deut. 7:4)]."

G. R. Simeon says, "Even if there is only one who entices him [to abandon the Lord]—lo, this one should not marry her."

H. If so, why is it said, *He should not multiply wives to himself?*

I. Even though they should be like Abigail [1 Sam. 25:3].

J. *He should not multiply horses to himself* (Deut. 17:16)—only enough for his chariot.

K. *Neither shall he greatly multiply to himself silver and gold* (Deut. 17:16)—only enough to pay his army.

L. *And he writes out a scroll of the Torah for himself* (Deut. 17:17)—

M. When he goes to war, he takes it out with him; when he comes back, he brings it back with him; when he is in session in court, it is with him; when he is reclining, it is before him,

N. As it is said, *And it shall be with him, and he shall read in it all the days of his life* (Deut. 17:19).

M. 2:4

A. [Others may] not (1) ride on his horse, (2) sit on his throne, (3) handle his scepter.

B. And [others may] (4) not watch him while he is getting a haircut, or (5) while he is nude, or (6) in the bathhouse,

C. since it is said, *You shall surely set him as king over you* (Deut. 17:15)—that reverence for him will be upon you.

M. 2:5

The main point, once more, is that the king stands subject to the Torah, and (systemically speaking) everybody knows who says what the Torah requires.[11] It follows that the king reigns but does not rule; the sages rule through him. When a war is obligatory (for example, for conquest of the Land), the sages' court makes the decision. When war is optional, the king calls out the army—again, on the initiative of the court of seventy-one! Policy making then scarcely belongs within the royal domain. True, the king remains in charge of public works, takes priority in collecting the spoils of war, maintains the army—but that is that. So far as we can see, the monarchy then takes charge of the infrastructure of the state, and even with that, in anything of consequence, he acts upon the instructions of the Sanhedrin run by the sages. How the king supports his army and administration we are not told, nor does the account tell us how legitimate violence belongs within the domain of the king acting on his own. All we hear is that in his person he is superior to the high priest—except as the high priest's genealogical and caste privileges intervene—and that both king and high priest obey sages.

Given that our evidence assumes the king governed at the instructions of sages, faithfully doing whatever they told him to do, it is not hard to understand why the system builders recognized scarcely any need to discuss the monarchy and its tasks, why they did not detail the monarchy's procedures, its modes of collecting

and disposing of taxes, dealing with foreign powers (a consideration utterly beyond the systemic imagination), maintaining and
using an army, maintaining the infrastructure of the state, the economy, and the institutions of culture and social order—all the things
kings were supposed to do. Indeed, if we seek in the initial statement of Judaism an account of the monarchy and the rules governing it, beyond the instructions of the Law of the Torah (Deut.
17:15 ff.), we look in vain, as we shall see in a moment. Since, as
we have seen, the (sages') court made decisions on war and peace,
civil order and suppression of sedition and revolution, the everyday governance of communities, and the administration of law and
justice, we must wonder why the system includes a king at all.

The one thing the Mishnah makes explicit is that the monarchy serves at the pleasure of the sages. This point appears indis-
putable in the following:

MISHNAH-TRACTATE SOTAH 7:8

    B. At the end of the first festival day of the Festival [of Sukkot],

    C. On the eighth year, [that is] at the end of the seventh year,

    D. They make him a platform of wood, set in the courtyard.

    E. And he sits on it,

    F. As it is said, *At the end of every seven years in the set time* (Deut.
31:10).

    G. The minister of the assembly takes a scroll of the Torah and
hands it to the head of the assembly, and the head of the assembly hands it to the prefect, and the prefect hands it to the
high priest, and the high priest hands it to the king, and the
king stands and receives it.

    H. But he reads sitting down.

    I. Agrippa the King stood up and received it and read it stand-
ing up, and sages praised him on that account.

    J. And when he came to the verse, *You may not put a foreigner over
you, who is not your brother* (Deut. 17:15), his tears ran down
from his eye.

    K. They said to him, "Do not be afraid, Agrippa, you are our
brother, you are our brother, you are our brother!"

L. He reads from the beginning of *These are the words* (Deut. 1:1) to *Hear O Israel* (Deut. 6:4), *Hear O Israel* (Deut. 6:4), *And it will come to pass, if you hearken* (Deut. 11:13), and *You shall surely tithe* (Deut. 14:22), and *When you have made an end of tithing* (Deut. 26:12–15), and the pericope of the king (Deut. 17:14–20), and the blessings and the curses (Deut. 27:15–26), and he completes the whole pericope.

M. With the same blessings with which the high priest blesses them [M. 7:7F], the king blesses them.

N. But he says the blessing for the festivals instead of the blessing for the forgiveness of sin.

M. 7:8

MISHNAH-TRACTATE NAZIR 3:6

A. Helene the Queen:

B. Her son went off to war and she said, "If my son comes home from war whole and in one piece, I shall be a Nazir for seven years."

C. Indeed her son did come home from war, and she was a Nazir for seven years.

D. Then at the end of the seven years, she went up to the Land. The House of Hillel instructed her to be a Nazir for another seven years.

E. Then at the end of the seven years, she contracted uncleanness.

F. So she turned out to be a Nazir for twenty-one years.

Both stories portray the monarchy as humbly obedient to sages' rule. The symbolic transaction in the former passage, with the king receiving the Torah, reading in it, and pledging his fealty to it—hence also to those who could tell him what it meant—underlines the principal message. The story about the queen is of the same sort. But the symbolic transaction of having the king read in the Torah, which the sage mastered and the king did not (if he did, he would be a sage), with the king humbly obeying the sages' instructions and gladly accepting, even obsequiously seeking, their approval—that transaction contains the entire story of administration. In the particular case at hand, the sages ("they") then complete their part of the transaction, setting aside the rule of the Torah for the king, who is a foreigner but whose rule they approve. Since sages are explicitly represented as placing their own politics above the Law of the Torah, the true picture, as sages portray matters, emerges.

The same point about sages' paramount status in the politics of state and administration applies to the priesthood. It is expressed with surpassing simplicity in the following:

MISHNAH-TRACTATE NEGAIM 3:1

    A. All are suitable to examine plagues, but the actual declaration of uncleanness and cleanness is in the hands of a priest.

    B. They say to him, "Say, 'Unclean,'" and he says, "Unclean;"

    C. "Say, 'Clean,'" and he says, "Clean."

MISHNAH-TRACTATE PARAH 3:8

    A. They would render the priest who burns the cow unclean, because of the Sadducees, so that they should not say, "It is done by one on whom the sun has set."

    B. They [sages] placed their hands on him and say to him, "My lord, High Priest, immerse now," and he descended, immersed, emerged, dried off [and proceeded with the rite of burning the red cow].

MISHNAH-TRACTATE YOMA 1:3, 5

    A. [Seven days before the Day of Atonement] they handed [the high priest] over to elders belonging to the court, and they read for him the prescribed rite of the Day of Atonement.

    B. And they say to him, "My lord, high priest, you read it with your own lips, lest you have forgotten, or never even learned it to begin with."

M. Yoma 1:3

    A. The elders of the court handed him over to the elders of the priesthood, who brought him up to the upper chamber of Abtinas.

B. And they imposed an oath on him and took their leave and went along.

C. This is what they said to him: "My lord, high priest, we are agents of the court, and you are our agent and agent of the court.

D. "We abjure you by Him who caused His name to rest upon this house that you will not vary in any way from all that we have instructed you."

M. Yoma 1:5

I cannot imagine a clearer way of saying that the priests run the Temple, but the sages run the priests. The picture of the dumb priest waiting for the sage to tell him what to say (M. Neg.) and what to do on the holiest day of the year (M. Yoma) bears an element of contempt. This is reinforced by the account of how the unnamed "they" deliberately impart uncleanness to the high priest, have him immerse, then carry out the rite, because "they" maintain that the rite is carried out by a priest who is in the status of one who has immersed on that selfsame day and awaits sunset for the completion of the purification rite. Here again, control of the cult lies not only in pronouncing decisions but in the more critical matter of applying the uncleanness taboos. The high priest in his own view will have carried out the rite in a condition of cultic uncleanness and so be worthy of the death penalty. But he submits—so the picture at hand wants us to believe. So too, I find equally contemptuous the oath imposed upon the high priest not to disobey the Torah that the sages have taught him. A politics of sages' domination over the Temple cannot have come to more stunning expression than in this brief account.

But the portrait of matters proves somewhat more complicated for, as before, the systemic account does consider the simple fact that priests do not conform to the law. This is implicit at M. Yoma 1:5, and it is made explicit in connection with the rejection by priests of sages' opinions on matters of marriage. Here, priests upset both the rules of genealogy and the system. But sages sidestep the problem. They concede that, for now, priests control whom they accept in marriage (deciding the law of genealogy and caste in a way that sages do not approve), but their concession means little, for they assert that in the end, God will intervene and straighten matters out. Where it counts, sages will win. That is, whereas the politics explicitly takes account of disobedience, by calling God in time to come to set matters right, by painting a picture of sages' dominance with Heaven's assistance, it both accounts for interim competition and dismisses that competition. This seems to me little more than the message already set forth.

Mishnah-tractate Eduyyot 8:3, 7

A. Testified R. Joshua and R. Judah b. Beterah concerning a widow of an Israelite family suspected of contamination with unfit genealogical stock, that she is valid for marriage into the priesthood. For a woman deriving from an Israelite family suspect of contamination with unfit genealogical stock is herself valid for being declared unclean or clean, being put out or being brought near.

B. Said Rabban Gamaliel, "We should accept your testimony, but what shall we do? For Rabban Yohanan b. Zakkai decreed against calling courts into session for such a matter. For the priests pay attention to you when it comes to putting someone out but not when it comes to drawing someone near."

M. Ed. 8:3

A. Said R. Joshua, "I have a tradition from Rabban Yohanan b. Zakkai, who heard it from his master, and his master from his master, as a law revealed to Moses at Sinai,

B. "That Elijah is not going to come to declare unclean or to declare clean, to put out or to draw near, but only to put out those who have been brought near [to marriage into the priestly caste] by force and to draw near those who have been put out by force."

M. Ed. 8:7

Where the priesthood remains in full charge, therefore, it concerns only whom they will agree to take in marriage, which is to say, the priests govern the issues of genealogy on which their caste status and power rest. But the concession by the sages is merely formal, concerning who ultimately dictates whom priests will marry; power here is negative, and the sanction involves what priests will refuse to do and may not (so the politics allows) be forced to do.

All that has been said bears the implication that the Temple is represented as an institution of power in a this-worldly political sense. But is that actually the case? The examples at hand suggest otherwise, for the Temple is never represented as a political institution, nor the priesthood as a political class. The priesthood is acknowledged, conceded its role and its rights (in a fantasy of the Temple to be sure), but not accorded that command of power that the political classes in fact enjoy. In other words, the sages do not concede much. In the Mishnah's picture of the politics of its Israel, the Temple does not conduct political trials or impose this-worldly sanctions.[12] These are not political actions, and do not involve any kind of coercion exercised outside the framework of the caste itself. For what narrowly political, administrative tasks are represented as assigned to the priesthood? I find none conceded by the systemic account. And that observation conforms to the distinction between the monarchy and the priesthood, the king and the high priest. The king is political; the high priest is not. Both, to be sure, serve as surrogates and representatives of the sages, who now are represented as forming the institutions of state and as exercising all the power that mattered. Can we explain the distinctions before us by appealing to the everyday facts of history? Hardly. There was no Temple in Jerusalem, no king ruling Israel, when sages made up their system. The distinction then is systemic, important because of the message that, through the picture of the political institutions, the system wished to convey. And that message comes through repeatedly, and loud and clear.

Enough has been said to raise the question, Is there any identification of an ongoing and permanent administration—that is, an institution in which sages as such, not merely as controlling personnel, organize, make decisions, and effect power? The answer, as we should now predict, is negative. And it had to be, for sages' governance effected right attitude and right thought, and the triviality that sages differed from one another on this and that required no institutional formulation and expression. Right-thinking people may well disagree on details; they may even vote. But the system knows no institution in which the sages, formed into a party, for instance, work out their differences and come to a common position on public policy. If, as we have seen, the politics of this Judaism represent matters such that sages form the "party" that controls the state, where and how does that party come to institutional form and expression? The systemic statement is remarkably silent on that matter, yielding only the following:

MISHNAH-TRACTATE SHABBAT 1:4

    A. These are some of the laws which they stated in the upper room of Hananiah b. Hezekiah b. Gurion when they went up to visit him.

    B. They took a vote and the House of Shammai outnumbered the House of Hillel. And eighteen rules did they decree on that very day.

M. Shab. 1:4

The party knows no substantial institutions. People are supposed to meet casually on informal occasions, make up their minds, and vote. Other portrayals of the sages' agency ("party" seems anachronistic) in the decision-making process offer details of how decisions are reached. These suggest a somewhat more regular procedure. In the following, part of a larger set of controversy-materials, we have an example of debate and vote in practice, with the debate summarized as positions assigned to names.

MISHNAH-TRACTATE YADAYIM 4:1

  I A. On that day did they vote and decide concerning

     B. a foot-bath—

     C. which holds from two *logs* to nine *qabs* and which was cracked,

     D. that it is susceptible to uncleanness through *midras* uncleanness [as an object suitable for a chair or a couch, that is, for sitting or lying].

     E. For R. Aqiba says, "A foot-bath is according to its name."

The continuation of the passage shows us what matters in how the system portrays the decision-making process: sages debate and vote. And on what basis do they make up their minds? In the debate the appeal is to verses of Scripture, which serve to settle questions as readily as tradition.

Are sages in their debates then engaged in running the government and dictating the policies of the agencies of administration? Yes and no. The program of issues portrayed in the systemic writings is limited to matters that we should regard as extrapolitical, such as the personal standing of an Ammonite proselyte, the rule, as to tithing, of outlying territories, a law of the Temple. These are not decisions having to do with peace and war, economics and the disposition of power. But they are the kinds of decisions that, in the imagination of the system builders, Israel's politics retained authority and power to settle. Thus, although none of this has any bearing on the great institutions of state and government—monarchy, Temple, court—the theory of the management of political institutions nonetheless emerges with great force: The institutional structure and program make no place for sages, but in the politics of this Judaism as set forth by the Mishnah, sages run things.

The upshot is that, except for the court, the institutions set forth by the politics of this Judaism, both in heaven and on earth, really represent formalities, symbols of slight substance. The picture that we should have drawn from the mythic portrait of the whole is radically revised by the interposition of sages in all three institutional representations. The institutions make no place for sages, any more than the sanctions encompass actions effected by sages. But, we now realize, sages dominate all institutions of power, at least so their politics maintains. First of all, the king—never portrayed as the earthly counterpart to God, even though God is routinely called King—is represented as a mere puppet of sages. Second, the earthly court is represented as wholly staffed by sages and governed by the rules they have learned within their circles. And, third, the Temple priests are instructed by sages. So while the politics sets forth an institutional system in which heaven and earth and Temple collaborate in the disposition of power, the system does not work in such a way at all. So why include the priesthood and monarchy? Because, after all, Scripture does; the Mishnah encompasses the governance of the Temple (which its authorship assumes will be rebuilt), and also the restoration of the monarchy (I assume, of the house of David). The utopian vision encompasses everything and, then, concedes nothing. Sages will govern while the king reigns, and the high priest rules only in his holy precinct. And both king and priest rule fully in accord with sages' instructions.

As we look backward, we realize that the systemic document is remarkably reticent in telling us about institutions at all. But we know why. Since sages form the true systemic manipulators of power, telling king and priest what to do and wholly controlling the court—which served as executive, legislature, and judiciary—institutional differentiation would indicate precisely what our authorship wants to neglect. An analogy drawn from modern times may serve to place into perspective the somewhat odd institutional politics in hand. We distinguish between government and party, that is, the institutions of government—heaven, earth, Temple—and the party of sages that runs all three institutions and administers them. Then we have a dual system of power, the government and the party, with the latter forming an inner and governing structure in control of the institutions of the former. To say that the politics of this Judaism portrays a party government probably presents an anachronism, but it seems also a valid metaphor for what we do see before us. This is not to suggest that the politics of a judicial government, a kind of court-administration by judicial fiat, exhausts the institutional arrangements contemplated by Judaism. It is to say that the only political institution that matters is that court, unicameral in the deepest sense: executive, legislature, judiciary all at once.

And the court administration is unitary in a second sense, since it is made up of sages who serve interchangeably in the three roles in which power attains institutionalization. So all things depend on the personnel, and the institutional arrangements represent formalities. The political system focuses, therefore, on the forming of qualified and correct personalities, persons trained for the work by reason of right formation of intellect and attitude. And that draws us onward to the administration of the politics.

2

The Rabbinic Polemic Against Wealth

Tithing: Validating Wealth

Pisqa Ten of Pesiqta deRab Kahana, which deals with tithing, makes the polemic against wealth explicit. Its base-verse is Deut. 14:22. In this connection, at X:I.4, we find a very precise treatment of a principal concern of economics, which is proper estate management. Xenophon would not have made much sense of the following:

4. A. R. Levi interpreted the cited verse [*The miser is in a hurry to grow rich, never dreaming that want will overtake him* (Prov. 28:22)] to speak of those who do not set aside the required tithes as is proper.

B. For R. Levi said, "There is the case of one who would set aside his required tithes as was proper.

C. "Now the man had one field, which produced a thousand measures of grain. He would separate from it a hundred measures for tithe. From the field he would derive his livelihood all his days, and from it he would nourish himself all his life. When he was dying, he called his son and said to him, 'My son, pay attention to this field. Such and so has it produced, such and so we would separate from the crop for tithe, and from that field we derived my livelihood all my days, and from it we nourished myself all my days.'

D. "In the first year [following the father's death], the son sowed the field and it produced a thousand measures of grain, from which the son set aside a hundred measures for tithe. In the second year the son became niggardly and deducted ten measures, and the field produced a hundred measures less, and so he deducted ten and it produced a hundred less, until the field yielded only the amount that had originally been set aside as tithe.

E. "When the man's relatives realized it, [as a sign of rejoicing] they put on white garments and cloaked themselves in white and assembled at his house. He said to them, 'Why have you come to rejoice over that man who has been afflicted?'

F. "They said to him, 'God forbid! We have come only to rejoice with you. In the past you were the householder, and the Holy One, blessed be he, was the priest [collecting the tithes as his share of the crop]. Now you have been turned into the priest, and the Holy One, blessed be he, has become the householder [keeping back the larger share of the crop, nine tenths of the former yield, for himself]. [So we are rejoicing at your rise in caste status!]'"

G. Said R. Levi, "After he had deducted [the priests' share] year by year, yearly the field reduced its yield."

H. Therefore Moses admonished Israel, saying to them, [*Year by year*] you shall set aside a tithe [*of all the produce of your seed, of everything that grows on the land. You shall eat it in the presence of the Lord your God in the place which he will choose as a dwelling for his name—the tithe of your corn and new wine and oil, and the first-born of your cattle and sheep, so that for all time you may learn to fear the Lord your God*] (Deut. 14:22).

The message cannot be missed: obedience to the law of the Torah yields prosperity, and violation, want. The sarcasm of the relatives underlines the main point. What the householder prized he lost. His father had left the right message: obedience to God, giving God the proper share of the jointly owned property, will assure prosperity. That point is made explicitly at Pesiqta deRab Kahana

XI:X.1.B–C: "... *tithing, you shall tithe*—so that you will get rich. Said the Holy One, blessed be he, 'Give a tithe of what is mine, and we shall enrich what is yours.'"

THE CONTINGENCY OF WEALTH

A case in which wealth is made contingent, so that the outsider's high valuation of money is contrasted with the Israelite's low valuation of money and his high valuation of holiness:

GENESIS RABBAH XI:IV

4. A. Said R. Tanhuma, "There was a case in Rome that took place on the eve of the great fast [the Day of Atonement]. A certain tailor there went to buy himself a fish, and it happened that the governor's bondman was bidding for it too, and one bid for such and so, and the other bid for such and so, until the price reached twelve denars. And the tailor got it.

   B. "At dinner the governor said to his servant, 'Why did you not serve fish?'

   C. "He said to him, 'My lord, why should I keep the matter from you? Such and so a certain Jew did to me. Do you want me to bring you a fish that cost twelve denars?'

   D. "He said to him, 'Who is he?'

   E. "He said to him, 'Such and so, a Jew.'

   F. "He sent for him and summoned him, and he came. He said, 'Will a Jewish tailor eat a fish for twelve denars?'

   G. "He said to him, 'My lord, we have a day which effects atonement for us for all of the sins of the year, and should we not treasure it?'

   H. "He brought proof for his statement, and the governor let him go free."

What is important from our perspective is the contrast that is drawn between the incorrect and the correct evaluation of wealth. The gentile does not know what counts; the Israelite does. Then by scarce resources, in the passage at hand and countless counterparts, something other than gold is meant.

The polemic against wealth and comfort and in favor of a different value altogether is exemplified in the notion that the generation of the Flood sinned because it had too much prosperity:

GENESIS RABBAH XXXIV:XI.2

A. Said R. Aha, "'What is it that made them rebel against me? Was it not because they sowed but did not reap, produced offspring and did not have to bury them?

B. "Henceforward: 'Seedtime and harvest,' meaning that they will give birth and then have to bury their children.

C. "'Cold and heat,' meaning they have fever and ague.

D. "'Summer and winter,' meaning: 'I shall give the birds the right to attack their summer crops,' in line with this verse, 'And the ravenous birds shall summer upon them and all the beasts of the earth shall winter upon them' (Isa. 18:6)."

5. A. Said R. Isaac, "What is it that made them rebel against me? Was it not because they sewed but did not reap?"

B. For R. Isaac said, "Once every forty years they would sow a crop, and as they made their trip they would travel from one end of the world to the other in a brief span and cut down the cedars of Lebanon. And the lions and leopards made no more of an impression on them than did a louse on their skin."

C. How so? The climate for them was like the climate from Passover to Pentecost.

D. R. Simeon b. Gamaliel said in the name of R. Meir, and so said R. Dosa, "The latter half of Tishré, Marheshvan, and the first half of Kislev are for sowing, the second half of Kislev and Tebet and the first half of Shebat are winter, the latter half of Shebat and Adar and the first half of Nisan are the cold season, the second half of Nisan and Iyyar and the first half of Sivan are the harvest season, the second half of Sivan and Tammuz and the first half of Ab are summer, and latter half of Ab and Elul and the first half of Tishré are the hot season."

E. R. Judah counts from Marheshvan.

F. R. Simeon counts from Tishri.

Humankind had rebelled under conditions of prosperity, so now they will have to endure "hot and cold," "seedtime and harvest time," interpreted as misfortunes. Lust for money is condemned in countless ways, for people are supposed to place their trust not in real estate or movables or other things of material value at all.

And that brings us to consider the re-presentation of wealth in the successor documents and to seek a richer sample of opinion than the story that ended the preceding chapter and that, we maintain, frames the new economics of the successor system. A system that declares forbidden using the Torah as a spade with which to dig, as a means of making one's living, will have found proof for its position in the numerous allegations in wisdom literature that the value of wisdom, understood of course as the Torah, is beyond price: "Happy is the man who finds wisdom . . . for the gain from it is better than gain from silver, and its profit better than gold; she is more precious than jewels, and nothing you desire can compare with her" (Prov. 3:13–15). That and numerous parallels were not understood to mean that if people devoted themselves to the study of the Torah and the teaching thereof, they would not have to work anymore. Nor do the praises of wisdom specifically contrast Torah-learning with landownership. But in the successor writings, that is precisely what is commonplace. And the conclusion is drawn that one may derive one's living from study of the Torah, which is a spade with which to dig, as much as a real spade serves to dig in the earth to make the ground yield a living.

AUTHENTIC WEALTH: TORAH-LEARNING

The issue of scarce resources in the context of a society that highly valued honor and despised and feared shame was phrased not only in terms of material wealth but also of worldly repute. Knowledge of the Torah served as did coins, that is, to circulate the name of the holy man or woman (Abraham or Sarah, in this context), all figures to whom, quite naturally, heroic deeds of Torah-learning and Torah-teaching were attributed:

GENESIS RABBAH **XXXIX:XI.5**

A. R. Berekhiah in the name of R. Helbo: "[The promise that God will make Abram great] refers to the fact that his coinage had circulated in the world.

B. "There were four whose coinage circulated in the world.

C. "Abraham: 'And we will make you' (Gen. 12:2). And what image appeared on his coinage? An old man and an old woman on the obverse side, a boy and a girl on the reverse [Abraham, Sarah, Isaac and Rebekkah].

D. "Joshua: 'So the Lord was with Joshua and his fame was in all the land' (Josh. 6:27). That is, his coinage circulated in the world. And what image appeared on his coinage? An ox on the obverse, a wild-ox on the reverse: 'His firstling bullock, majesty is his, and his horns are the horns of a wild ox' (Deut. 33:17). [Joshua descended from Joseph.]

E. "David: 'And the fame of David went out into all lands' (1 Chron. 14:17). That is, his coinage circulated in the world. And what image appeared on his coinage? A staff and a wallet on the obverse, a tower on the reverse: 'Your neck is like the tower of David, built with turrets' (Song 4:4).

F. "Mordecai: 'For Mordecai was great in the king's house, and his fame went forth throughout all the provinces' (Esther 9:4). That is, his coinage circulated in the world. And what image appeared on his coinage? Sackcloth and ashes on the obverse, a golden crown on the reverse."

"Coinage" is meant to be jarring, to draw an ironic contrast between true currency, which is the repute that is gained through godly service, and worldly currency; kings use their coins to make their persons and policies known; so do the saints. But this is not, by itself, a saying that assigns to Torah the value equivalent to coins.

But, of course, it cannot make such an assignment, since the value imputed to Torah study and teaching compares not to (mere) currency—which, in the context of Aristotelian and Mishnaic economics, bore the merely contingent value of a commodity—but only to land. So can we find in the successor writings clear affirmations, beyond the one now cited concerning Tarfon and Aqiba, that compare land with the Torah? For one thing, the Torah serves as Israel's deed to the land, and, it must follow, knowledge of the Torah is what demonstrates one's right to possess the one resource found worth having:

GENESIS RABBAH I.II.1

1. A. R. Joshua of Sikhnin in the name of R. Levi commenced [discourse by citing the following verse]: "'He has declared to his people the power of his works, in giving them the heritage of the nations' (Ps. 111:6).

   B. "What is the reason that the Holy One, blessed be he, revealed to Israel what was created on the first day and what on the second?

   C. "It was on account of the nations of the world. It was so that they should not ridicule the Israelites, saying to them, 'Are you not a nation of robbers [having stolen the land from the Canaanites]?'

   D. "It allows the Israelites to answer them, 'And as to you, is there no spoil in your hands? For surely: "The Caphtorim, who came forth out of Caphtor, destroyed them and dwelled in their place" (Deut. 2:23)!

   E. "'The world and everything in it belongs to the Holy One, blessed be he. When he wanted, he gave it to you, and when he wanted, he took it from you and gave it to us.'

   F. "That is in line with what is written, '. . . in giving them the heritage of the nations, he has declared to his people the power of his works' (Ps. 111:6). [So as to give them the land, he established his right to do so by informing them that he had created it.]

   G. "He told them about the beginning: 'In the beginning God created . . .' (Gen. 1:1)."

While pertinent, the passage is hardly probative; all we have here is the linkage of Torah to land, but for merely instrumental purposes. Not only so, but the conception of riches in the conventional philosophical sense certainly persisted. "Abram was very rich in cattle" is understood quite literally, interpreted in line with Psalm 105:37: "He brought them forth with silver with gold, and there was none that stumbled among his tribes."[1] Along these same lines, "Jacob's riches" of Genesis 30:43 are understood to be material and concrete: sixty thousand dogs, for example.[2] One may interpret the story of the disinheritance of Eliezer b. Hyrcanus on account of his running off to study the Torah with Yohanan ben Zakkai as a contrasting tale, therefore. The father intended to disinherit the son from his property because he had gone to study the Torah but then, impressed by his achievements, gives him the whole estate.[3] But that would require us to read into the story a symbolic transaction that is not explicit. So, too, the allegation that "Torah" is represented by bread does not require, and perhaps does not even sustain, the interpretation that Torah-learning forms a scarce resource that provides bread and that is worth bread and that serves as does bread: .

GENESIS RABBAH LXX:V.1

    A. ". . . will give me bread to eat and clothing to wear:"

    B. Aqilas the proselyte came to R. Eliezer and said to him, "Is all the gain that is coming to the proselyte going to be contained in this verse: '. . . and loves the proselyte, giving him food and clothing' (Deut. 10:18)?"

    C. He said to him, "And is something for which the old man [Jacob] beseeched going to be such a small thing in your view namely, '. . . will give me bread to eat and clothing to wear'? [God] comes and hands it over to [a proselyte] on a reed [and the proselyte does not have to beg for it]."

    D. He came to R. Joshua, who commenced by saying words to appease him: "'Bread' refers to Torah, as it is said, 'Come, eat of my bread' (Prov. 9:5). 'Clothing' refers to the cloak of a disciple of sages.

    E. "When a person has the merit of studying the Torah, he has the merit of carrying out a religious duty. [So the proselyte receives a great deal when he gets bread and clothing, namely, entry into the estate of disciples].

F. "And not only so, but his daughters may be chosen for marriage into the priesthood, so that their sons' sons will offer burnt-offerings on the altar. [So the proselyte may also look forward to entry into the priests' caste. That statement will now be spelled out.]

G. "'Bread' refers to the show-bread.'

H. "'Clothing' refers to the garments of the priesthood.'

I. "So lo, we deal with the sanctuary.

J. "How do we know that the same sort of blessing applies in the provinces? 'Bread' speaks of the dough-offering [that is separated in the provinces], while 'clothing' refers to the first fleece [handed over to the priest]."

Here too, we may reasonably interpret the passage in a merely symbolic way: "bread" stands for Torah-learning, because just as bread sustains the body, so Torah-learning sustains the soul. That and similar interpretations offer plausible alternatives to the conception that Torah-learning now forms that scarce resource that defines value in the way in which land for Aristotle or Israelite-occupied land in the Land of Israel for the Mishnah forms the final arbiter in the identification of scarce resources.

LAND AS WEALTH

But there are passages that are quite explicit: land is wealth, or Torah is wealth, but not both; owning land is power and studying Torah permits (re)gaining power. To take the first of the two propositions in its most explicit formulation:

LEVITICUS RABBAH XXX:I.4

A. R. Yohanan was going up from Tiberias to Sepphoris. R. Hiyya bar Abba was supporting him. They came to a field. He said, "This field once belonged to us, but we sold it in order to acquire merit in the Torah."

B. They came to a vineyard, and he said, "This vineyard once belonged to us, but we sold it in order to acquire merit in the Torah."

C. They came to an olive grove, and he said, "This olive grove once belonged to us, but we sold it in order to acquire merit in the Torah."

D. R. Hiyya began to cry.

E. Said R. Yohanan, "Why are you crying?"

F. He said to him, "It is because you left nothing over to support you in your old age."

G. He said to him, "Hiyya, my disciple, is what we did such a light thing in your view? We sold something which was given in a spell of six days [of creation] and in exchange we acquired something which was given in a spell of forty days [of revelation].

H. "The entire world and everything in it was created in only six days, as it is written, 'For in six days the Lord made heaven and earth' [Exod. 20:11].

I. "But the Torah was given over a period of forty days, as it was said, 'And he was there with the Lord for forty days and forty nights' [Exod. 34:28].

J. "And it is written, 'And we remained on the mountain for forty days and forty nights'" (Deut. 9:9).

5. A. When R. Yohanan died, his generation recited concerning him [the following verse of Scripture]: "If a man should give all the wealth of his house for the love" (Song 8:7), with which R. Yohanan loved the Torah, "he would be utterly destitute" (Song 8:7) . . .

C. When R. Eleazar b. R. Simeon died, his generation recited concerning him [the following verse of Scripture]: "Who is this who comes up out of the wilderness like pillars of smoke, perfumed with myrrh and frankincense, with all the powders of the merchant?" (Song 3:6).

D. What is the meaning of the clause, "With all the powders of the merchant"?

E. [Like a merchant who carries all sorts of desired powders,] he was a master of Scripture, a repeater of Mishnah traditions, a writer of liturgical supplications, and a liturgical poet.

The sale of land for the acquisition of "merit in the Torah" introduces two principal systemic components, merit and Torah.[4] For our purpose, the importance of the statement lies in the second of the two, which deems land the counterpart—and clearly the opposite—of the Torah.

Now one can sell a field and acquire "Torah," meaning, in the context established by the exchange between Tarfon and Aqiba, the opportunity to gain leisure to (acquire the merit gained by) the study of the Torah. That the sage has left himself nothing for his support in old age makes explicit the material meaning of the statement, and the comparison of the value of land, created in six days, and the Torah, created in forty days, is equally explicit. The comparison of knowledge of Torah to the merchandise of the merchant simply repeats the same point, but in a lower register. So too does the this-worldly power of study of the Torah make explicit in another framework the conviction that study of the Torah yields material and concrete benefit, not just spiritual renewal. Thus R. Huna states, "All of the exiles will be gathered together only on account of the study of Mishnah-teachings."[5]

SUPPORTING TORAH-SAGES

Not only so, but the sage devoted to study of the Torah has to be supported because he can no longer perform physical work. Study of the Torah deprives him of physical strength, and that contrast and counterpart represented by land and working of the land as against Torah and the study of the Torah comes to symbolic expression in yet another way:

LEVITICUS RABBAH XI:XXII.1

A. R. Eleazar bar Simeon was appointed to impress men and beasts into forced labor [in the corvée]. One time Elijah, of blessed memory, appeared to him in the guise of an old man. Elijah said to him, "Get me a beast of burden."

B. Eleazar said to him, "What do you have as a cargo [to load on the beast]?"

C. He said to him, "This old skin-bottle of mine, my cloak, and me as rider."

D. He said, "Take a look at this old man! we [personally] can take him and carry him to the end of the world, and he says to us to get a beast ready!"

E. What did he do? He loaded him on his back and carried him up mountains and down valleys and over fields of thorns and fields of thistles.

F. In the end [Elijah] began to bear down on him. He said to him, "Old man, old man! Make yourself lighter, and if you don't, I'll toss you off."

G. [Elijah] said to him, "Now do you want to take a bit of a rest?"

H. He said to him, "Yes."

I. What did he do? [Elijah] took him to a field and set him down under a tree and gave him food and drink. When he had eaten and drunk, he [Elijah] said to him, "All this running about—what is in it for you? Would it not be better for you to take up the vocation of your fathers?"

J. He said to him, "And can you teach it to us?"

K. He said to him, "Yes."

L. And there are those who say that for thirteen years Elijah of blessed memory taught him until he could recite even Sifra [the exegesis of Leviticus, which is particularly difficult].

M. But once he could recite that document, [he had so lost his strength that] he could not lift up even a cloak.

2. A. The household of Rabban Gamaliel had a member who could carry forty *seahs* [of grain] to the baker [on his back].

B. He said to him, "All this vast power do you possess, and you do not devote yourself to the study of Sifra."

C. When he could recite that document, they say that even a single *seah* of grain he was unable to bear.

D. There are those who say that if someone else did not take it off him, he would not have been able to take it off himself.

These stories about how a mark of the sage is physical weakness are included only because they form part of the (in this instance, secondary) composition on Eleazar b. Simeon. But they do form part of a larger program of contrasting Torah study with landownership, intellectual prowess with physical power, the superiority of the one over the other. No wonder sages would in time claim that their power protected cities, which then needed neither police nor walls. These were concrete claims, affecting the rational utilization of scarce resources as much as the use and distribution of land constituted an expression of a rationality concerning scarce resources, their preservation and increase.

In alleging that the pertinent verses of Proverbs were assigned a quite this-worldly and material sense, so that study of the Torah really was worth more than silver, we say no more than the successor compilations allege in so many words. Thus we find the following, which faces head-on the fact that masters of the Torah are paid for studying the Torah, so confirming the claim that the Torah now served as a spade with which to dig:

PESIQTA DERAB KAHANA XXVII:I

1. A. R. Abba bar Kahana commenced [discourse by citing the following verse]: *Take my instruction instead of silver, and knowledge rather than choice gold (Prov. 8:10)."*

   B. Said R. Abba bar Kahana, *"Take the instruction of the Torah instead of silver.*

   C. "Take the instruction of the Torah and not silver.

   D. *"Why do you weigh out money? [Because there is no bread]* (Isa. 55:2).

   E. "'Why do you weigh out money to the sons of Esau [Rome]? [It is because] *there is no bread,* because you did not sate yourselves with the bread of the Torah.

   F. *"And [why] do you labor? Because there is no satisfaction* (Isa. 55:2).

   G. *"Why do you labor* while the nations of the world enjoy plenty? *Because there is no satisfaction,* that is, because you have not sated yourselves with the bread of the Torah and with the wine of the Torah.

   H. "For it is written, *Come, eat of my bread, and drink of the wine we have mixed* (Prov. 9:5)."

2. A. R. Berekhiah and R. Hiyya, his father, in the name of R. Yosé b. Nehorai: "It is written, *we shall punish all who oppress him* (Jer. 30:20), even those who collect funds for charity [and in doing so, treat people badly], except [for those who collect] the wages to be paid to teachers of Scripture and repeaters of Mishnah traditions.

B. "For they receive [as a salary] only compensation for the loss of their time, [which they devote to teaching and learning rather than to earning a living].

C. "But as to the wages [for carrying out] a single matter in the Torah, no creature can pay the [appropriate] fee in reward."

The obvious goal, the homily at 1.E, surely stands against my claim that we deal with allegations of concrete and material value: the imputation to the learning of the Torah of the status of "scarce resources." But, as a matter of fact, the whole of No. 2 makes the contrary position explicit: wages are paid to Torah-teachers. The following makes the same point:

Y. Nedarim 4:3.II

A. It is written, "Behold, we have taught you statutes and ordinances" [Deut. 4:5].

B. Just as we do so without pay, so you must do so without pay.

C. Is it possible that the same rule applies to teaching Scripture and translation [cf. M. Ned. 4:3D]?

D. Scripture says "statutes and ordinances."

E. Statutes and ordinances must you teach without pay, but you need not teach Scripture and translation without pay.

F. And yet we see that those who teach Mishnah collect their pay.

G. Said R. Judah b. R. Ishmael, "It is a fee for the use of their time [which they cannot utilize to earn a living for themselves] which they collect."

True, this transformation of Torah study into something of real worth is rationalized as salary in compensation for loss of time. But the same rationalization clearly did not impress the many masters of the initial system who insisted that one must practice a craft in order to make a living and study the Torah only in one's leisure time. We see the contrast in the two positions quite explicitly in what follows. The contrast between the received position and that before us is found at the following:

Y. PEAH 1:1.VII (Brooks)

D. It is forbidden to a person to teach his son a trade, in as much as it is written, "And you shall meditate therein day and night" (Joshua 1:8.)

E. But has not R. Ishmael taught, "You shall choose life" (Deut. 30:19)—this refers to learning [Torah] and practicing a trade as well. [One studies the Torah and also a trade.]

There is no harmonizing the two views by appeal to the rationalization before us. In fact, study of the Torah substituted for practicing a craft, and it was meant to do so, as A alleges explicitly. In all, therefore, the case in favor of the proposition that Torah has now become a material good, and, further, that Torah has now been transformed into the ultimate scarce resource—explicitly substituting for real estate, even in the Land of Israel—is firmly established.

That ultimate value—Torah study—surely bears comparison with other foci of value, such as prayer, using money for building synagogues, and the like. It is explicitly stated that spending money on synagogues is a waste of money, while spending money supporting Torah-masters is the right use of scarce resources. Further, we find the claim, synagogues and schoolhouses—communal real estate—in fact form the property of sages and their disciples, who may dispose of them just as they want, as any owner may dispose of his property according to his unfettered will. In Y. Sheqalim we find the former allegation, Y. Megillah the latter:

Y. SHEQALIM 5:4.II

A. R. Hama bar Haninah and R. Hoshaia the Elder were strolling in the synagogues in Lud. Said R. Hama bar Haninah to R. Hoshaia, "How much money did my forefathers invest here [in building these synagogues]!"

B. He said to him, "How many lives did your forefathers invest here! Were there not people who were laboring in Torah [who needed the money more]?"

C. R. Abun made the gates of the great hall [of study]. R. Mana came to him. He said to him, "See what we have made!"

D. He said to him, "'For Israel has forgotten his Maker and built palaces'! (Hos. 8:14). Were there no people laboring in Torah [who needed the money more]?"

Y. Sotah 9:13.VI

C. A certain rabbi would teach Scripture to his brother in Tyre, and when they came and called him to do business, he would say, "I am not going to take away from my fixed time to study. If the profit is going to come to us, let it come in due course [after my fixed time for study has ended]."

Y. Megillah 3:3:V

A. R. Joshua b. Levi said, "Synagogues and schoolhouses belong to sages and their disciples."

B. R. Hiyya bar Yosé received [guests] in the synagogue [and lodged them there].

C. R. Immi instructed the scribes, "If someone comes to you with some slight contact with Torah-learning, receive him, his asses, and his belongings."

D. R. Berekhiah went to the synagogue in Beisan. He saw someone rinsing his hands and feet in a fountain [in the courtyard of the synagogue]. He said to him, "It is forbidden to you [to do this]."

E. The next day the man saw [Berekhiah] washing his hands and feet in the fountain.

F. He said to him, "Rabbi, is it permitted to you and forbidden to us?"

G. He said to him, "Yes."

H. He said to him, "Why?"

I. He said to him, "Because this is what R. Joshua b. Levi said: 'Synagogues and schoolhouses belong to sages and their disciples.'"

Not all acts of piety, we see, are equal, and the one that takes precedence over all others (just as was alleged at Mishnah-tractate Peah 1:1) is study of the Torah. But the point now is a much more concrete one, and that is, through study of the Torah, sages and their disciples gain possession, as a matter of fact, over communal real estate, which they may utilize in any way they wish; and that is a quite concrete claim indeed, as the same story alleges.

SAGES AS GUARDIANS OF THE COMMONWEALTH

No wonder, then, that people in general are expected to contribute their scarce resources for the support of sages and their disciples. Moreover, society at large was obligated to support sages, and the sages' claim upon others was enforceable by Heaven. Those who gave sages' disciples money so that they would not have to work would get it back from Heaven, and those who did not would lose what they had:

Y. SOTAH 7:4.IV

F. R. Aha in the name of R. Tanhum b. R. Hiyya: "If one has learned, taught, kept, and carried out [the Torah], and has ample means in his possession to strengthen the Torah and has not done so, lo, such a one still is in the category of those who are cursed." [The meaning of "strengthen" here is to support the masters of the Torah.]

G. R. Jeremiah in the name of R. Hiyya bar Ba, "[If] one did not learn, teach, keep, and carry out [the teachings of the Torah], and did not have ample means to strengthen [the masters of the Torah] [but nonetheless did strengthen them], lo, such a one falls into the category of those who are blessed."

H. And R. Hannah, R. Jeremiah in the name of R. Hiyya: "The Holy One, blessed be he, is going to prepare a protection for those who carry out religious duties [of support for masters of Torah] through the protection afforded to the masters of Torah [themselves].

I. "What is the Scriptural basis for that statement? 'For the protection of wisdom is like the protection of money'" (Qoh. 7:12).

J. "And it says, '[The Torah] is a tree of life to those who grasp it; those who hold it fast are called happy'" (Prov. 3:18).

Such contributions form the counterpart to taxes, that is, scarce resources taken away from the owner by force for the purposes of the public good, that is, the ultimate meeting point of economics and politics, the explicit formation of distributive, as against market, economics. Then what is distributed and to whom and by what force forms the centerpiece of the systemic political economy, and the answer is perfectly simple: all sorts of valued things are taken away from people and handed over for the support of sages:

Pesiqta deRab Kahana V:IV.2

A. "A man's gift makes room for him and brings him before great men" (Prov. 18:16).

B. M'SH B: R. Eliezer, R. Joshua, and R. Aqiba went to the harborside of Antioch to collect funds for the support of sages.

C. [In Aramaic:] A certain Abba Yudan lived there.

D. He would carry out his religious duty [of philanthropy] in a liberal spirit, but had lost his money. When he saw our masters, he went home with a sad face. His wife said to him, "What's wrong with you, that you look so sad?"

E. He repeated the tale to her: "Our masters are here, and we don't know what we shall be able to do for them."

F. His wife, who was a truly philanthropic woman—what did she say to him? "You only have one field left. Go, sell half of it and give them the proceeds."

G. He went and did just that. When he was giving them the money, they said to him, "May the Omnipresent make up all your losses."

H. Our masters went their way.

I. He went out to plough. While he was ploughing the half of the field that he had left, the Holy One, blessed be he, opened his eyes. The earth broke open before him, and his cow fell in and broke her leg. He went down to raise her up, and found a treasure beneath her. He said, "It was for my gain that my cow broke her leg."

J. When our masters came back, [in Aramaic:] they asked about a certain Abba Yudan and how he was doing. They said, "Who can gaze on the face of Abba Yudan [which glows with prosperity]—Abba Yudan, the owner of flocks of goats, Abba Yudan, the owner of herds of asses, Abba Yudan, the owner of herds of camels."

K. He came to them and said to them, "Your prayer in my favor has produced returns and returns on the returns."

L. They said to him, "Even though someone else gave more than you did, we wrote your name at the head of the list."

M. Then they took him and sat him next to themselves and recited in his regard the following verse of Scripture: "A man's gift makes room for him and brings him before great men" (Prov. 18:16).

Now what is at stake in the scarce resource represented by Torah study? It cannot be a (merely) spiritual benefit, when, in consequence of giving money to sages so that they will not have to work, we get rich. Not only so, but the matter of position is equally in play: We get rich and we also enjoy the standing of sages, sitting next to them. So far as social position intersects with wealth, we find in the Torah that wealth that, in this systemic context, serves to tells us what we mean by scarce resources: source of this-worldly gain in practical terms, source of public prestige in social terms, validation of the use of force—in context, psychological force—for taking away scarce (material) resources in favor of a superior value. The entire system comes to expression in this story: its economics, its politics and, as a matter of fact, its philosophy. But all three are quite different from what they were in the initial structure and system.

No wonder then that sages protect cities. So it is claimed that sages are the guardians of cities, and later on that would yield the further allegation that sages do not have to pay taxes to build walls around cities, since their Torah study protects the cities:

Pesiqta deRab Kahana XV:V.1

A. R. Abba bar Kahana commenced discourse by citing the following verse: *"Who is the man so wise that he may understand this? To whom has the mouth of the Lord spoken, that he may declare it? Why is the land ruined and laid waste like a wilderness, [so that no one passes through? The Lord said, It is because they forsook my*

Torah *which we set before them; they neither obeyed me nor conformed
to it. They followed the promptings of their own stubborn hearts; they
followed the Baalim as their forefathers had taught them. Therefore
these are the words of the Lord of Hosts the God of Israel: we will feed
this people with wormwood and give them bitter poison to drink. We
will scatter them among nations whom neither they nor their forefathers have known; we will harry them with the sword until we have
made an end of them]* (Jer. 9:16)."

B. It was taught in the name of R. Simeon b. Yohai, "If you see
towns uprooted from their place in the Land of Israel, know
that [it is because] the people did not pay the salaries of teachers of children and Mishnah-instructors.

C. "What is the verse of Scripture that indicates it? *Why is the
land ruined and laid waste like a wilderness, [so that no one passes
through?]* What is written just following? *It is because they forsook my Torah [which we set before them; they neither obeyed me nor
conformed to it.]*

2. A. Rabbi Judah the Patriarch sent R. Yosé and R. Ammi to go and
survey the towns of the Land of Israel. They would go into a
town and say to the people, "Bring me the guardians of the
town."

B. The people would bring out the head of the police and the
local guard.

C. [The sages] would say, "These are not the guardians of the
town, they are those who destroy the town. Who are the
guardians of the town? They are the teachers of children and
Mishnah-teachers, who keep watch by day and by night, in
line with the verse, *And you shall meditate in it day and night*
(Josh. 1:8)."

D. And so Scripture says, *If the Lord does not build the house, in vain
the builders labor* (Ps. 127:1).

7. A. Said R. Abba bar Kahana, "No philosophers in the world ever
arose of the quality of Balaam ben Beor and Abdymos of
Gadara. The nations of the world came to Abdymos of Gadara.
They said to him, 'Do you maintain that we can make war
against this nation?'

B. "He said to them, 'Go and make the rounds of their synagogues and their study houses. So long as there are there chil-

dren chirping out loud in their voices [and studying the Torah],
then you cannot overcome them. If not, then you can con-
quer them, for so did their father promise them: *The voice is
Jacob's voice* (Gen. 27:22), meaning that when Jacob's voice
chirps in synagogues and study houses, *The hands are* not *the
hands of Esau* [so Esau has no power].

C. "'So long as there are no children chirping out loud in their
voices [and studying the Torah] in synagogues and study
houses, *The hands are the hands of Esau* [so Esau has power].'"

The reference to Esau—that is, Rome—of course links the whole
to the contemporary context and alleges that if the Israelites will
support those who study the Torah and teach it, then their cities
will be safe, and, still more, the rule of Esau/Rome will come to an
end; then the Messiah will come, so the stakes are not trivial.

3

TELEOLOGY AND THE PERSONALITY OF THE SAGE

WHERE RABBINIC JUDAISM CHANGED

The one important, explicit, and articulated statement of the teleology of Rabbinic Judaism makes its appearance in stories about sages, and, in particular, in those stories that accord personality to the undifferentiated names that occur in the earlier documents. What we shall see is that it is when the sage acquires a personality, in the post-Constantinian writings, that the sage also makes statements about the purpose of life, the meaning of death, and the study of the Torah. To understand how striking a phenomenon is represented by the individuation of sages, we have first of all to compare the Rabbinic Judaic with the Christian interest in biography and then follow the documents as they unfold, with the later ones assigning personalities to names mentioned in the earlier ones.

But in the documents that took shape later on, the Rabbinic authors and compilers produced stories about individual sages; most of them appear in the post-Constantinian compilations. While the Mishnah rarely tells stories about sages and, when it does, uses those stories in the setting of legal precedents, the post-Constantinian compilations contain large quantities of stories about sages told for other-than-legal purposes. The received forms of biographical sayings and stories are attested in various compilations, but, best of all, the Bavli's pages. They were made up of compositions—completed units of thought—and composites as well. Twin biographical principles define the poles around which they coalesce: either as strings of stories about great sages of the past or as collections of sayings and comments drawn together solely because the same name stands behind all the collected sayings.

Restricting our attention to the Bavli alone suffices for the present purpose. There, we note, that document as a whole lays itself out as a commentary to the Mishnah. So the framers wished us to think that whatever they wanted to tell us would take the form of Mishnah commentary. But a second glance indicates that the Bavli is made up of enormous composites, themselves closed prior to inclusion in the Bavli. Some of these composites—around 35 to 40 percent of those that comprise important tractates of the Bavli—were selected and arranged along lines dictated by a logic other than that deriving from the requirements of Mishnah commentary. Accordingly, the decision that the framers of the Bavli reached was to adopt the two redactional principles inherited from the antecedent century or so and to reject the one already rejected by their predecessors, even while honoring it. They organized the Bavli around the Mishnah.

But they adapted and included vast tracts of antecedent materials organized as scriptural commentary. These they inserted whole and complete, not at all in response to the Mishnah's program. And, finally, while making provision for small-scale compositions built on biographical principles, preserving both strings of sayings from a given master (and often a given tradent of a given master) as well as tales about authorities of the preceding half-millennium, they never created redactional compositions, of a sizable order, that focused upon given authorities. But sufficient materials certainly lay at hand to allow doing so. In the three decisions, two of what to do and one of what not to do, the final compositors of the Bavli indicated what they proposed to accomplish: to give final form and fixed expression through their categories of the organization of all knowledge, to the Torah as it had been known, sifted, searched, approved, and handed down, even from the remote past to their own day.

COMPOSITIONS AND COMPOSITES FOCUSED ON INDIVIDUAL SAGES

In the discourse that focuses on the sage—e.g., a paragraph of thought, a story—things that a given authority said are strung together or tales about a given authority are told at some length. Whoever composed and preserved units of discourse on the Mishnah and on Scripture ultimately preserved in the two Talmuds did the same for the sage. What that fact means is simple. In the circles responsible for making up and writing down completed units of discourse, three distinct categories of interest defined the task: (1) exegesis of the Mishnah, (2) exegesis of Scripture, and (3) preservation and exegesis, in exactly the same reverential spirit, of the words and deeds of sages. Not only so, but the kind of analysis to which Mishnah and Scripture exegesis were subjected also applied to the exegesis of sage-stories.

That fact may be shown in three ways. First, just as Scripture supplied proof-texts, so deeds or statements of sages provided proof-texts. Second, just as a verse of Scripture or an explicit statement of the Mishnah resolved a disputed point, so what a sage said or did might be introduced into discourse as ample proof for settling a dispute. And third, it follows that just as Scripture or the Mishnah laid down Torah, so what a sage did or said laid down Torah. In the dimensions of the applied and practical reason by which the law unfolded, the sage found a comfortable place in precisely the taxonomic categories defined, to begin with, by both the Mishnah and Scripture.

Let us examine a few substantial examples of the sorts of sustained discourse in biographical materials turned out by circles of sages. What we shall see is an important fact. Just as these circles composed units of discourse about the meaning of a Mishnah passage, a larger theoretical problem of law, the sense of scriptural verse, and the sayings and doings of scriptural heroes seen as sages, so they did the same for living sages themselves.

In the simplest example we see that two discrete sayings of a sage are joined together. The principle of conglomeration, therefore, is solely the name of the sage at hand. One saying has to do with overcoming the impulse to do evil, and the other has to do with the classifications of sages' program of learning. What the two subjects have in common is slight. But to the framer of the passage, that fact meant nothing. For he thought that compositions joined by the same tradent and authority—the rabbis, Levi and Simeon—should be made up.

B. Berakhot 4b.XXIII

    A. Said R. Levi bar Hama said R. Simeon b. Laqish, "A person should always provoke his impulse to do good against his impulse to do evil,

    B. "as it is said, 'Provoke and do not sin' (Ps. 4:5).

    C. "If [the good impulse] wins, well and good. If not, let him take up Torah study,

    D. "as it is said, 'Commune with your own heart' (Ps. 4:5).

    E. "If [the good impulse] wins, well and good. If not, let him recite the Shema,

    F. "as it is said, 'upon your bed' (Ps. 4:5).

    G. "If [the good impulse] wins, well and good. If not, let him remember the day of death,

    H. "as it is said, 'And keep silent. Sela' (Ps. 4:5)."

    I. And R. Levi bar Hama said R. Simeon b. Laqish said, "What is the meaning of the verse of Scripture, 'And I will give you the tables of stone, the law and the commandment, which I have written, that you may teach them' (Exod. 24:12).

    J. "'The tables' [here] refers to the Ten Commandments.

    K. "'Torah' refers to Scripture.

    L. "'Commandment' refers to Mishnah.

    M. "'Which I have written' refers to the Prophets and the Writings.

    N. "'That you may teach them' refers to the Gemara.

    O. "This teaches that all of them were given to Moses from Sinai."

The frame of the story at hand links A–H and I–O in a way unfamiliar to those accustomed to the principles of conglomeration in legal and biblical-exegetical compositions. In the former, a given problem or principle of law will tell us why one item is joined to some other. In the latter, a single verse of Scripture will account for the joining of two or more otherwise discrete units of thought. Here one passage, A–H, takes up Psalm 4:5; the other, I–O, Exodus 24:12. The point of the one statement hardly goes over the ground of the other. So the *sole* principle by which one item has joined the other is biographical: a record of what a sage said about topics that are, at best, contiguous, if related at all.

A second way of stringing together materials illustrative of the lives and teachings of sages is to join incidents involving a given authority or (as in the following case) two authorities believed to have stood in close relationship with one another—disciple and master, for instance. Often these stories go over the same ground in the same way. In the following, the two farewell stories make essentially the same point but in quite different language. What joins the stories is not only the shared theme but the fact that Eliezer is supposed to have studied with Yohanan b. Zakkai.

B. SANHEDRIN 68A.II

A. Our rabbis have taught on Tannaite authority:

B. When R. Eliezer fell ill, his disciples came in to pay a call on him. They said to him, "Our master, teach us the ways of life, so that through them we may merit the world to come."

C. He said to them, "Be attentive to the honor owing to your fellows, keep your children from excessive reflection, and set them among the knees of disciples of sages, and when you pray, know before whom you stand, and on that account you will merit the life of the world to come."

D. And when R. Yohanan b. Zakkai fell ill, his disciples came in to pay a call on him. When he saw them, he began to cry. His disciples said to him, "Light of Israel! Pillar at the right hand! Mighty hammer! On what account are you crying?"

E. He said to them, "If I were going to be brought before a mortal king, who is here today and tomorrow gone to the grave, who, should he be angry with me, will not be angry forever, and, if he should imprison me, will not imprison me forever, and if he should put me to death, whose sentence of death is not for eternity, and whom I can appease with the right words or bribe with money, even so, I should weep.

F. "But now that I am being brought before the King of kings of kings, the Holy One, blessed be he, who endures forever and ever, who, should he be angry with me, will be angry forever, and if he should imprison me, will imprison me forever, and if he should put me to death, whose sentence of death is for eternity, and whom I cannot appease with the right words or bribe with money,

G. "and not only so, but before me are two paths, one to the Garden of Eden and the other to Gehenna, and I do not know by which path I shall be brought,

H. "and should I not weep?"

I. They said to him, "Our master, bless us."

J. He said to them, "May it be God's will that the fear of Heaven be upon you as much as the fear of mortal man."

K. His disciples said, "Just so much?"

L. He said to them, "Would that it were that much. You should know that, when a person commits a transgression, he says, 'I hope no man sees me.'"

M. When he was dying, he said to them, "Clear out utensils from the house, because of the uncleanness [of the corpse, which I am about to impart when I die], and prepare a throne for Hezekiah king of Judah, who is coming."

The links between B–C and D–M are clear. First, we have stories about sages' farewells. Second, people took for granted, because of the lists of M. Abot 2:2 ff., that Eliezer was a disciple of Yohanan b. Zakkai. Otherwise, it is difficult to explain the joining of the stories, since they scarcely make the same point, go over the same matters, or even share a common literary or rhetorical form or preference. But a framer of a composition of lives of saints, who is writing a tractate on how saints die, will have found this passage a powerful one indeed.

Yet another approach to the utilization of tales about sages was to join together stories on a given theme but told about different sages. A tractate or a chapter of a tractate on a given theme—for example, suffering and its reward—can have emerged from the sort of collection that follows. The importance of the next item is that the same kinds of stories about different sages are strung together to make a single point.

B. Berakhot 5B.XXXI

A. R. Hiyya bar Abba became ill. R. Yohanan came to him. He said to him, "Are these sufferings precious to you?"

B. He said to him, "I don't want them, I don't want their reward."

C. He said to him, "Give me your hand."

D. He gave him his hand, and [Yohanan] raised him up [out of his sickness].

E. R. Yohanan became ill. R. Hanina came to him. He said to him, "Are these sufferings precious to you?"

F. He said to him, "I don't want them. I don't want their reward."

G. He said to him, "Give me your hand."

H. He gave him his hand and [Hanina] raised him up [out of his sickness].

I. Why so? R. Yohanan should have raised himself up?

J. They say, "A prisoner cannot get himself out of jail."

B. Berakhot 5B.XXXII

A. R. Eliezer became ill. R. Yohanan came to see him and found him lying in a dark room. [The dying man] uncovered his arm, and light fell [through the room]. [Yohanan] saw that R. Eliezer was weeping. He said to him, "Why are you crying? Is it because of the Torah that you did not learn sufficiently? We have learned: 'All the same are the ones who do much and do little, so long as each person will do it for the sake of Heaven.'

B. "Is it because of insufficient income? Not everyone has the merit of seeing two tables [Torah and riches, as you have. You have been a master of Torah and also have enjoyed wealth].

C. "Is it because of children? Here is the bone of my tenth son [whom I buried, so it was no great loss not to have children, since you might have had to bury them]."

D. He said to him, "I am crying because of this beauty of mine which will be rotting in the ground."

E. He said to him, "For that it certainly is worth crying," and the two of them wept together.

F. He said to him, "Are these sufferings precious to you?"

G. He said to him, "I don't want them, I don't want their reward."

H. He said to him, "Give me your hand."

I. He gave him his hand, and [Yohanan] raised him up [out of his sickness].

B. BERAKHOT 5B.XXXIII

A. Four hundred barrels of wine turned sour on R. Huna. R. Judah, brother of R. Sala the Pious, and rabbis came to see him (and some say it was R. Ada bar Ahba and rabbis). They said to him, "The master should take a good look at his deeds."

B. He said to them, "And am I suspect in your eyes?"

C. They said to him, "And is the Holy One, blessed be he, suspect of inflicting a penalty without justice?"

D. He said to them, "Has anybody heard anything bad about me? Let him say it."

E. They said to him, "This is what we have heard: the master does not give to his hired hand [the latter's share of] vine twigs [which are his right]."

F. He said to them, "Does he leave me any! He steals all of them to begin with."

G. They said to him, "This is in line with what people say: 'Go steal from a thief but taste theft too!' [Simon: If you steal from a thief, you also have a taste of it.]"

H. He said to them, "I pledge that I'll give them to him."

I. Some say that the vinegar turned back into wine, and some say that the price of vinegar went up so he sold it off at the price of wine.

The foregoing composite makes the same point several times: "Not them, not their reward." Sufferings are precious, but sages are prepared to forgo the benefits. The formally climactic entry at XXXIII makes the point that, if bad things happen, the victim has deserved punishment. In joining these several stories about sages—two involving Yohanan, the third entirely separate—the compositor of the passage made his point by juxtaposing two like biographical snippets to a distinct one. Collections of stories about saints can have served quite naturally when formed into tractates on pious virtues, expressing these virtues through strong and pictorial language such as is before us.

The foregoing sources have shown two important facts. First, a principle of composition in the sages' circles was derived from interest in the teachings associated with a given sage, as well as in tales and stories told about a sage or groups of sages. The first of the passages shows us the simplest composition of sayings, the latter, an equivalent conglomeration of related stories. Up to this point, therefore, the reader will readily concede that biographical materials on sages, as much as Mishnah exegesis and Scripture exegesis, came forth out of circles of sages. But I have yet to show that such materials attained sufficient volume and cogency from large-scale compilations—conglomerates so substantial as to sustain entire books.

COLLECTIONS OF SAYINGS ASSIGNED TO INDIVIDUAL SAGES

Had the framers of large-scale Rabbinic compositions wished, they could readily have made up tractates devoted to diverse sayings of a given authority (or, tradent-and-authority). What follows to demonstrate the possibility are two enormous compositions, which together can have made up as much as half of a Talmud chapter in volume. If anyone had wanted to compose a chapter around Rabbinical authorities' names, he is thus shown to have had the opportunity.

The first shows us a string of sayings not only in a single set of names but also on discrete subjects. We also see how such a string of sayings could form the focus of exactly the kind of critical analysis and secondary amplification to which any other Talmudic passage would be subjected. So there can have been not only a Talmud based on the Mishnah and a Midrash-compilation, comprising compositions based on the Scripture, but also a life of a saint (a holy life?) based on a set of rabbis' sayings. Here is the Talmud that can have served a collection of sayings of Yohanan-in-the-name-of-Simeon b. Yohai.

B. BERAKHOT 7B–8A.LIX

A. [7B] Said R. Yohanan in the name of R. Simeon b. Yohai, "From the day on which the Holy One, blessed be he, created the world, there was no man who called the Holy One, blessed be he, 'Lord,' until Abraham came along and called him Lord.

B. "For it is said, 'And he said, O Lord, God, whereby shall I know that I shall inherit it' (Gen. 15:8)."

C. Said Rab, "Daniel too was answered only on account of Abraham.

D. "For it is said, 'Now therefore, O our God, hearken to the prayer of your servant and to his supplications and cause your face to shine upon your sanctuary that is desolate, for the Lord's sake' (Dan. 9:17).

E. "'For your sake' is what he should have said, but the sense is, 'For the sake of Abraham, who called you Lord.'"

B. BERAKHOT 7B–8A.LX

A. And R. Yohanan said in the name of R. Simeon b. Yohai, "How do we know that people should not seek to appease someone when he is mad?

B. "As it is said, 'My face will go and then I will give you rest' (Exod. 33:14)."

B. BERAKHOT 7B–8A.LXI

A. And R. Yohanan said in the name of R. Simeon b. Yohai, "From the day on which the Holy One, blessed be he, created his world, there was no one who praised the Holy One, blessed be he, until Leah came along and praised him.

B. "For it is said, 'This time I will praise the Lord' (Gen. 29:35)."

C. As to Reuben, said R. Eleazar, "Leah said, 'See what is the difference [the name of Reuben yielding *reu* ("see") and *ben* ("between")] between my son and the son of my father-in-law.

D. "The son of my father-in-law, even knowingly, sold off his birthright, for it is written, 'And he sold his birthright to Jacob' (Gen. 25:33).

E. "See what is written concerning him: 'And Esau hated Jacob' (Gen. 27:41), and it is written, 'And he said, is he not rightly named Jacob? for he has supplanted me these two times' (Gen. 27:36).

F. "My son, by contrast, even though Joseph forcibly took away his birthright, as it is written, 'But for as much as he defiled his father's couch, his birthright was given to the sons of Joseph' (1 Chron. 5:1), did not become jealous of him, for it is written, 'And Reuben heard it and delivered him out of their hand' (Gen. 37:21)."

G. As to the meaning of the name of Ruth, said R. Yohanan, "It was because she had the merit that David would come forth from her, who saturated (RWH) the Holy One, blessed be he, with songs and praises."

H. How do we know that a person's name affects [his life]?

I. Said R. Eleazar, "It is in line with the verse of Scripture: 'Come, behold the works of the Lord, who has made desolations in the earth' (Ps. 46:9).

J. "Do not read 'desolations' but 'names' [which the same root-letters yield]." [The Hebrew letters that bear the vowels to indicate the sound for "desolations" may be given different vowels, which yield the sound for "names."]

B. BERAKHOT 7B–8A.LXII

A. And R. Yohanan said in the name of R. Simeon b. Yohai, "Bringing a child up badly is worse in a person's house than the war of Gog and Magog.

B. "For it is said, 'A Psalm of David, when he fled from Absalom, his son' (Ps. 3:1), after which it is written, 'Lord how many are my adversaries become, many are they that rise up against me' (Ps. 3:2).

C. "By contrast, in regard to the war of Gog and Magog it is written, 'Why are the nations in an uproar? And why do the peoples mutter in vain?' (Ps. 2:1).

D. "But it is not written in that connection, 'How many are my adversaries become.'"

E. "A Psalm of David, when he fled from Absalom, his son (Ps. 3:1):

F. "'A Psalm of David'? It should be, 'A lamentation of David'!

G. Said R. Simeon b. Abishalom, "The matter may be compared to the case of a man against whom an outstanding bond was issued. Before he had paid it, he was sad. After he had paid it, he was glad.

H. "So too with David, when the Holy One had said to him, 'Behold, I will raise up evil against you out of your own house,' (2 Sam. 2:11), he was sad.

I. "He thought to himself, 'Perhaps it will be a slave or a bastard child, who will not have pity on me.'

J. "When he saw that it was Absalom, he was happy. On that account, he said a psalm."

B. BERAKHOT 7B–8A.LXIII

A. And R. Yohanan said in the name of R. Simeon b. Yohai, "It is permitted to contend with the wicked in this world,

B. "for it is said, 'Those who forsake the Torah praise the wicked, but those who keep the Torah contend with them' (Prov. 28:4)."

C. It has been taught on Tannaite authority along these same lines:

D. R. Dosetai bar Matun says, "It is permitted to contend with the wicked in this world, for it is said, 'Those who forsake the Torah praise the wicked, but those who keep the Torah contend with them' (Prov. 28:4)."

E. And if someone should whisper to you, "But is it not written, 'Do not contend with evildoers, nor be envious against those who work unrighteousness' (Ps. 37:1)," say to him, "Someone whose conscience bothers him thinks so.

F. "In fact, 'Do not contend with evildoers' means, do not be like them, 'nor be envious against those who work unrighteousness,' means, do not be like them.

G. "And so it is said, 'Let your heart not envy sinners, but fear the Lord all day' (Prov. 23:17)."

H. Is this the case? And lo, R. Isaac has said, "If you see a wicked person for whom the hour seems to shine, do not contend with him, for it is said, 'His ways prosper at all times' (Ps. 10:5).

I. "Not only so, but he wins in court, as it is said, 'Your judgments are far above, out of his sight' (Ps. 10:5).

J. "Not only so, but he overcomes his enemies, for it is said, 'As for all his enemies, he snorts at them' (Ps. 10:5)."

K. There is no contradiction. The one [Isaac] addresses one's own private matters [in which case one should not contend with the wicked], but the other speaks of matters having to do with Heaven [in which case one should contend with them].

L. And if you wish, I shall propose that both parties speak of matters having to do with heaven. There is, nonetheless, no contradiction. The one [Isaac] speaks of a wicked person on whom the hour shines, the other of a wicked person on whom the hour does not shine.

M. And if you wish, I shall propose that both parties speak of a wicked person on whom the hour shines, and there still is no contradiction.

N. The one [Yohanan, who says the righteous may contend with the wicked] speaks of a completely righteous person, the other [Isaac] speaks of someone who is not completely righteous.

O. For R. Huna said, "What is the meaning of this verse of Scripture: 'Why do you look, when they deal treacherously, and hold your peace, when the wicked swallows up the man that is more righteous than he' (Hab. 1:13)?

P. "Now can a wicked person swallow up a righteous one?

Q. "And lo, it is written, 'The Lord will not leave him in his hand' (Ps. 37:33). And it is further written, 'No mischief shall befall the righteous' (Prov. 12:21).

R. "The fact therefore is that he may swallow up someone who is more righteous than he, but he cannot swallow up a completely righteous man."

S. And if you wish, I shall propose that, when the hour shines for him, the situation is different.

B. BERAKHOT 7B–8A.LXIV

A. And R. Yohanan said in the name of R. Simeon b. Yohai, "Beneath anyone who establishes a regular place for praying do that person's enemies fall.

B. "For it is said, 'And I will appoint a place for my people Israel, and I will plant them, that they may dwell in their own place and be disquieted no more, neither shall the children of wickedness afflict them any more as at the first' (2 Sam. 7:10)."

C. R. Huna pointed to a contradiction between two verses of Scripture: "It is written, 'To afflict them,' and elsewhere, 'To exterminate them' (1 Chron. 17:9).

D. "To begin with, merely to afflict them, but, at the end, to exterminate them."

B. BERAKHOT 7B–8A.LXV

A. And R. Yohanan said in the name of R. Simeon b. Yohai, "Greater is personal service to Torah than learning in Torah [so doing favors for a sage is of greater value than studying with him].

B. "For it is said, 'Here is Elisha, the son of Shaphat, who poured water on the hands of Elijah' (2 Kings 3:11).

C. "It is not said, 'who learned' but 'who poured water.'

D. "This teaches that greater is service to Torah than learning in Torah."

It is not difficult to pick up the main beams of the foregoing construction, since they are signified by Yohanan-Simeon sayings, LIX.A, LX.A, LXI.A, LXII.A, LXIII.A, LXIV.A, LXV.A—seven entries in line. The common theme is not prayer; no other topic is treated in a cogent way either. The sort of inner coherence to which any student of the Bavli is accustomed does not pass before us. Rather we have a collection of wise thoughts on diverse topics, more in the manner of Proverbs than in the style of the great intellects behind the sustained reasoning in passages of the Bavli and much of the Yerushalmi as well. What is interesting is that, at a later stage, other pertinent materials have been inserted, for example, Rab's at LIX.C–E, and so on down. There is no reason to imagine that these sayings were made up in response to Yohanan-Simeon's statement. Quite to the contrary, framed in their own terms, the sayings were presumably tacked on at a point at which the large-scale construction of Yohanan-Simeon was worked over for a purpose beyond the one intended by the original compositor. For what he wanted to do he did, which is compose a collection of Yohanan-Simeon sayings. If he hoped that his original collection would form part of a larger composition on Yohanan, he surely was disappointed. But even if he imagined that he would make up material for compositions of lives and sayings of saints, he cannot have expected his little collection to end up where and how it did, as part of a quite different corpus of writing from one in which a given authority had his say or in which stories were told in some sort of sensible sequence about a particular sage. The type of large-scale composition, for which our imagined compositor did his work, in the end never came into being in the Rabbinic canon.

In the following, still longer example I begin with the passage to which the entire composition, organized in the name of a tradent and a sage, is attached. At B. Berakhot 6B/1:1 XLI, we have a statement that a synagogue should have a regular quorum. Then the next passage, 1:1 XLII, makes the secondary point that a person should pray in a regular place—a reasonable amplification of the foregoing. That is, just as there should be a quorum routinely organized in a given location, so should an individual routinely attach himself to a given quorum. This statement is given by Helbo in Huna's name. What follows is a sizable set of sayings by Helbo in Huna's name, all of them on the general theme of prayer but none of them on the specific point at hand. Still more interesting, just as in the foregoing, the passage as a whole was composed so that the Helbo-Huna materials themselves are expanded and enriched with secondary accretions. For instance, at XLIII the base materials are given glosses of a variety of types. All in all, we see what we may call a little tractate in the making. But, as we shall hardly have to repeat, no one in the end created a genre of Rabbinic literature to accommodate the vast collections of available compositions on sages' sayings and doings.

B. BERAKHOT 6B.XLI

A. Said R. Yohanan, "When the Holy One, blessed be he, comes to a synagogue and does not find ten present, he forthwith becomes angry.

B. "For it is said, 'Why when I came was there no one there? When I called, there was no answer' (Isa. 50:2)."

B. BERAKHOT 6B.XLII

A. Said R. Helbo said R. Huna, "For whoever arranges a regular place for praying, the God of Abraham is a help, and when he dies, they say for him, 'Woe for the humble man, woe for the pious man, one of the disciples of Abraham, our father.'

B. "And how do we know in the case of Abraham, our father, that he arranged a regular place for praying?

C. "For it is written, 'And Abraham got up early in the morning in the place where he had stood' (Gen. 19:27).

D. "'Standing' refers only to praying, for it is said, 'Then Phinehas stood up and prayed' (Ps. 106:30)."

E. Said R. Helbo to R. Huna, "He who leaves the synagogue should not take large steps."

F. Said Abayye, "That statement applies only when one leaves, but when he enters, it is a religious duty to run [to the synagogue].

G. "For it is said, 'Let us run to know the Lord' (Hos. 6:3)."

H. Said R. Zira, "When in the beginning I saw rabbis running to the lesson on the Sabbath, I thought that the rabbis were profaning the Sabbath. But now that I have heard what R. Tanhum said R. Joshua b. Levi said,

I. "namely, 'A person should always run to take up a matter of law, and even on the Sabbath, as it is said, "They shall walk after the Lord who shall roar like a lion [for he shall roar, and the children shall come hurrying]" (Hos. 11:10),'

J. "I too run."

B. BERAKHOT 6B.XLIII

A. Said R. Zira, "The reward for attending the lesson is on account of running [to hear the lesson, not necessarily on account of what one has learned.]"

B. Said Abayye, "The reward for attending the periodic public assembly [of rabbis] is on account of the crowding together."

C. Said Raba [to the contrary], "The reward for repeating what one has heard is in reasoning about it."

D. Said R. Papa, "The reward for attending a house of mourning is on account of one's preserving silence there."

E. Said Mar Zutra, "The reward for observing a fast day lies in the acts of charity one performs on that day."

F. Said R. Sheshet, "The reward for delivering a eulogy lies in raising the voice."

G. Said R. Ashi, "The reward for attending a wedding lies in the words [of compliment paid to the bride and groom]."

B. Berakhot 6B.XLIV

A. Said R. Huna, "Whoever prays behind the synagogue is called wicked,

B. "as it is said, 'The wicked walk round about' (Ps. 12:9)."

C. Said Abayye, "That statement applies only in the case of one who does not turn his face toward the synagogue, but if he turns his face toward the synagogue, we have no objection."

D. There was a certain man who would say his prayers behind the synagogue and did not turn his face toward the synagogue. Elijah came by and saw him. He appeared to him in the guise of a Tai Arab.

E. He said to him, "Are you now standing with your back toward your master?" He drew his sword and killed him.

F. One of the rabbis asked R. Bibi bar Abayye, and some say, R. Bibi asked R. Nahman bar Isaac, "What is the meaning of the verse, 'When vileness is exalted among the sons of men' (Ps. 12:9)?"

G. He said to him, "This refers to matters that are exalted, which people treat with contempt."

H. R. Yohanan and R. Eleazar both say, "When a person falls into need of the help of other people, his face changes color like the kerum-bird, for it is said, 'As the kerum was to be reviled among the sons of men' (Ps. 12:9)."

I. What is the meaning of "kerum-bird?"

J. When R. Dimi came, he said, "There is a certain bird among the coast towns, called the kerum. When the sun shines, it turns many colors."

K. R. Ammi and R. Assi both say, "[When a person turns to others for support], it is as if he is judged to suffer the penalties of both fire and water.

L. "For it is said, 'When you caused men to ride over our heads, we went through fire and through water' (Ps. 66:12)."

B. BERAKHOT 6B.XLV

A. And R. Helbo said R. Huna said, "A person should always be attentive at the afternoon prayer.

B. "For lo, Elijah was answered only at the afternoon prayer.

C. "For it is said, 'And it came to pass at the time of the offering of the late afternoon offering, that Elijah the prophet came near and said, "Hear me, O Lord, hear me"' (1 Kings 18:36–37)."

D. "Hear me" so fire will come down from heaven.

E. "Hear me" that people not say it is merely witchcraft.

F. R. Yohanan said, "[A person should also be attentive about] the evening prayer.

G. "For it is said, 'Let my prayer be set forth as incense before you, the lifting up of my hands as the evening sacrifice' (Ps. 141:2)."

H. R. Nahman bar Isaac said, "[A person should also be attentive about] the morning prayer.

I. "For it is said, 'O Lord, in the morning you shall hear my voice, in the morning I shall order my prayer to you, and will look forward' (Ps. 5:4)."

B. BERAKHOT 6B.XLVI

A. And R. Helbo said R. Huna said, "Whoever enjoys a marriage banquet and does not felicitate the bridal couple violates five 'voices.'

B. "For it is said, 'The voice of joy and the voice of gladness, the voice of the bridegroom and the voice of the bride, the voice of those who say, "Give thanks to the Lord of hosts"' (Jer. 33:11)."

C. And if he does felicitate the couple, what reward does he get?

D. Said R. Joshua b. Levi, "He acquires the merit of the Torah, which was handed down with five voices.

E. "For it is said, 'And it came to pass on the third day, when it was morning, that there were voices [thus two], and lightnings, and a thick cloud upon the mount, and the voice of a horn, and when the voice of the horn waxed louder, 'Moses spoke and God answered him by a voice.' (Exod. 19:16, 19) [thus five voices in all]."

F. Is it so [that there were only five voices]?

G. And lo, it is written, "And all the people saw the voices" (Exod. 20:15). [So this would make seven voices.]

H. These voices came before the giving of the Torah [and do not count].

I. R. Abbahu said, "It is as if the one [who felicitated the bridal couple] offered a thanksgiving offering.

J. "For it is said, 'Even of them that bring thanksgiving offerings into the house of the Lord' (Jer. 33:11)."

K. R. Nahman bar Isaac said, "It is as if he rebuilt one of the ruins of Jerusalem.

L. "That is because it is said, 'For I will cause the captivity of the land to return as at the first, says the Lord' (Jer. 33:11)."

B. Berakhot 6B.XLVII

A. And R. Helbo said R. Huna said, "The words of any person in whom is fear of Heaven are heard.

B. "For it is said, 'The end of the matter, all having been heard: fear God and keep his commandments, since this is the whole man' (Qoh. 12:13)."

C. What is the meaning of the phrase, "For this is the whole man" (Qoh. 12:13)?

D. Said R. Eleazar, "Said the Holy One, blessed be he, 'The entire world has been created only on account of this one.'"

E. R. Abba bar Kahana said, "This one is worth the whole world."

F. Simeon b. Zoma says, "The entire world was created only to accompany this one."

B. Berakhot 6B.XLVIII

 A. And R. Helbo said R. Huna said, "Whoever knows that his fellow regularly greets him should greet the other first.

 B. "For it is said, 'Seek peace and pursue it' (Ps. 34:15).

 C. "If he greeted him and the other did not reply, the latter is called a thief.

 D. "For it is said, 'It is you who have eaten up the vineyard, the spoil of the poor is in your houses' (Isa. 3:14)."

What we noted in connection with the Yohanan-Simeon collection needs no restatement here. The scope and dimensions of the passage prove impressive. Again we must wonder for what sort of composition the framer of the Helbo-Huna collection planned his writing. Whatever it was, it hardly fit the ultimate destination of his work.

Names Without Personalities: Tractate Abot

In tractate Abot—which came to closure about a half-century after the Mishnah and served as a prologue for the Mishnah, enriching the presentation of the Mishnah's authorities through assigning to them wise sayings, in addition to the practical laws that the Mishnah attributes to them—we see how sages are portrayed without personality. In Chapter 1's list of names there is a clear logic of fixed association in play. The names of the listed sages form a coherent pattern. What is attributed to the sages exhibits a certain topical coherence but in substance is random and episodic. Major authorities of the Mishnah stand in a chain of tradition to Sinai; hence, the Mishnah contains the Torah of Sinai. The order of the names is therefore deliberate and unites what is attributed, though the sentences themselves bear slight connections among themselves:

 1:2. Simeon the Righteous was one of the last survivors of the great assembly. He would say: On three things does the world stand: On the Torah, and on the Temple service, and on deeds of loving-kindness.

1:3. Antigonus of Sokho received [the Torah] from Simeon the Righteous. He would say: Do not be like servants who serve the master on condition of receiving a reward, but [be] like servants who serve the master not on condition of receiving a reward. And let the fear of Heaven be upon you.

1:4. Yosé ben Yoezer of Zeredah and Yosé ben Yohanan of Jerusalem received [the Torah] from them. Yosé ben Yoezer says: Let your house be a gathering place for sages. And wallow in the dust of their feet, and drink in their words with gusto.

1:5. Yosé ben Yohanan of Jerusalem says: Let your house be open wide. And seat the poor at your table ["make the poor members of your household"]. And don't talk too much with women. (He referred to a man's wife, all the more so is the rule to be applied to the wife of one's fellow. In this regard did sages say: So long as a man talks too much with a woman, he brings trouble on himself, wastes time better spent on studying the Torah, and ends up an heir of Gehenna.)

1:6. Joshua ben Perahyah and Nittai the Arbelite received [the Torah] from them. Joshua ben Perahyah says: Set up a master for yourself. And get yourself a companion-disciple. And give everybody the benefit of the doubt.

1:7. Nittai the Arbelite says: Keep away from a bad neighbor. And don't get involved with a bad person. And don't give up hope of retribution.

1:8A. Judah ben Tabbai and Simeon ben Shetah received [the Torah] from them.

1:8B. Judah ben Tabbai says: Don't make yourself like one of those who advocate before judges [while you yourself are judging a case]. And when the litigants stand before you, regard them as guilty. But when they leave you, regard them as acquitted (when they have accepted your judgment).

1:9. Simeon ben Shetah says: Examine the witnesses with great care. And watch what you say, lest they learn from what you say how to lie.

1:10. Shemaiah and Abtalyon received [the Torah] from them. Shemaiah says: Love work. Hate authority. Don't get friendly with the government.

1:11. Abtalyon says: Sages, watch what you say, lest you become liable to the punishment of exile, and go into exile to a place of bad water, and disciples who follow you drink bad water and die, and the name of Heaven be thereby profaned.

1:12. Hillel and Shammai received [the Torah] from them. Hillel says: Be disciples of Aaron, loving peace and pursuing grace, loving people and drawing them near to the Torah.

1:13A. He would say [in Aramaic]: A name made great is a name destroyed, and one who does not add, subtracts.

1:13B. And who does not learn is liable to death. And the one who uses the crown, passes away.

1:14. He would say: If I am not for myself, who is for me? And when I am for myself, what am I? And if not now, when?

1:15. Shammai says: Make your learning of the Torah a fixed obligation. Say little and do much. Greet everybody cheerfully.

1:16. Rabban Gamaliel says: Set up a master for yourself. Avoid doubt. Don't tithe by too much guesswork.

1:17. Simeon his son says: All my life I grew up among the sages, and I found nothing better for a person [the body] than silence. And the learning is not the thing, but the doing. And whoever talks too much causes sin.

1:18. Rabban Simeon ben Gamaliel says: On three things does the world stand: on justice, on truth, and on peace. As it is said, Execute the judgment of truth and peace in your gates. (Zech 8:16)

The intent of the list is not only to establish the link to Sinai; the fixed associative list bears a second polemic, which emerges in the pairs of names and how they are arranged:

Moses
Joshua
Elders

Prophets
Men of the Great Assembly
Simeon the Righteous
Antigonus of Sokho

1. Yosé ben Yoezer	Yosé b. Yohanan
2. Joshua b. Perahyah	Nittai the Arbelite
3. Judah b. Tabbai	Simeon b. Shetah
4. Shemaiah	Abtalyon
5. Hillel	Shammai
Gamaliel	

Simeon his son [that is, Simeon b. Gamaliel]
Rabban Simeon b. Gamaliel

Once the pairs end, we find Gamaliel, who is (later on) represented as the son of Hillel, and then Gamaliel and Simeon, his son, Hillel's grandson.

The cogency of the list emerges when we realize that the names Gamaliel, then Simeon, continued through this same family, of primary authorities, through Gamaliel II, ruler of the Jewish community after the destruction of the Second Temple in 70 and into the second century, then his son, Simeon b. Gamaliel, ruler of the Jewish community after the defeat of Bar Kokhba in 135—and also, as it happens, the father of Judah the Patriarch, this same Judah the Patriarch who sponsored the Mishnah. Judah the Patriarch stands in the chain of tradition to Sinai. So not only the teachings of the sages of the Mishnah, but also the political sponsor of the document, who also was numbered among the sages, formed part of this same tradition. The list itself bears the message that the patriarch and sages employed by him carry forward the tradition of Sinai.

GIVING INDIVIDUALITY TO NAMES: THE TALMUD TO TRACTATE ABOT

In 250 Mishnah-tractate Abot, The Fathers, delivered its message through aphorisms assigned to named sages. A few centuries later—the date is indeterminate but it is possibly c. 500—the Fathers According to Rabbi Nathan, a vast secondary expansion of that same tractate, endowed those anonymous names with flesh-and-blood form, recasting the tractate by adding a sizable number of narratives. The authorship of the Mishnah-tractate, the Fathers, c. 250, presented its teachings in the form of aphorisms, rarely finding it necessary to supply those aphorisms with a narrative setting, and never resorting to narrative for the presentation of its propositions. The testamentary authorship, The Fathers According to Rabbi Nathan, provided an amplification and supplement to The Fathers and introduced into its treatment of the received tractate a vast corpus of narratives of various sorts. In this way, the later authorship indicated that it found in narrative in general, and stories about sages in particular, modes of discourse for presenting its message that the earlier authorship did not utilize. And the choice of the medium bore implicit meanings, also, for the message that would emerge in the later restatement of the received tractate.

To call The Fathers According to Rabbi Nathan the Talmud of The Fathers leads to the false expectation that the successor document subjects the principal one to sustained analytical reading. But the character of The Fathers does not sustain analysis, since the compilation presents no theses for argumentation, only wise sayings. The work of The Fathers according to Rabbi Nathan was defined by the fact that the authorship of The Fathers presented the message of sages solely in aphoristic form. Apothegms bore the entire weight of that authorship's propositions, and—quite consistently—what made one saying cogent with others fore and aft was solely the position of the authority behind that saying: here, not there. The framers of the successor writing vastly augmented The Fathers by recasting aphorisms in narrative form, and, more important, according to the names of sages listed in the prior writing the rudiments of biography.

Given a saying of an apothegmatic character, whether or not that saying is drawn from The Fathers, the authorship of the Fathers According to Rabbi Nathan will do one of the following:

1. give a secondary expansion, including an exemplification, of the wise saying at hand;

2. cite a proof-text of Scripture in that same connection;

3. provide a parable to illustrate the wise saying (as often as not instead of the proof-text).

These three exercises in the structuring of their document—selecting materials and organizing them in a systematic way—the authors of The Fathers According to Rabbi Nathan learned from the framers of The Fathers. In addition they contributed two further principles of structuring their document:

4. add a sizable composition of materials that intersect with the foregoing, either by amplifying on the proof-text without regard to the wise saying served by the proof-text, or by enriching discourse on a topic introduced in connection with the base-saying;

5. tack on a protracted story of a sage and what he said and did, which story may or may not exemplify the teaching of the apophthegm at hand.

The Fathers According to Rabbi Nathan presents two types of materials and sets them forth in a fixed order. The document contains (1) amplifications of sayings in The Fathers as well as (2) materials not related to anything in the original document. The order in which The Fathers According to Rabbi Nathan arranges its types of material becomes immediately clear. First, that authorship presents amplifications of the prior document, and, only second, does it tack on its own message. The Fathers According to Rabbi Nathan first of all presents itself as continuous with the prior document, and then shows itself to be connected to it. That is the strategy of both Talmuds in connecting with the Mishnah. And where the authorship gives us compositions that are essentially new in rhetoric, logic and topic, it is in that second set of materials that we find what is fresh. Let me spell out matters as they will soon become clear. Where the authorship of the later document has chosen (1) to cite and amplify sayings in the earlier one, that exercise comes first. There may be additional amplification, and what appears to augment often turns out to be quite new and to enter the second of our two categories, in the form of (i) proof-texts drawn from Scripture, or (ii) parables, (iii) other sorts of stories, sometimes involving named sages, that illustrate the same point, and (iv) sequences of unadorned sayings, not in The Fathers, that make the same point. These come later in a sequence of discourses in The Fathers According to Rabbi Nathan. Where an appendix of secondary materials on a theme introduced in the primary discourse occurs, it will be inserted directly after the point at which said theme is located in the counterpart, in the later document, to that passage in the earlier one, and only afterward will the exposition of the saying in The Fathers proceed to a further point. This general order predominates throughout.

The authorship of The Fathers According to Rabbi Nathan clearly found inadequate the mode of intelligible discourse and the medium of expression selected by the framers of the document they chose to extend. The later writers possessed a message they deemed integral to that unfolding Torah of Moses at Sinai. They resorted to a mode of intelligible discourse, narrative, that conveyed propositions with great clarity, deeming the medium—again, narrative—a vehicle for conveying propositions from heart to heart. Not only so, but among the narratives utilized in their composition, they selected one for closest attention and narrative development. The sage-story took pride of place in its paramount position in The Fathers According to Rabbi Nathan, and that same subclassification of narrative bore messages conveyed, in the document before us, in no other medium. The framers made ample use of formerly neglected matters of intellect, aesthetics, and theology, specifically, to compose their ideas through a mode of thought and cogent thought, so as to construct intelligible discourse through a medium, meant to speak with immediacy and power to convey a message of critical urgency. Three traits define the sage-story in this document.

1. The story about a sage has a beginning, middle, and end, and the story about a sage also rests not only on verbal exchanges ("he said to him . . . , he said to him . . ."), but on (described) action.

2. The story about a sage unfolds from a point of tension and conflict to a clear resolution and remission of the conflict.

3. The story about a sage rarely invokes a verse of Scripture and never serves to prove a proposition concerning the meaning of a verse of Scripture.

What about Scripture stories? The traits of stories about scriptural figures and themes prove opposite:

1. In the story about a scriptural hero there is no beginning, middle, and end, and little action. The burden of the narrative is carried by "he said to him . . . , he said to him . . . ." Described action is rare and plays slight role in the unfolding of the narrative. Often the narrative consists of little more than a setting for a saying, and the point of the narrative is conveyed not through what is told but through the cited saying.

2. The story about a scriptural hero is worked out as a tableau, with description of the components of the stationary tableau placed at the center. There is little movement, no point of tension that is resolved.

3. The story about a scriptural hero always invokes verses from Scripture and makes the imputation of meaning to those verses the center of interest.

So the Fathers According to Rabbi Nathan systematically enriches The Fathers with a variety of narratives, each with its own conventions. When the narrators wish to talk about sages, they invoked one set of narrative conventions, deemed appropriate to that topic, and when they turned to make up stories about scriptural heroes and topics, they appealed to quite different narrative conventions.

The topical program of The Fathers According to Rabbi Nathan in particular emerges only in identifying topics treated in the successor compilations but not in the principal one. Points of emphasis in The Fathers lacking all counterpart in restatement and development in the Fathers According to Rabbi Nathan are three. First, the study of the Torah alone does not suffice. One has also to make an honest living through work. In what is peculiar to The Fathers According to Rabbi Nathan we find not that point but its opposite: one should study the Torah and other things will take care of themselves—a claim of a more supernatural character than the one in The Fathers. A second point of clear interest in the earlier document to which, in the later one, we find no response tells sages to accommodate their wishes to those of the community at large, to accept the importance of the government, to work in community, to practice self-abnegation and restraint in favor of the wishes of others. The sage here is less a supernatural figure than a political leader, eager to conciliate and reconcile the other. The third and most important, indicative shift in the later document imparts to the teleological question an eschatological answer altogether lacking in the earlier one.

PERSONALITY AND TELEOLOGY

If we were to ask the authorship of Abot to spell out their teleology, they would draw our attention to the numerous sayings about this life's being a time of preparation for the life of the world to come, on the one side, and to judgment and eternal life, on the other. The focus is on the individual and how he or she lives in this world and prepares for the next. The category is the individual, and, commonly in the two documents before us when we speak of the individual, we also tend to find the language of "this world" and "the world to come," *olam hazzeh, olam habba*. The sequence of sayings about this world and the next form a stunning contrast to the ones about this *age* and the next age, *olam hazzeh, le'atid labo*. In general, though not invariably, the shift in language draws in its wake a shift in social category, from individual to social entity of group, nation, or people. The word *olam* bears two meanings, "world," and "age." In context, when we find the word bearing the sense of "world," the category under discussion is the private person, and where the required sense, in English, is "age," then—as a rough rule of thumb—what is promised is for the nation.

We can tell that the definitive category is social, therefore national, when at stake is the fate not of the private person but of holy Israel. The concern then is what will happen to the nation in time to come, meaning the coming age, not the coming life of the resurrection. The systemic teleology shifts its focus to the holy people, and, alongside, to the national history of the holy people—now and in the age to come. So in the movement from *this world* and *the world to come*, to *this age* and *the age to come*, often expressed as *the coming future, le'atid labo,* we note an accompanying categorical shift in the definitive context: from individual and private life of home and family, to society and historical, public life. That shift then characterizes the teleological movement, as much as the categorical change. And, as we see, it is contained both in general and in detail in the differences we have noticed between The Fathers and The Fathers According to Rabbi Nathan.

The national-eschatological interest of the later document, with its focus on living only in the Land of Israel, on the one side, and its contrast between this age, possessed by the gentiles, and the age to come, in which redeemed Israel will enjoy a paramount position, which has no counterpart in the earlier composition, emerges not only in sayings but also in stories about the critical issue, the destruction of Jerusalem and the loss of the Temple, along with the concomitant matter, associated with the former stories, about repentance and how it is achieved at this time.

Yet a further point of development lies in the notion that study of the Torah combined with various virtues—e.g., good deeds, fear of sin—suffices, with a concomitant assurance that making a living no longer matters. Here too the new medium of the later document—the stories about sages—bears the new message. For that conviction emerges not only explicitly, e.g., in the sayings of Hananiah about the power of Torah study to take away many sources of suffering, Judah b. Ilai's that one should treat words of the Torah as the principal, earning a living as trivial, and so on. but also in the detail that both Aqiba and Eliezer began poor but through their mastery of Torah ended rich.

The Fathers According to Rabbi Nathan differs from The Fathers in one aspect so fundamental as to change the face of the base document completely. While the earlier authorship took slight interest in lives and deeds of sages, the later one contributed in a systematic and orderly manner the color and life of biography to the named but faceless sages of The Fathers. The stories about sages make points that correspond to positions taken in statements of viewpoints peculiar to The Fathers According to Rabbi Nathan. The Fathers presents an ideal of the sage as model for the everyday life of the individual, who must study the Torah and also work, and through the good life prepare now for life after death, while The Fathers According to Rabbi Nathan has a different conception of the sage, of the value and meaning of the study of the Torah, and of the center of interest—and also has selected a new medium for the expression of its distinctive conception. To spell this out:

1. The sage is now—in the Fathers According to Rabbi Nathan—not a judge and teacher alone but also a supernatural figure.

2. Study of the Torah in preference to making a living promises freedom from the conditions of natural life.

3. Israel as the holy people seen as a supernatural social entity takes center stage.

And these innovative points are conveyed not only in sayings but in stories about sages.

What follows is that the medium not only carries a new message but also forms a component of that new message. The sage as a supernatural figure now presents Torah-teachings through what he does, not only through what he says. Therefore telling stories about what sages did and the circumstances in which they made their sayings forms part of the Torah, in a way in which, in the earlier document, it clearly did not. The interest in stories about sages proves therefore not merely literary or formal; it is more than a new way of conveying an old message. Stories about the sages are told because sages stand for a message that can emerge only in stories and not in sayings alone. So we turn to a close reading of the stories themselves to review that message and find out why through stories in particular the message now emerges. For what we see is nothing short of a new mode of revelation, that is, of conveying and imparting God's will in the Torah.

People told stories because they wanted to think about history, and, in their setting, history emerged in an account of what happened, with an implicit message of the meaning of events conveyed in the story as well. They further conceived of the social entity, Israel, as an extended family, children of a single progenitor, Abraham, with his son and grandson, Isaac and Jacob. Consequently, when they told stories, they centered on family history. That accounts in general for the details of what the authorship of The Fathers According to Rabbi Nathan have chosen to add to the topical program of The Fathers. The sage in the system of The Fathers According to Rabbi Nathan constituted the supernatural father, who replaced the natural one; events in the life of the sage constituted happenings in the history of the family-nation, Israel. So history blended with family, and family with Torah study. The national, salvific history of the nation-family, Israel, took place in such events as the origins of the sage, i.e., his beginnings in Torah study; the sagacity of the sage, the counterpart to what we should call social history; the doings of the sage in great turnings in the family's history, including, especially, the destruction of the Temple, now perceived as final and decisive; and the death of the sage, while engaged in Torah study. And these form the four classifications of story in this document.

THE BIRTH OF THE SAGE AS HOLY MAN

Of interest to readers of this Introduction will be the contrast between sage-story and Gospel-story. That is readily drawn when we compare Matthew's story of the birth of Jesus with the stories about the origins of Aqiba and Eliezer in The Fathers According to Rabbi Nathan. The interest of the former is well known. "Now the birth of Jesus Christ took place in this way" (Matt. 2:18): the birth of the child was announced to the virgin-mother, Mary. Herod was told that the king of the Jews has been born. The Magi worshiped the infant. Herod killed the newborn babes; Joseph and Mary fled to Egypt. When Herod died, Joseph and Mary returned. And so on. The well-known story covers a variety of details. Stories about sages present us with a counterpart to not a single detail of Matthew's story; there is no birth legend comparable, for example, to the birth of Samuel or Joseph either. The counterpart is structural: telling the tale of the starting point.

The Fathers According to Rabbi Nathan contains stories not of the birth but of "the origins" as masters of the Torah of two sages, Aqiba and Eliezer. By "origins," the storytellers mean the beginnings of the Torah study of a famed authority. Life begins at birth, but when we wish to tell sage-stories, beginnings are measured differently. The sage begins life when he begins Torah study. And the sages whose origins are found noteworthy both began in mature years, not in childhood (despite the repeated emphasis of The Fathers upon the unique value of beginning Torah study in childhood). The proposition implicit in origins-stories then is that any male may start his Torah study at any point in life and hope for true distinction in the Torah community. But that does not account for the germ of the story, the critical tension that creates an event worthy of narrative, that poses a question demanding an answer, a problem requiring a solution through a tale with a beginning, middle, and end.

While told each in its own terms and subject to differentiation from the other, the stories make essentially the same point, which is that one can begin Torah study in mature years and progress to the top. When one does so, one also goes from poverty to wealth through public recognition of one's mastery of the Torah, and a range of parallel propositions along the same lines. The supernatural relationship, which has superseded the natural ones to wife and father, generates glory and honor, riches and fame, for the sage, and, through reflection, for the natural family as well. That is the point of the stories of the origins of sages, which take up what is clearly a pressing question and answer it in a powerful way. (I give in boldface type citations of language in The Fathers.)

The Fathers According to Rabbi Nathan VI:IV.1

> A. Another comment on the statement, **And wallow in the dust of their feet:**
> B. This refers to R. Eliezer.
> C. . . . **and drink in their words with gusto:**
> D. This refers to R. Aqiba.

This pericope serves as a prologue to the vast stories to follow. first on Aqiba, then on Eliezer.

VI:V.1 A. How did R. Aqiba begin [his Torah study]?

B. They say: He was forty years old and had never repeated a tradition [that is to say, he was completely illiterate and had never studied the Torah or learned its traditions.] One time he was standing at the mouth of a well. He thought to himself, "Who carved out this stone?"

C. They told him, "It is the water that is perpetually falling on it every day."

D. They said to him, "Aqiba, do you not read Scripture? *The water wears away stones* (Job. 4:19)?"

E. On the spot R. Aqiba constructed in his own regard an argument *a fortiori*: now if something soft can [Goldin:] wear down something hard, words of Torah, which are as hard as iron, how much the more so should wear down my heart, which is made of flesh and blood."

F. On the spot he repented [and undertook] to study the Torah.

G. He and his son went into study session before a children's teacher, saying to him, "My lord, teach me Torah."

H. R. Aqiba took hold of one end of the tablet, and his son took hold of the other end. The teacher wrote out for him *Alef Bet* and he learned it, *Alef Tav* and he learned it, *the Torah of the Priests* [the books of Leviticus and Numbers] and he learned it. He went on learning until he had learned the entire Torah.

I. He went and entered study sessions before R. Eliezer and before R. Joshua. He said to them, "My lords, open up for me the reasoning of the Mishnah."

J. When they had stated one passage of law, he went and sat by himself and said, "Why is this *alef* written? why is this *bet* written? Why is this statement made?" He went and asked them and, in point of fact, [Goldin:] reduced them to silence.

Clearly, our opening component in the *magnalia Aqibae* is a narrative. The tone and program establish the mood of narrative: he was ... he had ... he did .... But how shall we classify the narrative, and by what criteria? One important criterion is whether the narrative describes a situation or tells about something that happened, with a beginning, middle, and end. The one is at rest, the other in movement. These constitute questions with objective answers. Do we have a tableau or a story, or, for that matter, a parable, or any of those other types of narratives we have already classified? By the simple criterion that a story has a beginning, middle, and end—which dictate points of narrative tension—and a clearly delineated program of action, we have a story. The components do more than merely set up pieces in a static tableau. They flow from one to the next and yield movement—hence narrative action.

What about the Scripture story? The blatant differences require slight amplification. We note that verses of Scripture scarcely intervene, and there is no focus on the exegesis of a verse of Scripture. At D, Aqiba and his interlocutors do not interpret the verse but simply draw upon its statement of fact. A sage-story, as I said, following the pattern determined by Aristotle, has a beginning, middle, and end: movement from tension to resolution. In the present story there is a beginning: he had not studied; a middle, he went and studied; and an end, following Goldin's persuasive rendering, "he reduced them to silence." True, the action takes place mainly in what Aqiba thought, rather than in what he did. But in the nature of things, the action of going to study the Torah forms the one genuinely dramatic deed that is possible with the present subject matter. The beginning then works its way out at B–F. The middle is at G–H: Aqiba was so humble as to study with his own son. Then at I–J we have a climax and conclusion: Aqiba proved so profound in his question-asking that he reduced the great authorities to silence. That conclusion hardly flows from A–H, but it is absolutely necessary to make the entire sequence into a cogent story. Otherwise we have merely bits and pieces of an uncompleted narrative.

Let us proceed to what follows in the context of the telling of the story of Aqiba's origins. Here we shall see most strikingly how, given the opportunity for a sustained narrative of the life of a man, the framers of The Fathers According to Rabbi Nathan do not exploit the occasion. Rather than dealing with other tales about the man, they focus upon the theme that he has served to realize in his own life, Torah study.

> VI:V.2 A. R. Simeon b. Eleazar says, "I shall make a parable for you. To what is the matter comparable? To a stonecutter who was cutting stone in a quarry. One time he took his chisel and went and sat down on the mountain and started to chip away little sherds from it. People came by and said to him, 'What are you doing?'
>
> B. "He said to them, 'Lo, I am going to uproot the mountain and move it into the Jordan River.'"
>
> C. "They said to him, 'You will never be able to uproot the entire mountain.'
>
> D. "He continued chipping away at the mountain until he came to a huge boulder. He quarried underneath it and unearthed it and uprooted it and tossed it into the Jordan.'
>
> E. "He said to the boulder, 'This is not your place, but that is your place.'
>
> F. "Likewise this is what R. Aqiba did to R. Eliezer and to R. Joshua."

The parable without F simply says that with patience one may move mountains. The parable by itself—not applied—amplifies or at least continues VI:V.1.E, the power of words of Torah to wear down the hard heart of a human being. But the parable proves peculiar to the preceding story, since the add-on, E, F, applies the parable to VI:V.1.J, the humiliation of Joshua and Eliezer. We may wonder whether, without the announcement at A that we have a parable, the parabolic character of the tale would have impressed us. The answer is that the general traits of a parable—an anonymous illustration in concrete and everyday terms of an abstract proposition—do occur in A–D, at which point the parable worked out its proposition: "he continued chipping away." Even E, without F, can remain within the limits of the announced proposition of the parable, that is, the power of patience and persistence. So only F is jarring. It clearly serves the redactor's purpose. It does not transform the parable into a story (!), since it does not impose upon the prior narrative that particularity and concrete onetimeness that form the indicative traits of the story alone. In all, we may dismiss from the evidence of the story the present complement to the foregoing.

> VI:V.3 A. Said R. Tarfon to him, "Aqiba, in your regard Scripture says, *He stops up streams so that they do not trickle, and what is hidden he brings into the light* (Job 28:11).
>
> B. "Things that are kept as mysteries from ordinary people has R. Aqiba brought to light."

"He said to him" does not make a story, and what is said does not bear the marks of a story, whole or in part.

> VI:V.4 A. Every day he would bring a bundle of twigs [Goldin: straw], half of which he would sell in exchange for food, and half of which he would use for a garment.
>
> B. His neighbors said to him, "Aqiba, you are killing us with the smoke. Sell them to us, buy oil with the money, and by the light of a lamp do your studying."
>
> C. He said to them, "I fill many needs with that bundle, first, I repeat traditions [by the light of the fire I kindle with] them, second, I warm myself with them, third, I sleep on them."
>
> VI:V.5 A. In time to come R. Aqiba is going to impose guilt [for failing to study] on the poor [who use their poverty as an excuse not to study].
>
> B. For if they say to them, "Why did you not study the Torah," and they reply, "Because we were poor," they will say to them, "But was not R. Aqiba poorer and more poverty-stricken?"
>
> C. If they say, "Because of our children [whom we had to work to support]," they will say to them, "Did not R. Aqiba have sons and daughters?"
>
> D. So they will say to them, "Because Rachel, his wife, had the merit [of making it possible for him to study, and we have

no equivalent helpmates; our wives do not have equivalent merit at their disposal]."

It is hard to classify VI:V.4 as other than a narrative setting for a conversation. But the conversation makes no point by itself. In fact the whole forms a prologue to VI:V.5, which does make a powerful point.

VI:V.6 A. It was at the age of forty that he went to study the Torah. Thirteen years later he taught the Torah in public.

B. They say that he did not leave this world before there were silver and golden tables in his possession,

C. and before he went up onto his bed on golden ladders.

D. His wife went about in golden sandals and wore a golden tiara of the silhouette of the city [Jerusalem].

E. His disciples said to him, "My lord, you have shamed us by what you have done for her [since we cannot do the same for our wives]."

F. He said to them, "She bore a great deal of pain on my account for [the study of] the Torah."

This item completes the foregoing, the narrative of how Rachel's devotion to Aqiba's study of the Torah produced a rich reward. The "they said to him . . . he said to him . . ." sequences do not comprise a story or even establish much of a narrative framework. The upshot is that for Aqiba we have a sequence of narratives but only one story, that at the beginning. The composite does not hang together very well, but it does make a few important points.

This brings us to the story of the origins, in the Torah, of Eliezer. Let us turn directly to the account:

VI:VI.1 A. How did R. Eliezer ben Hyrcanus begin [his Torah study]?

B. He had reached the age of twenty-two years and had not yet studied the Torah. One time he said, "I shall go and study the Torah before Rabban Yohanan ben Zakkai."

C. His father Hyrcanus said to him, "You are not going to taste a bit of food until you have plowed the entire furrow.":

D. He got up in the morning and plowed the entire furrow.

E. They say that that day was Friday. He went and took a meal with his father-in-law.

F. And some say that he tasted nothing from the sixth hour on Friday until the sixth hour on Sunday.

The narrative is rather strange, since none of the actions is given a motivation. That immediately evident difference between Eliezer's and Aqiba's story will later on prove still more striking than it does now. But it suffices to note the points in which the two stories diverge in narrative technique. While in the case of Aqiba, we know why the great master originally determined to study the Torah, in the instance of Eliezer we do not. All we know is that at the mature age of twenty-two, he determined to study in the session of Yohanan ben Zakkai. My judgment is that the storyteller has in mind the task of explaining Eliezer's origins as Yohanan's disciple, not working out the inner motivation of the disciple. That accounts, also, for the random details, none of which fits together with the next. I see only a sequence of unintegrated details: he was twenty-two and decided to study the Torah. His father said, "Do not eat until you plow the furrow." He plowed the furrow. Then he went and ate with his father-in-law. Some say he did not eat until Sunday. These details, scarcely connected, produce no effect either of narrative or of a propositional character.

VI:VI.2 A. On the way he saw a rock. He picked it up and took it and put it into his mouth.

B. And some say that what he picked up was cattle dung.

C. He went and spent the night at his hostel.

Even if we read VI:VI.2 as part of VI:VI.1, all we have is more unintegrated details. Nothing in VI:VI.1-2 points to a cogent narrative, let alone a story. All we have are odd bits of information about what someone "said." The whole conglomerate does serve, however, to set the stage for VI:VI.3. The details necessary to understand what is coming have now made their appearance, and the climax is before us: he went and studied, and, because he had not eaten, produced bad breath. Yohanan recognized the bad breath and said, "Just as you suffered, so you will enjoy a reward."

VI:VI.3 A. He went and entered study session before Rabban Yo-hanan ben Zakkai in Jerusalem.

B. Since a bad odor came out of his mouth, Rabban Yo-hanan ben Zakkai said to him, "Eliezer my son, have you taken a meal today?"

C. He shut up.

D. He asked him again, and he shut up again.

E. He sent word and inquired at his hostel, and asked, "Has Eliezer eaten anything with you?"

F. They sent word to him, "We thought that he might be eating with my lord."

G. He said, "For my part, I thought that he might be eating with you. Between me and you, we should have lost R. Eliezer in the middle."

H. He said to him, "Just as the odor of your mouth has gone forth, so will a good name in the Torah go forth for you."

VI:VI.4 A. Hyrcanus, his father, heard that he was studying the Torah with Rabban Yohanan ben Zakkai. He decided, "I shall go and impose on Eliezer my son a vow not to de-rive benefit from my property."

B. They say that that day Rabban Yohanan ben Zakkai was in session and expounding [the Torah] in Jerusalem, and all the great men of Israel were in session before him. [Eliezer] heard that [his father] was coming. He set up guards, say-ing to them, "If he comes to take a seat, do not let him."

C. He came to take a seat and they did not let him.

D. He kept stepping over people and moving forward until he came to Ben Sisit Hakkesset and Naqdimon b. Gurion and Ben Kalba Sabua. He sat among them, trembling.

E. They say, On that day Rabban Yohanan ben Zakkai looked at R. Eliezer, indicating to him, "Cite an appro-priate passage and give an exposition."

F. He said to him, "I cannot cite an appropriate passage."

G. He urged him, and the other disciples urged him.

H. He went and cited an opening passage and expounded matters the like of which no ear had ever heard.

I. And at every word that he said, Rabban Yohanan ben Zakkai arose and kissed him on his head and said, "My lord, Eliezer, my lord, you have taught us truth."

J. As the time came to break up, Hyrcanus his father stood up and said, "My lords, I came here only to impose a vow on my son, Eliezer, not to derive benefit from my possession. Now all of my possessions are given over to Eliezer my son, and all my other sons are disinherited and will have no share in them."

We have a beginning: Hyrcanus plans to go and place Eliezer under vow that would ban the son from all contact with, or benefit from, his family; he would say something like "Qorban, all my possessions are forbidden to you as though they were holy, an offering to the Lord in the Temple." That would then prevent Eliezer from deriving any benefit from his father's estate and would cut him off from his family. That is a considerable and weighty act, as we can well imagine. So the stated plan of disinheritance through a ferocious vow not only begins the story, but it also creates an enormous tension. A dramatic setting is then portrayed: do not let the father sit down at the back, so that the father will sit among the greatest men of Jerusalem (B–D). Yohanan then calls upon Eliezer to speak, and, after appropriate urging, he does. The tension is resolved at the climax, which also is the conclusion. I cannot think of a more perfect story, since every detail contributes to the whole, and the storyteller's intent—to underline the reward coming to the disciple, even though his family originally opposes his joining the sage—is fully realized. We note, therefore, that the conglomerate of narratives involving both Aqiba and Eliezer in fact rest in each case on a single story, and that story forms the redactional focus, permitting the aggregation of further materials, not all of them of a finished character, and some of them not stories at all.

Let us now stand back and review the whole composite involving both Aqiba and Eliezer, which, in the aggregate, makes the point that one can start Torah study in mature years. VI:IV.1 serves only as a preface to the autonomous materials collected on the theme of how two famous masters began their studies late in life, having had no prior education. Both figures, moreover, started off poor but got rich when they became famous. These are Eliezer and Aqiba. There is no clear connection between the materials and the original saying. Perhaps the reference to wallowing in the dust of their feet in connection with Eliezer is meant to link up to the detail that he put a piece of dirt or cow dung in his mouth, but that seems to me farfetched. We refer first to Eliezer, then to Aqiba, but tell the stories in reverse order.

The diverse stories on Aqiba are hardly harmonious, since one set knows nothing of his wife, while the other introduces her as the main figure. The first set, No. 2 ff., emphasizes how slow and steady wins the race. The lesson is that if one persists, one may ultimately best one's masters. No. 3 goes over the same matter, now with a parable to make the point that if one persists, he can uproot mountains. This seems to me appropriately joined to the foregoing, with the notion that the sage is the mountain now made explicit. Tarfon then goes over the same matter in yet another way, No. 4. No. 5 then goes over the theme of studying in poverty. No. 5 seems to me a rather pointless story, but it leads to No. 6, which presents its own message explicitly. I treat No. 6 as distinct from No. 5 because it introduces the distinct theme of Aqiba's wife, and that has nothing to do with studying in poverty, but rather, the wife's toleration of the husband's long absences. No. 7 then carries forward the second theme of the foregoing, Aqiba's wealth later on and how he lavished it on Rachel. I find puzzling the failure of the storyteller to take an interest in the source of Aqiba's great wealth. The sequence on Eliezer goes over a recurrent theme, but is as incoherent as the foregoing. No. 1 presents a number of problems of continuity, since 1.1A–D are simply gibberish, there being no clear relationship between C and B. How 1.E–F fit in I cannot say. One may make a good case for treating VI:VI.1 and

VI:VI.2 as continuous. But because of the detail of 9.A, on the way
he saw a rock, it seems to me that we are on good ground in treating the latter as a fragment of yet another story, rather than as a
bridge. VI:VI.3 is on its own coherent and complete, a cogent and
readily comprehended statement on its own. VI:VI.4 also works
well, beginning to end. The details given in D then account for the
appendix that follows, VI:VII–X.

CHRISTIAN AND JUDAIC PORTRAITS OF THE HOLY MAN: SIMILARITIES AND DIFFERENCES

The most striking difference between Christianity and Rabbinic
Judaism emerges when we ask about documents of biography, sustained collections of sayings and stories about named sages, formed
into compilations. These are the documents we do not have in
Rabbinic literature, but that the other heir to the Hebrew Scriptures of ancient Israel, Christianity, produced in abundance. In the
post-Constantinian documents, however, the Rabbinic compositors added a rich body of tales about sages, according to them personalities, even individuality, lacking in the Mishnah and its associated documents. In this respect, Rabbinic Judaism changed and
drew closer to Christianity's initial and ongoing interest in the personality of the holy man, in the model of Jesus himself.

The Gospels, about a single individual, legitimated writing not
only about, but by named persons, and few authoritative documents of Christianity lack an attributed author (whatever the ac-
tualities of authorship). For the entire cadre of sages, we do not
have a single biography devoted to an individual, or even the raw
materials for a sustained and systematic biography. We do not possess a single document produced by a clearly identifiable individual author, a single coherent composite of any consequence at all
that concerns itself with a named figure. The counterpart writings
for Christianity, the Gospels, the letters of Paul—not to mention
the huge collections of signed, personal, individual writings of
Church Fathers—show us the documents we do not have in Rabbinic literature. The theory of authorship accounts for that fact. A
document to warrant recognition—thus to be accorded authority,

to be written and copied, or memorized and handed on as tradition—had to attain the approval of the sages' consensus.

That meant, every document in Rabbinic literature emerged anonymously, under public sponsorship and authorship, stripped of all marks of individual, therefore idiosyncratic, origin. Personality and individuality stood for schism, and Rabbinic literature in its very definition and character aims at the opposite, forming as it does the functional counterpart to the creeds and decisions of church councils. Framed in mythic terms, the literature aimed to make this theological statement: sages stood in a chain of tradition from Sinai, and the price of inclusion was the acceptance of the discipline of tradition—anonymity, reasoned argument to attain for a private view the public status of a consensus statement. The very definition of tradition that comes to expression in the character of Rabbinic literature—God's revelation to Moses at Sinai received and handed on unimpaired and intact in a reliable process of instruction by masters to disciples—accounts for the public, anonymous character of Rabbinic writing.

Not a line in the entire Rabbinic literature even suggests that schismatic writing existed, even though named statements of individual authorities are preserved on every page of that literature. The point that is proven is simple. People disagreed within a permitted agendum, and the protocol of disagreement always began with the premise of concurrence on all that counted. That was, as we saw, the very goal of Rabbinic dialectics: the rationality of dispute, the cogency of theology and of law as a whole. As every named saying we have examined has already shown us, dissenting views too found their properly labeled position in Rabbinic literature, preserved in the name of the private person who registered dissent in accord with the rules governing the iron-consensus of the collegium as a whole.

4

ZEKHUT AND THE RABBINIC THEOLOGY OF HISTORY

RABBINIC JUDAISM: THE SYSTEMIC CENTER

In expanding our view of the comparison and contrast between Rabbinic Judaism and formative Christianity, we have implied that the systemic center of each, meriting juxtaposition with that of the other, ought to prove congruent, thus Torah or Gospel, Christ or Messiah-sage. But that implication is unintended and we have now to amplify the matter.

If at this point we had to identify the center of the Rabbinic-Judaic system, we should naturally point to that composite formed by Torah study, the figure of the sage, and the sage-Messiah. It would follow that the source of supernatural power, the Torah, the identity of those with access to it, the sage, and the systemic teleology, the Messiah-sage, would take concrete form in the symbol of the Torah and the myth of the revelation of the Torah in two media, oral and written. But that theory would not survive a simple test: do we find stories that reject the centrality of Torah study altogether but substitute a different virtue from learning, a different ideal from that of study of the Torah, and a different hero from the sage-Messiah? And when we find a word defying all translation, a category to which the system itself attaches the status of uniqueness, is that word, is that category, Torah-learning? For indeed, we do. Not only so, but these same stories find their heroic figures in two sorts of persons to whom the system centered on the Torah accords little place or importance. The first such sort is the ignorant man, and the second, the woman. Centrality accorded in such stories—embedded in the heart of the Rabbinic literature, in the Talmud of the Land of Israel, for example—to the ignorant and the feminine represents a systemic reversal, the outsider standing at the center, the disenfranchised exercising valued power, in the case of the woman and the ignorant man, respectively. Then the message of those stories must come to the fore to attest to the Rabbinic account of the meaning and end of events, such as a theology of history defines.

At the systemic center stands not Torah-learning and Torah-power but a different sort of supernatural locus entirely, for which a word stands that is as difficult to translate as the word "Torah." Not only so, but, the further we investigate the traits and properties of that word, the more impressed we become by the unique status enjoyed by that category or by the person assigned to that category. Just as in Christianity, we come to the systemic center when we speak of Christ, meaning, not a messiah, such as the Mishnah reveals, but The Messiah, the only one. So in Rabbinic Judaism when we come to the conception at hand, we find ourselves dealing with what stands beyond all comparisons, analogies, and contrasts. The word *zekhut,* bearing a variety of closely related meanings, dictated by context, stands at the systemic center, the point at which systemic reversals prove plausible, the key to the explanation of the here and now and also times past and times to come.

Zekhut stands for the empowerment, of a supernatural character, that derives from the virtue of one's ancestry or from one's own virtuous deeds of a very particular order. No single word in English bears the same meaning, nor can I identify a synonym for *zekhut* in the canonical writings in the original either. As we noted, the difficulty of translating a word of systemic consequence with a single word in some other language (or in the language of the system's documents themselves) tells us we deal with what is unique, beyond comparison and therefore contrast and comprehension.[1] What is most particular to, distinctive of, the systemic structure and its functioning requires definition through circumlocution: "the heritage of virtue and its consequent entitlements."[2] The word *zekhut* for the successor system forms the systemic counterpart to the *mythologoumenon* of the Resurrection of Jesus Christ, unique son of God, for important Christianities.

DEFINING ZEKHUT

Zekhut, scarce or common as our capacity for uncoerced action dictated, puissant or supine as our strength to refrain from deeds of worldly power decided, accomplished the systemic integration of the successor documents. That protean conception formed into a cogent political economy for the social order of Israel the economics and the politics that transformed powerlessness into power, disinheritance into wealth. Acts of will consisting of submission, on one's own, to the will of Heaven endowed Israel with a lien and entitlement upon Heaven. What we cannot by will impose, we can by will evoke. What we cannot accomplish through coercion, we can achieve through submission. God will do for us what we cannot do for ourselves, when we do for God what God cannot make us do. In a wholly concrete and tangible sense—love God with all the heart, the soul, the might—we have. That systemic statement justifies classifying the successor system as religious in as profound and complete a way as the initial system had been wholly and restrictedly philosophical.

It must follow that *zekhut,* not Torah, in a single word defines the generative myth, the critical symbol of the successor Judaism. The signal that the Torah formed a mere component in a system that transcended Torah study and defined its structure in some way other than by appeal to the symbol and activity of the Torah comes from a simple fact. Ordinary folk, not disciples of sages, have access to *zekhut* entirely outside of study of the Torah. In stories not told about rabbis, a single remarkable deed, exemplary for its deep humanity, sufficed to win for an ordinary person the *zekhut*—"the heritage of virtue and its consequent entitlements"— that elicits the same marks of supernatural favor enjoyed by some rabbis on account of their Torah study.

Accordingly, the systemic centrality of *zekhut* in the structure, the critical importance of the heritage of virtue together with its supernatural entitlements—these emerge in a striking claim. It is framed in extreme form—another mark of the unique place of *zekhut* within the system. Even though a man was degraded, one action sufficed to win for him that heavenly glory to which rabbis in lives of Torah study aspired. The mark of the system's integration around *zekhut* lies in its insistence that all Israelites, not only sages, could gain *zekhut* for themselves (and their descendants). The rabbinical storyteller whose writing we shall consider assuredly identifies with this lesson, since it is the point of his story and its climax.

In all three instances that follow, defining what the individual must do to gain *zekhut,* the point is that the deeds of the heroes of the story make them worthy of having their prayers answered, which is a mark of the working of *zekhut.* It is deeds beyond the strict requirements of the Torah, and even the limits of the law altogether, that transform the hero into a holy man, whose holiness served just like that of a sage marked as such by knowledge of the Torah. The following stories should not be understood as expressions of the mere sentimentality of the clerks concerning the lower orders, for they deny in favor of a single action of surpassing power sages' lifelong devotion to what the sages held to be the highest value, knowledge of the Torah:

Y. Taanit 1:4.I

    F. A certain man came before one of the relatives of R. Yannai. He said to him, "Rabbi, attain *zekhut* through me [by giving me charity]."

    G. He said to him, "And didn't your father leave you money?"

    H. He said to him, "No."

    I. He said to him, "Go and collect what your father left in deposit with others."

    J. He said to him, "I have heard concerning property my father deposited with others that it was gained by violence [so I don't want it]."

K. He said to him, "You are worthy of praying and having your prayers answered."

The point of K, of course, is self-evidently a reference to the possession of entitlement to supernatural favor, and it is gained, we see, through deeds that the law of the Torah cannot require but must favor: what one does on one's own volition, beyond the measure of the law. Here I see the opposite of sin. A sin is what one has done by one's own volition beyond all limits of the law. So an act that generates *zekhut* for the individual is the counterpart and opposite: what one does by one's own volition, that also is beyond all requirements of the law.

L. A certain ass driver appeared before the rabbis [the context requires: in a dream] and prayed, and rain came. The rabbis sent and brought him and said to him, "What is your trade?"

M. He said to them, "I am an ass driver."

N. They said to him, "And how do you conduct your business?"

O. He said to them, "One time I rented my ass to a certain woman, and she was weeping on the way, and I said to her, 'What's with you?' and she said to me, 'The husband of that woman [me] is in prison [for debt], and I wanted to see what I can do to free him.' So I sold my ass and I gave her the proceeds, and I said to her, 'Here is your money, free your husband, but do not sin [by becoming a prostitute to raise the necessary funds].'"

P. They said to him, "You are worthy of praying and having your prayers answered."

The ass-driver clearly has a powerful lien on Heaven, so that his prayers are answered, even while those of others are not. What he did to get that entitlement? He did what no law could demand: impoverished himself to save the woman from a "fate worse than death."

Q. In a dream of R. Abbahu, Mr. Pentakaka ["Five Sins"] appeared, who prayed that rain would come, and it rained. R. Abbahu sent and summoned him. He said to him, "What is your trade?"

R. He said to him, "Five sins does that man [I] do every day, [for I am a pimp:] hiring whores, cleaning up the theater, bringing home their garments for washing, dancing, and performing before them."

S. He said to him, "And what sort of decent thing have you ever done?"

T. He said to him, "One day that man [I] was cleaning the theater, and a woman came and stood behind a pillar and cried. I said to her, 'What's with you?' And she said to me, 'That woman's [my] husband is in prison, and I wanted to see what I can do to free him,' so I sold my bed and cover, and I gave the proceeds to her. I said to her, 'Here is your money, free your husband, but do not sin.'"

U. He said to him, "You are worthy of praying and having your prayers answered."

Q moves us still further, since the named man has done everything sinful that one can do, and, more to the point, he does it every day. So the singularity of the act of *zekhut*, which suffices if done only one time, encompasses its power to outweigh a life of sin—again, an act of *zekhut* as the mirror-image and opposite of sin. Here again, the single act of saving a woman from a "fate worse than death" has sufficed.

V. A pious man from Kefar Imi appeared [in a dream] to the rabbis. He prayed for rain and it rained. The rabbis went up to him. His householders told them that he was sitting on a hill. They went out to him, saying to him, "Greetings," but he did not answer them.

W. He was sitting and eating, and he did not say to them, "You break bread too."

X. When he went back home, he made a bundle of faggots and put his cloak on top of the bundle [instead of on his shoulder].

Y. When he came home, he said to his household [wife], "These rabbis are here [because] they want me to pray for rain. If I pray and it rains, it is a disgrace for them, and if not, it is a profanation of the name of Heaven. But come, you and I will go up [to the roof] and pray. If it rains, we shall tell them, 'We are not worthy to pray and have our prayers answered.'"

Z. They went up and prayed and it rained.

AA. They came down to them [and asked], "Why have the rabbis troubled themselves to come here today?"

BB. They said to him, "We wanted you to pray so that it would rain."

CC. He said to them, "Now do you really need my prayers? Heaven already has done its miracle."

DD. They said to him, "Why, when you were on the hill, did we say hello to you, and you did not reply?"

EE. He said to them, "I was then doing my job. Should I then interrupt my concentration [on my work]?"

FF. They said to him, "And why, when you sat down to eat, did you not say to us 'You break bread too'?"

GG. He said to them, "Because I had only my small ration of bread. Why would I have invited you to eat by way of mere flattery [when I knew I could not give you anything at all]?"

HH. They said to him, "And why when you came to go down, did you put your cloak on top of the bundle?"

II. He said to them, "Because the cloak was not mine. It was borrowed for use at prayer. I did not want to tear it."

JJ. They said to him, "And why, when you were on the hill, did your wife wear dirty clothes, but when you came down from the mountain, did she put on clean clothes?"

KK. He said to them, "When I was on the hill, she put on dirty clothes, so that no one would gaze at her. But when I came home from the hill, she put on clean clothes, so that I would not gaze on any other woman."

LL. They said to him, "It is well that you pray and have your prayers answered."

The pious man of V, finally, enjoys the recognition of the sages by reason of his lien upon Heaven, able as he is to pray and bring rain. What has so endowed him with *zekhut*? Acts of punctiliousness of a moral order: concentrating on his work, avoiding an act of dissimulation, integrity in the disposition of a borrowed object, his wife's concern not to attract other men and her equal concern to make herself attractive to her husband. None of these stories refers explicitly to *zekhut;* all of them tell us about what it means to enjoy not an entitlement by inheritance but a lien accomplished by one's own supererogatory acts of restraint.

Zekhut integrates what has been differentiated. Holding together learning, virtue, and supernatural standing, by explaining how Torah study transforms the learning man, *zekhut* further makes implausible those points of distinction between economics, and politics that bore the systemic message of the initial philosophy. Hierarchical classification, with its demonstration of the upward-reaching unity of all being, gives way to a different, and more compelling proposition: the unity of all being within the heritage of *zekhut,* to be attained equally and without differentiation in all the principal parts of the social order. The definition of *zekhut* therefore carries us to the heart of the integrating and integrated religious system of Judaism.

The word *zekhut* bears a variety of meanings, as Jastrow summarizes the data,[3] and the pertinence of each possible meaning is to be determined in context: (1) acquittal, plea in favor of the defendant; (2) doing good, blessing; (3) protecting influence of good conduct, merit; (4) advantage, privilege, benefit. The first meaning pertains solely in juridical (or metaphorically juridical) contexts; the second represents a very general and imprecise use of the word, since a variety of other words bear the same meaning. Only the third and the fourth meanings pertain, since they are particular to this word, on the one side, and also religious, on the other. That is to say, only through using the word *zekhut* do authors of compositions and authorships of composites express the sense given at No. 3. Moreover, it will rapidly become clear, in context that No. 4 is not to be distinguished from No. 3, since "protecting influence of good conduct" when the word *zekhut* appears always yields "advantage, privilege, benefit." It follows that, for the purposes of systemic analysis, passages in which the word *zekhut* bears the sense, in Jastrow's words, of "the protecting influence of good conduct" which yields "advantage, privilege, or benefit" will tell us how the word *zekhut* functions.

My simple definition emphasizes "heritage," because the advantages or privileges conferred by *zekhut* may be inherited and also passed on; it stresses "entitlements" because advantages or privileges always, invariably result from receiving *zekhut* from ancestors or acquiring it on one's own; and I use the word "virtue" to refer to those supererogatory acts that demand a reward because they form matters of choice, the gift of the individual and his or her act of free will, an act that is at the same time (1) uncompelled, e.g., by the obligations imposed by the Torah, but (2) also valued by the Torah. The systemic importance of the conception of *zekhut* derives from its capacity to unite the generations in a heritage of entitlements; *zekhut* is fundamentally a historical category and concept, in that, like all historical systems of thought, it explains the present in terms of the past, and the future in terms of the present.[4]

Because *zekhut* is something one may receive as an inheritance, out of the distant past, *zekhut* imposes upon the definition of the social entity, "Israel," a genealogical meaning. It furthermore imparts a distinctive character to the definitions of way of life. So the task of the political component of a theory of the social order, which is to define the social entity by appeal to empowerment, and of the economic component, which is to identify scarce resources by specification of the rationality of right management, is accomplished in a single word, which stands for a conception, a symbol, and a myth. All three components of this religious theory of the social order turn out to present specific applications, in context, for the general conception of *zekhut*. For the first source of *zekhut* derives from the definition of Israel as family; the entitlements of supernatural power deriving from virtue then are inherited from Abraham, Isaac, and Jacob. The second source is personal: the power one can gain for one's own heirs, moreover, by virtuous deeds. *Zekhut* deriving from either source is to be defined in context: what can you do if you have *zekhut* that you cannot do if you do not have *zekhut,* and to whom can you do it. The answer to that question tells you the empowerment of *zekhut*.

Now in the nature of things, a theory of power or violence that is legitimately exercised falls into the category of a politics, and a conception of the scarce resource, defined as supernatural power that is to be rationally managed, falls into the category of an economics. That is why in the concept of *zekhut,* we find the union of economics and politics into a political economy: a theory of the whole society in its material and social relationships as expressed in institutions that permanently are given the right to impose order through real or threatened violence and in the assignment of goods and benefits, as systemically defined, to be sure, through a shared rationality.

ZEKHUT IN DOCUMENTARY CONTEXT

Since I have identified as systemically active not the conception but the word and its usages, we shall focus not on general situations, e.g., in which one receives some sort of benefit by reason of an inheritance from some other person, but upon specific usages of the word at hand. That focus is required not only by the logic of this study, but also by the difficulty of knowing what belongs and what does not belong when *zekhut* bears the confusing translation of "merit," and when "merit" promiscuously refers to pretty much anything that one gets *not* by one's own merit or just desserts at all, but despite what one has done. Scripture, for example, knows that God loves Israel because he loved the patriarchs (Deut. 4:37); the memory or deeds of the righteous patriarchs and matriarchs appear in a broad range of contexts, e.g., "Remember your servants, Abraham, Isaac, and Jacob" (Exod. 32:13), for Moses, and "Remember the good deeds of David, your servant" (2 Chr. 6:42), for David. At stake throughout is giving people what they do not merit, to be sure. But in these contexts, "remembering" what X did as an argument in behalf of favor for Y does not invoke the word *zekhut,* and the context does not require use of that word either.[5] Accordingly, our problem of definition requires limitation to precise usages of a given word. Were we to propose to work our way back from situations that seem to exhibit conceptual affinities to the concept represented by the word under consideration—cases, for instance, in which someone appeals to what is owing the fathers in behalf of the children—we shall not accomplish the goal at hand, which is one of definition of a word that in this system, in these documents in particular, bears a very particular meaning, and, more to the point, carries out a highly critical role.

At M. San. 4:1, 5:4, 5:5, and 6:1 we find *zekhut* in the sense of "acquittal," as against conviction; at M Ket 13:6 the sense is, "right," as in "right of ownership;" at M Git 8:8 the sense is not "right of ownership" in a narrow sense, but "advantage," in a broader one of prerogative: "It is not within the power of the first husband to render void the right of the second." These usages of course bear no point in common with the sense of the word later on. But the evidence of the Mishnah seems to me to demonstrate that the sense of *zekhut* paramount in the successor documents is not original to them. The following usage at M. Qid. 4:14 seems to me to invite something very like the sense that I have proposed here. So states M. Qid. 4:14E–I:

> R. Meir says, "A man should always teach his son a clean and easy trade. And let him pray to him to whom belong riches and possessions. For there is no trade which does not involve poverty or wealth. For poverty does not come from one's trade, nor does wealth come from one's trade. But all is in accord with a man's *zekhut*."

Quite how to translate our key word in this passage is not self-evident. The context permits a variety of possibilities. The same usage seems to me to be located at M. Sot. 3:4, 3:5, and here there is clear indication of the presence of a conception of an entitlement deriving from some source other than one's own deed of the moment:

MISHNAH-TRACTATE SOTAH 3:4–5

3:4. E. There is the possibility that *zekhut* suspends the curse for one year, and there is the possibility that *zekhut* suspends the curse for two years, and there is the possibility that *zekhut* suspends the curse for three years.

    F. On this basis Ben Azzai says, "A man is required to teach Torah to his daughter.

G. "For if she should drink the water, she should know that [if nothing happens to her], *zekhut* is what suspends [the curse from taking effect]."

3:5 A. R. Simeon says, "*Zekhut* does not suspend the effects of the bitter water.

B. "And if you say, '*Zekhut* does suspend the effects of the bitter water,' you will weaken the effect of the water for all the women who have to drink it.

C. "And you give a bad name to all the women who drink it who turned out to be pure.

D. "For people will say, 'They are unclean, but *zekhut* suspended the effects of the water for them.'"

E. Rabbi says, "*Zekhut* does suspend the effects of the bitter water. But she will not bear children or continue to be pretty. And she will waste away, and in the end she will have the same [unpleasant] death."

Now if we insert for *zekhut* at each point, "the heritage of virtue and its consequent entitlements," (thus replacing "For people will say, 'They are unclean, but *zekhut* suspended the effects of the water for them,'" with "For people will say, 'They are unclean, but the heritage of virtue and its consequent entitlements suspended the effects of the water for them'"), we have good sense. That is to say, the woman may not suffer the penalty to which she is presumably condemnable, not because her act or condition (e.g., her innocence) has secured her acquittal or nullified the effects of the ordeal, but because she enjoys some advantage extrinsic to her own act or condition. She may be guilty, but she may also possess a benefice deriving by inheritance, hence, heritage of virtue, and so be entitled to a protection not because of her own, but because of someone else's action or condition.

That meaning may be sustained by the passage at hand, even though it is not required by it; still, it seems to me plausible that the word *zekhut* in the Mishnah bears not only a juridical but a religious sense. But, if, as I think, it does, that usage is not systemically critical, or even very important. If we search the pages of the Mishnah for places in which, absent the word *zekhut,* the concep-

tion in hand is present, we find none—not one. For example, there
simply is no reference to gaining *zekhut* through doing one's duty—
e.g., in reciting the *Shema* or studying the Torah—and references
to studying the Torah—e.g., at M. Peah 1:1—do not encompass
the conception that, in doing so, one gains an advantage or entitlement for either one's own descendants or for all Israel. On that
basis we are on firm ground in holding the twin-positions (1) that
the word bore, among its meanings, the one important later on,
and also (2) that the word played no systemic role, in the philosophical system adumbrated by the Mishnah, commensurate with
the importance accorded to the word and its sense in the religious
system that took shape and came to expression in the successor
writings.

The evidence of tractate Abot is consistent with that of the
Mishnah. The juridical sense of *zekhut* occurs at 1:6, "Judge everybody as though to be acquitted," more comprehensibly translated,
"And give everybody the benefit of the doubt," forming a reasonably coherent match with the usages important in Mishnah-tractate Sanhedrin. In Abot, however, we have clear evidence for the
sense of the word that seems to me demanded later on. At M. Abot
2:2 we find the following:

Tractate Abot 2:2

    C. "And all who work with the community—let them work with
    them for the sake of Heaven.

    D. "For the (1) *zekhut* of their fathers strengthens them, and their
    [fathers'] (2) righteousness stands forever.

    E. "And as for you, I credit you with a great reward, as if you had
    done [all of the work required by the community on your own
    merit alone]."

Here there is no meaning of *zekhut* possible other than that I have
given above: "the heritage of virtue and its consequent entitlements." The reference to an advantage that one gains by reason of
inheritance out of one's fathers' righteousness is demanded by the
parallel between *zekhut* of clause (1) and *righteousness* of clause (2).
Whatever the conceivable ambiguity of the Mishnah, none is sus-

tained by the context at hand, which is explicit in language and pellucid in message. That the sense is exactly the same as the one I have proposed is shown at the following passages, which seem to me to exhibit none of the possible ambiguity that characterized the usage of *zekhut* in the Mishnah:

Tractate Abot 5:18

A. He who causes *zekhut* to the community never causes sin.

B. And he who causes the community to sin—they never give him a sufficient chance to attain penitence.

Here the contrast is between causing *zekhut* and causing sin, so *zekhut* is the opposite of sin. The continuation is equally clear that a person attained *zekhut* and endowed the community with *zekhut,* or sinned and made the community sin:

C. Moses attained *zekhut* and bestowed *zekhut* on the community.

D. So the *zekhut* of the community is assigned to his [credit],

E. as it is said, "He executed the justice of the Lord and his judgments with Israel" (Deut. 33:21).

F. Jeroboam sinned and caused the community to sin.

G. So the sin of the community is assigned to his [debit],

H. as it is said, "For the sins of Jeroboam which he committed and wherewith he made Israel to sin" (1 Kings 15:30).

The appropriateness of interpreting the passage in the way I have proposed will now be shown to be self-evident. All that is required is to substitute for *zekhut* the proposed translation:

C. Moses attained the heritage of virtue and bestowed its consequent entitlements on the community.

D. So the heritage of virtue end its entitlements enjoyed by the community are assigned to his [credit],

The sense then is simple. Moses through actions of his own (of an unspecified sort) acquired *zekhut,* which is the credit for such actions that accrued to him and bestowed upon him certain supernatural entitlements; and he for his part passed on as an inheritance that credit, a lien on Heaven for the performance of these same supernatural entitlements: *zekhut,* pure and simple.

If we may now define *zekhut* as the initial system explicated in tractate Abot has used the word, we must pay close attention to the antonymic structure before us. The juridical opposites are guilty as against innocent, the religious ones, as we have now seen, sin as against the opposite of sin. That seems to me to require our interpreting *zekhut* as

1. an action, as distinct from a (mere) attitude; that
2. is precisely the opposite of a sinful one; it is, moreover, an action that
3. may be done by an individual or by the community at large, and one that
4. a leader may provoke the community to do (or not do).

The contrast of sin to *zekhut* requires further attention. Since, in general, two classes that are compared to begin with, if different, must constitute opposites, the ultimate definition of *zekhut* requires us to ask how *zekhut* is precisely the opposite of sin. For one thing, as we recall, Scripture is explicit that the burden of sins cannot be passively inherited, willy-nilly, but, to form a heritage of guilt, must be actively accepted and renewed; the children cannot be made to suffer for the sins of the parents unless they repeat them. Then *zekhut,* being a mirror image, can be passively inherited, not by one's own merit[6] but by one's good fortune alone. But what constitutes these *actions* that form mirror images of sins? Answers to that critical question must emerge from the systemic documents before us, since they do not occur in those of the initial system.

That simple fact, too, attests to the systemic centrality of *zekhut:* it defines a principal point of exegesis. For the question left open by the Mishnah's merely episodic, and somewhat opaque, reference to the matter and the incomplete evidence provided by its principal apologetic's representation as well, alas, is the critical issue. Precisely what actions generate *zekhut,* and which ones do not? To find answers to those questions, we have to turn to the

successor documents, since not a single passage in the Mishnah
or in tractate Abot provides me with information on the matter of
what I must do to secure for myself or my descendants a lien on
Heaven, that is, an entitlement to supernatural favor and even action of a miraculous order.

ZEKHUT AND THE RABBINIC THEOLOGY OF HISTORY

We turn first to the conception of the *zekhut* that has been accumulated by the patriarchs and passed on to Israel, their children.
The reason is that the single distinctive trait of *zekhut,* as we have
seen it to this point, is its transitive quality: one need not earn or
merit the supernatural power and resource represented by the
things you can do if you have *zekhut* but cannot do if you do not
have it. One can inherit that entitlement from others, dead or living. Moses not only attains *zekhut* but he also imparts *zekhut* to the
community of which he is leader, and the same is so for any Israelite. That conception is broadened in the successor documents
into the deeply historical notion of *zekhut Abot,* empowerment of
a supernatural character to which Israel is entitled by reason of
what the patriarchs and matriarchs in particular did long ago. That
conception forms the foundation for the paramount sense of *zekhut*
in the successor system: the Israelite possesses a lien on Heaven
by reason of God's love for the patriarchs and matriarchs, God's
appreciation for certain things they did, and God's response to
those actions not only in favoring them but also in entitling their
descendants to do or benefit from otherwise unattainable miracles.
Zekhut, as we noted earlier, explains the present—particularly what
is odd and unpredictable in the present—by appeal to the past,
hence forms a distinctively historical conception.

Within the historically grounded metaphor of Israel as a family expressed by the conception of *zekhut Abot,* Israel was a family,
the children of Abraham, Isaac, and Jacob, or children of Israel, in
a concrete and genealogical sense. Israel hence fell into the genus,
family, as the particular species of family generated by Abraham
and Sarah. The distinguishing trait of that species was that it possessed the inheritance, or heritage, of the patriarchs and matri-

archs, and that inheritance, consisting of *zekhut,* served the descendants and heirs as protection and support. It follows that the systemic position of the conception of *zekhut* to begin with lies in its power to define the social entity, and hence, *zekhut* (in the terms of the initial category-formation, the philosophical one) forms a fundamentally political conception[7] and only secondarily an economic and philosophical one.

But *zekhut* serves, in particular, that counterpart category that speaks of not legitimate but illegitimate violence, not power but weakness. In context, time and again, we observe that *zekhut* is the power of the weak. People who through their own merit and capacity can accomplish nothing, can accomplish miracles through what others do for them in leaving a heritage of *zekhut..* And, not to miss the stunning message of the triplet of stories cited above, *zekhut* also is what the weak and excluded and despised can do that outweighs in power what the great masters of the Torah have accomplished. In the context of a system that represents Torah as supernatural, that claim of priority for *zekhut* represents a considerable transvaluation of power, as much as of value. And, by the way, *zekhut* also forms the inheritance of the disinherited: what you receive as a heritage when you have nothing in the present and have gotten nothing in the past, that scarce resource that is free and unearned but much valued. So let us dwell on the definitive character of the transferability of *zekhut* in its formulation, *zekhut* Abot, the *zekhut* handed on by the ancestors, the transitive character of the concept and its standing as a heritage of entitlements.

It is in the successor documents that the concept of *zekhut* is joined with *Abot,* that is, the *zekhut* that has been left as Israel's family inheritance by the patriarchs or ancestors, yielding the very specific notion, defining the systemic politics, its theory of the social entity, of Israel not as a (mere) community (e.g., as in tractate Abot's reference to Moses's bestowing *zekhut* upon the community) but as a family, with a history that takes the form of a genealogy, precisely as Genesis has represented that history.[8] Now *zekhut* was joined to the metaphor of the genealogy of patriarchs and matriarchs and served to form the missing link, explaining how the inheritance and heritage were transmitted from them to their heirs.

Consequently, the family, called "Israel," could draw upon the family estate, consisting of the inherited *zekhut* of matriarchs and patriarchs in such a way as to benefit today from the heritage of yesterday. This notion involved very concrete problems. If "Israel, the family" sinned, it could call upon the "*zekhut*" accumulated by Abraham and Isaac at the binding of Isaac (Genesis 22) to win forgiveness for that sin. True, "fathers will not die on account of the sin of the sons," but the children may benefit from the *zekhut* of the forebears. That concrete expression of the larger metaphor imparted to the metaphor a practical consequence, moral and theological, that was not at all neglected.

A survey of Genesis Rabbah proves indicative of the character and use of the doctrine of *zekhut,* because that systematic reading of the Book of Genesis dealt with the founders of the family and made explicit the definition of Israel as family. What we shall see is that *zekhut* draws in its wake the notion of the inheritance of an ongoing (historical) family, that of Abraham and Sarah, and *zekhut* worked itself out in the moments of crisis of that family in its larger affairs. So the Israelites later on enjoy enormous *zekhut* through the deeds of the patriarchs and matriarchs. That conception comes to expression in what follows:

Genesis Rabbah LXXVI:V

2. A. ". . . for with only my staff I crossed this Jordan, and now I have become two companies:"

   B. R. Judah bar Simon in the name of R. Yohanan: "In the Torah, in the Prophets, and in the Writings we find proof that the Israelites were able to cross the Jordan only on account of the *zekhut* achieved by Jacob:

   C. "In the Torah: '. . . for with only my staff I crossed this Jordan, and now I have become two companies.'

   D. "In the prophets: 'Then you shall let your children know, saying, "Israel came over this Jordan on dry land"' (Josh. 4:22), meaning our father, Israel.

   E. "In the Writings: 'What ails you, O you sea, that you flee? You Jordan, that you burn backward? At the presence of the God of Jacob' (Ps. 114:5 ff.)."

Here is a perfect illustration of my definition of *zekhut* as an entitlement I enjoy by reason of what someone else—an ancestor—has done; and that entitlement involves supernatural power. Jacob did not only leave *zekhut* as an estate to his heirs. The process is reciprocal and ongoing. *Zekhut* deriving from the ancestors had helped Jacob himself:

GENESIS RABBAH LXXVII:III.3

A. "When the man saw that he did not prevail against Jacob, [he touched the hollow of his thigh, and Jacob's thigh was put out of joint as he wrestled with him]" (Gen. 32:25):

B. Said R. Hinena bar Isaac, "[God said to the angel,] 'He is coming against you with five "amulets" hung on his neck, that is, his own *zekhut,* the *zekhut* of his father and of his mother and of his grandfather and of his grandmother.

C. "'Check yourself out, can you stand up against even his own *zekhut* [let alone the *zekhut* of his parents and grandparents].'

D. "The matter may be compared to a king who had a savage dog and a tame lion. The king would take his son and sic him against the lion, and if the dog came to have a fight with the son, he would say to the dog, 'The lion cannot have a fight with him, are you going to make out in a fight with him?'

E. "So if the nations come to have a fight with Israel, the Holy One, blessed be he, says to them, 'Your angelic prince could not stand up to Israel, and as to you, how much the more so!'"

The collectivity of *zekhut,* not only its transferability, is illustrated here as well: what an individual does confers *zekhut* on the social entity. It is, moreover, a matter of the legitimate exercise of supernatural power. And the reciprocity of the process extended in all directions. Accordingly, what we have in hand is first and foremost a matter of the exercise of legitimate violence, hence a political power. *Zekhut* might project not only backward, deriving from an ancestor and serving a descendant, but forward as well. Thus Joseph accrued so much *zekhut* that the generations that came before him were credited with his zekhut:

Genesis Rabbah LXXXIV:V.2

A. "These are the generations of the family of Jacob. Joseph [being seventeen years old, was shepherding the flock with his brothers]" (Gen. 37:2):

B. These generations came along only on account of the *zekhut* of Joseph.

C. Did Jacob go to Laban for any reason other than for Rachel?

D. These generations thus waited until Joseph was born, in line with this verse: "And when Rachel had borne Joseph, Jacob said to Laban, 'Send me away'" (Gen. 30:215).

E. Who brought them down to Egypt? It was Joseph.

F. Who supported them in Egypt? It was Joseph.

G. The sea split open only on account of the *zekhut* of Joseph: "The waters saw you, O God" (Ps. 77:17). "You have with your arm redeemed your people, the sons of Jacob and Joseph" (Ps. 77:16).

H. R. Yudan said, "Also the Jordan was divided only on account of the *zekhut* of Joseph."

The passage at hand asks why only Joseph is mentioned as the family of Jacob. The inner polemic is that the *zekhut* of Jacob and Joseph would more than suffice to overcome Esau. Not only so, but Joseph survived because of the *zekhut* of his ancestors:

Genesis Rabbah LXXXVII:VIII.1

A. "She caught him by his garment . . . but he left his garment in her hand and fled and got out of the house. [And when she saw that he had left his garment in her hand and had fled out of the house, she called to the men of her household and said to them, 'See he has brought among us a Hebrew to insult us; he came in to me to lie with me, and I cried out with a loud voice, and when he heard that I lifted up my voice and cried, he left his garment with me and fled and got out of the house']" (Gen. 39:13–15):

B. He escaped through the *zekhut* of the fathers, in line with this verse: "And he brought him forth outside" (Gen. 15:5).

C. Simeon of Qitron said, "It was on account of bringing up the bones of Joseph that the sea was split: 'The sea saw it and fled' (Ps. 114:3), on the *zekhut* of this: '. . . and fled and got out.'"

Zekhut, we see, is both personal and national. B refers to Joseph's enjoying the *zekhut* he had inherited, C referring to Israel's enjoying the zekhut that they gained through their supererogatory loyalty to that same *zekhut*-rich personality. How do we know that the *zekhut* left as a heritage by ancestors is in play? Here is an explicit answer:

GENESIS RABBAH LXXIV:XII.1

A. "If the God of my father, the God of Abraham and the Fear of Isaac, had not been on my side, surely now you would have sent me away empty-handed. God saw my affliction and the labor of my hand and rebuked you last night" (Gen. 31:41–42):

B. Zebedee b. Levi and R. Joshua b. Levi:

C. Zebedee said, "Every passage in which reference is made to 'if' tells of an appeal to the *zekhut* accrued by the patriarchs."[9]

D. Said to him R. Joshua, "But it is written, 'Except we had lingered' (Gen. 43:10) [a passage not related to the *zekhut* of the patriarchs]."

E. He said to him, "They themselves would not have come up except for the *zekhut* of the patriarchs, for if it were not for the *zekhut* of the patriarchs, they never would have been able to go up from there in peace."

✿

133

✿

The issue of the *zekhut* of the patriarchs comes up in the reference to the God of the fathers. The conception of the *zekhut* of the patriarchs is explicit, not general. It specifies what later benefit to the heir, Israel the family, derived from which particular action of a patriarch or matriarch.

GENESIS RABBAH XLIII:VIII.2

A. "And Abram gave him a tenth of everything" (Gen. 14:20):

B. R. Judah in the name of R. Nehorai: "On the strength of that blessing the three great pegs on which the world depends, Abraham, Isaac, and Jacob, derived sustenance.

C. "Abraham: 'And the Lord blessed Abraham in *all* things' (Gen. 24:1) on account of the *zekhut* that 'he gave him a tenth of *all* things' (Gen. 14:20).

D. "Isaac: 'And I have eaten of *all*' (Gen. 27:33), on account of the *zekhut* that 'he gave him a tenth of *all* things' (Gen. 14:20).

E. "Jacob: 'Because God has dealt graciously with me and because I have all' (Gen. 33:11) on account of the *zekhut* that 'he gave him a tenth of *all* things' (Gen. 14:20).

GENESIS RABBAH XLIII:VIII.3

A. Whence did Israel gain the *zekhut* of receiving the blessing of the priests?

B. R. Judah said, "It was from Abraham: '*So* shall your seed be' (Gen. 15:5), while it is written in connection with the priestly blessing: '*So* shall you bless the children of Israel' (Num. 6:23)."

C. R. Nehemiah said, "It was from Isaac: 'And I and the lad will go *so* far' (Gen. 22:5), therefore said the Holy One, blessed be he, '*So* shall you bless the children of Israel' (Num. 6:23)."

D. And rabbis say, "It was from Jacob: 'So shall you say to the house of Jacob' (Exod. 19:3) (in line with the statement, '*So* shall you bless the children of Israel' (Num. 6:23)."

No. 2 links the blessing at hand with the history of Israel. Now the reference is to the word "all," which joins the tithe of Abram to the blessing of his descendants. Since the blessing of the priest is at hand, No. 3 treats the origins of the blessing. The picture is clear. "Israel" constitutes a family as a genealogical and juridical fact. It inherits the estate of the ancestors. It hands on that estate. It lives by the example of the matriarchs and patriarchs, and its history exemplifies events in their lives. And *zekhut* forms that entitlement that one generation may transmit to the next, in a way in which the heritage of sin is not to be transmitted except by reason of the deeds of the successor generation. The good that one does lives onward, the evil is interred with the bones.

To conclude this brief survey of *zekhut* as the medium of historical existence, that is, the *zekhut* deriving from the patriarchs, or *zekhut Abot,* let me present a statement of the legitimate power—sufficient to achieve salvation, which, in this context, always bears a political dimension—imparted by the *zekhut* of the ancestors. That *zekhut* will enable them to accomplish the political goals of Israel: its attaining self-rule and avoiding government by gentiles. This statement appeals to the binding of Isaac as the source of the *zekhut,* deriving from the patriarchs and matriarchs, which will in the end lead to the salvation of Israel. What is important here is that the *zekhut* that is inherited joins together with the *zekhut* of one's own deeds; one inherits the *zekhut* of the past, and, moreover, if one does what the progenitors did, one not only receives an entitlement out of the past, one secures an entitlement on one's own account. So the difference between *zekhut* and sin lies in the sole issue of transmissibility:

Genesis Rabbah LVI:II.5

A. Said R. Isaac, "And all was on account of the *zekhut* attained by the act of prostration.

B. "Abraham returned in peace from Mount Moriah only on account of the *zekhut* owing to the act of prostration: '. . . and we will worship [through an act of prostration] and come [then, on that account] again to you' (Gen. 22:5).

C. "The Israelites were redeemed only on account of the *zekhut* owing to the act of prostration: And the people believed . . . then they bowed their heads and prostrated themselves' (Exod. 4:31).

D. "The Torah was given only on account of the *zekhut* owing to the act of prostration: 'And worship [prostrate themselves] you afar off' (Exod. 24:1).

E. "Hannah was remembered only on account of the *zekhut* owing to the act of prostration: 'And they worshiped before the Lord' (1 Sam. 1:19).

F. "The exiles will be brought back only on account of the *zekhut* owing to the act of prostration: 'And it shall come to pass in that day that a great horn shall be blown and they shall come that were lost . . . and that were dispersed . . . and they shall worship the Lord in the holy mountain at Jerusalem' (Isa. 27:13).

G. "The Temple was built only on account of the *zekhut* owing to the act of prostration: 'Exalt you the Lord our God and worship at his holy hill' (Ps. 99:9).

H. "The dead will live only on account of the *zekhut* owing to the act of prostration: 'Come let us worship and bend the knee, let us kneel before the Lord our maker' (Ps. 95:6)."

The entire history of Israel flows from its acts of worship ("prostration") beginning with that performed by Abraham at the binding of Isaac. Every sort of advantage Israel has ever gained came about through that act of worship done by Abraham and imitated thereafter. Israel constitutes a family and inherits the *zekhut* laid up as a treasure for the descendants by the ancestors. It draws upon that *zekhut* but, by doing the deeds they did, it also enhances its heritage of *zekhut* and leaves to the descendants greater entitlement than they would enjoy by reason of their own actions. But their own actions—here, prostration in worship—generate *zekhut* as well.

Accordingly, as I claimed at the outset, *zekhut* may be personal or inherited. The *zekhut* deriving from the prior generations is collective and affects all Israel. But one's own deeds can generate *zekhut* for oneself, with the simple result that *zekhut* is as much personal as it is collective. Specifically, Jacob reflects on the power that Esau's own *zekhut* had gained for Esau. He had gained that *zekhut* by living in the Land of Israel and also by paying honor and respect to Isaac. Jacob then feared that, because of the *zekhut* gained by Esau, he, Jacob, would not be able to overcome him. So *zekhut* worked on its own; it was a credit gained by proper action, which went to the credit of the person who had done that action. What made the action worthy of evoking Heaven's response with an act of supernatural favor is that it was an action not to be required but if done to be rewarded, an act of will that cannot be coerced but must be honored. In Esau's case, it was the simple fact that he had remained in the Holy Land:

Genesis Rabbah LXXVI:II

2. A. "Then Jacob was greatly afraid and distressed" (Gen. 32:7): [This is Jacob's soliloquy:] "Because of all those years that Esau was living in the Land of Israel, perhaps he may come against me with the power of the *zekhut* he has now attained by dwelling in the Land of Israel.

    B. "Because of all those years of paying honor to his father, perhaps he may come against me with the power of the *zekhut* he attained by honoring his father.

    C. "So he said: 'Let the days of mourning for my father be at hand, then I will slay my brother Jacob' (Gen. 27:41).

    D. "Now the old man is dead."

The important point, then, is that *zekhut* is not only inherited as part of a collective estate left by the patriarchs. It is also accomplished by an individual in his or her own behalf. By extension, we recognize, the successor system opens a place for recognition of the individual, both man and woman as a matter of fact, within the system of *zekhut*. As we shall now see, what a man or a woman does may win for that person an entitlement on Heaven for supernatural favor of some sort. So there is space, in the system, for a private person, and the individual is linked to the social order through the shared possibilities of generating or inheriting an entitlement on Heaven.[10]

✡
137
✝

Zekhut and Israel's Salvation, Now and Then

For if we now ask, what are the sorts of deeds that generate *zekhut*, we realize that those deeds produce a common result of gaining for their doer, as much as for the heirs of the actor, an entitlement for heavenly favor and support when needed. And that fact concerning gaining and benefiting from *zekhut* brings us to the systemic message to the living generation, its account of what now is to be done. And that message proves acutely contemporary, for its stress is on the power of a single action to create sufficient *zekhut* to outweigh a life of sin. Then the contrast between sin and *zekhut* gains greater depth still. One sin of sufficient weight condemns, one act of *zekhut* of sufficient weight saves; the entire issue of entitlements out of the past gives way, then, when we realize what is actually at stake.

We recall that Torah study is one—but only one—means for an individual to gain access to that heritage, to get *zekhut.* There are other equally suitable means, and, not only so, but the merit gained by Torah study is no different from the merit gained by acts of a supererogatory character. If one gets *zekhut* for studying the Torah, then we must suppose there is no holy deed that does not generate its share of *zekhut.* But when it comes to specifying the things one does to get *zekhut,* the documents before us speak of what the Torah does not require but does recommend: not what we are commanded to do in detail, but what the right attitude, formed within the Torah, leads us to do on our own volition:

Y. Taanit 3:11.IV

C. There was a house that was about to collapse over there [in Babylonia], and Rab set one of his disciples in the house, until they had cleared out everything from the house. When the disciple left the house, the house collapsed.

D. And there are those who say that it was R. Adda bar Ahwah.

E. Sages sent and said to him, "What sort of good deeds are to your credit [that you have that much merit]?"

F. He said to them, "In my whole life no man ever got to the synagogue in the morning before I did. I never left anybody there when I went out. I never walked four cubits without speaking words of Torah. Nor did I ever mention teachings of Torah in an inappropriate setting. I never laid out a bed and slept for a regular period of time. I never took great strides among the associates. I never called my fellow by a nickname. I never rejoiced in the embarrassment of my fellow. I never cursed my fellow when I was lying by myself in bed. In the marketplace I never walked over to someone who owed me money.

G. "In my entire life I never lost my temper in my household."

H. This was meant to carry out that which is stated as follows: "I will give heed to the way that is blameless. Oh when wilt thou come to me? I will walk with integrity of heart within my house" (Ps. 101:2).

What I find striking in this story is that mastery of the Torah is only one means of attaining the merit that enabled the sage to keep the house from collapsing. For what the sage did to gain such remarkable merit is not to master such and so many tractates of the Mishnah. Nor does the storyteller refer to carrying out the commandments of the Torah as specified. It was rather acts that expressed courtesy, consideration, restraint. These acts, which no specification can encompass in detail, produced the right attitude, one of gentility, that led to gaining merit. Acts rewarded with an entitlement to supernatural power are those of self-abnegation or the avoidance of power over others—not taking great strides among the associates, not using a nickname, not rejoicing in the embarrassment of one's fellow, not singling out one's debtor—and the submission to the will and the requirement of self-esteem of others.

Here, in a moral setting, we find the politics replicated: the form of power that the system promises derives from the rejection of power that the world recognizes—legitimate violence replaced by legitimation of the absence of the power to commit violence or of the failure to commit violence. Not exercising power over others, that is, the counterpart politics, moreover, produced that scarcest of all resources, supernatural favor, by which the holy man could hold up a tottering building. Here then we find politics and economics united in the counterpart category formed of *zekhut*: the absence of power yielding supernatural power, the valuation of the intangible, Torah, yielding supernatural power. It was, then, that entitlement to supernatural favor that formed the systemic center.

What about what we have to do to secure an inheritance of *zekhut* for our heirs? Here is a concrete example of how acts of worth or *zekhut* accrue to the benefit of the heirs of those that do them. What makes it especially indicative is that here gentiles have the power to acquire zekhut for their descendants, which is coherent with the system's larger interest in not only Israel (as against the faceless, undifferentiated outsider) but the gentiles as well. Here we see that the successor system may hold within the orbit of its generative conception even the history of the gentiles:

Genesis Rabbah C:VI.1

A. "When they came to the threshing floor of Atad, which is beyond the Jordan, they lamented there with a very great and sorrowful lamentation, and he made a mourning for his father seven days" (Gen. 50:10):

B. Said R. Samuel bar Nahman, "We have reviewed the entire Scripture and found no other place called Atad. And can there be a threshing floor for thorns [the Hebrew word for thorn being *atad*]?

C. "But this refers to the Canaanites. It teaches that they were worthy of being threshed like thorns. And on account of what *zekhut* were they saved? It was on account of the acts of kindness that they performed for our father, Jacob [on the occasion of the mourning for his death]."

D. And what were the acts of kindness that they performed for our father, Jacob?

E. R. Eleazar said, "[When the bier was brought up there,] they unloosened the girdle of their loins."

F. R. Simeon b. Laqish said, "They untied the shoulder-knots."

G. R. Judah b. R. Shalom said, "They pointed with their fingers and said, 'This is a grievous mourning to the Egyptians' (Gen. 50:11).

H. Rabbis said, "They stood upright."

I. Now is it not an argument *a fortiori:* now if these, who did not do a thing with their hands or feet, but only because they pointed their fingers, were saved from punishment, Israel, which performs an act of kindness [for the dead] whether they are adults or children, whether with their hands or with their feet, how much the more so [will they enjoy the *zekhut* of being saved from punishment]!

J. Said R. Abbahu, "Those seventy days that lapsed between the first letter and the second match the seventy days that the Egyptians paid respect to Jacob. [Seventy days elapsed from Haman's letter of destruction until Mordecai's letter announcing the repeal of the decree (cf. Est. 3:12, 8:9). The latter letter, which permitted the Jews to take vengeance on their would-be destroyers, should have come earlier, but it was delayed seventy days as a reward for the honor shown by the Egyptians to Jacob."[11]

The Egyptians gained *zekhut* by honoring Jacob in his death, so Abbahu. This same point then registers for the Canaanites. The connection is somewhat farfetched, that is, through the reference to the threshing floor, but the point is a strong one. And the explanation of history extends not only to Israel's, but also the Canaanites', history.

If the Egyptians and the Canaanites, how much the more so Israelites! What is it that Israelites as a nation do to gain a lien on Heaven for themselves or entitlements of supernatural favor for their descendants? Here is one representative answer to that question:

GENESIS RABBAH LXXIV:XII.1

A. "If the God of my father, the God of Abraham and the Fear of Isaac, had not been on my side, surely now you would have sent me away empty-handed. God saw my affliction and the labor of my hand and rebuked you last night" (Gen. 31:41–42):

B. Zebedee b. Levi and R. Joshua b. Levi:

C. Zebedee said, "Every passage in which reference is made to 'if' tells of an appeal to the *zekhut* accrued by the patriarchs."[12]

D. Said to him R. Joshua, "But it is written, 'Except we had lingered' (Gen. 43:10) [a passage not related to the *zekhut* of the patriarchs]."

E. He said to him, "They themselves would not have come up except for the *zekhut* of the patriarchs, for it if it were not for the *zekhut* of the patriarchs, they never would have been able to go up from there in peace."

F. Said R. Tanhuma, "There are those who produce the matter in a different version." [It is given as follows:]

G. R. Joshua and Zebedee b. Levi:

H. R. Joshua said, "Every passage in which reference is made to 'if' tells of an appeal to the *zekhut* accrued by the patriarchs except for the present case."

I. He said to him, "This case too falls under the category of an appeal to the *zekhut* of the patriarchs."

So much for *zekhut* that is inherited from the patriarchs, a now familiar notion. But what about the deeds of Israel in the here and now?

J. R. Yohanan said, "It was on account of the *zekhut* achieved through sanctification of the divine name."

K. R. Levi said, "It was on account of the *zekhut* achieved through faith and the *zekhut* achieved through Torah.

Faith despite the here and now, study of the Torah—these are what Israel does in the here and now with the result that they gain an entitlement for themselves or their heirs.

L. "The *zekhut* achieved through faith: 'If I had not believed . . .' (Ps. 27:13).

M. "The *zekhut* achieved through Torah: 'Unless your Torah had been my delight' (Ps. 119:92)."

2. A. "God saw my affliction and the labor of my hand and rebuked you last night" (Gen. 31:41–42):

B. Said R. Jeremiah b. Eleazar, "More beloved is hard labor than the *zekhut* achieved by the patriarchs, for the *zekhut* achieved by the patriarchs served to afford protection for property only, while the *zekhut* achieved by hard labor served to afford protection for lives.

C. "The *zekhut* achieved by the patriarchs served to afford protection for property only: 'If the God of my father, the God of Abraham and the Fear of Isaac, had not been on my side, surely now you would have sent me away empty-handed.'

D. "The *zekhut* achieved by hard labor served to afford protection for lives: 'God saw my affliction and the labor of my hand and rebuked you last night.'"

Here is as good an account as any of the theology of *zekhut*. The issue of the *zekhut* of the patriarchs comes up in the reference to the God of the fathers. The conception of the *zekhut* of the patriarchs is explicit, not general. It specifies what later benefit to the heir, Israel the family, derived from which particular action of a patriarch or matriarch. But acts of faith and Torah study form only one medium; hard labor, that is, devotion to one's calling, defines that source of *zekhut* that is going to be accessible to those many Israelites unlikely to distinguish themselves either by Torah study and acts of faith, encompassing the sanctification of God's name, or by acts of amazing gentility and restraint.

The system here speaks to everybody, Jew and gentile, past and present and future; *zekhut* therefore defines the structure of the cosmic social order and explains how it is supposed to function. It is the encompassing quality of *zekhut*, its pertinence to past and future, high and low, rich and poor, gifted and ordinary, that marks as the systemic statement the message of *zekhut*, now fully revealed as the conception of reciprocal response between Heaven and Israel on earth, to acts of devotion beyond the requirements of the Torah but defined all the same by the Torah. As Scripture had said, God responds to the faith of the ancient generations by supernatural acts to which, on their own account, the moderns are not entitled, hence a heritage of entitlement. But those acts, now fully defined for us, can and ought to be done, also, by the living generation. And, as a matter of fact, no one today, at the time of the system builders, is exempt from the systemic message and its demands: even steadfastness in accomplishing the humble work of the everyday and the here and now.

The systemic statement made by the usages of *zekhut* speaks of relationship, function, the interplay of humanity and God. One's store of *zekhut* derives from a relationship, that is, from one's forebears. That is one dimension of the relationships in which one stands. *Zekhut* also forms a measure of one's own relationship with Heaven, as the power of one person, but not another, to pray and so bring rain attests. What sort of relationship does *zekhut*, as the opposite of sin, then posit? It is not one of coercion, for Heaven cannot force us to do those types of deeds that yield *zekhut*, and that, story after story suggests, is the definition of a deed that generates *zekhut*: doing what we ought to do but do not have to do. But then, we cannot coerce Heaven to do what we want done either, for example, by carrying out the commandments. These are obligatory, but do not obligate Heaven.

Whence then our lien on Heaven? It is through deeds of a supererogatory character—to which Heaven responds by deeds of a supererogatory character: supernatural favor to this one, who through deeds of ingratiation of the other or self-abnegation or restraint exhibits the attitude that in Heaven precipitates a counterpart attitude, hence generating *zekhut,* rather than to that one, who does not. The simple fact that rabbis cannot pray and bring rain, but a simple ass-driver can, tells the whole story. The relationship measured by *zekhut*—Heaven's response by an act of uncoerced favor to a person's uncoerced gift, e.g., act of gentility, restraint, or self-abnegation—contains an element of unpredictability for which appeal to the *zekhut* inherited from ancestors accounts. So while I cannot coerce Heaven, I can through *zekhut* gain acts of favor from Heaven, and that is by doing what Heaven cannot require of me. Heaven then responds to my attitude in carrying out my duties—and more than my duties. That act of pure disinterest—giving the woman my means of livelihood—is the one that gains for me Heaven's deepest interest.

So *zekhut* forms the political economy of the religious system of the social order put forward by the Talmud of the Land of Israel, Genesis Rabbah, Leviticus Rabbah, and related writings. Here we find the power that brought about the transvaluation of value, the reversal of the meaning of power and its legitimacy. *Zekhut* expresses and accounts for the economic valuation of the scarce resource of what we should call moral authority. *Zekhut* stands for the political valorization of weakness, that which endows the weak with a power that is not only their own but their ancestors'. It enables the weak to accomplish goals through not their own power, but their very incapacity to accomplish acts of violence—a transvaluation as radical as that effected in economics. And *zekhut* holds together both the economics and the politics of this Judaism: it makes the same statement twice.

Zekhut as the power of the powerless, the riches of the disinherited, the valuation and valorization of the will of those who have no right to will. In the context of Christian Palestine, Jews found themselves on the defensive. Their ancestry called into question, their supernatural standing thrown into doubt, their future denied, they called themselves "Israel," and the land, "the Land of Israel." But what power did they possess, legitimately, if need be through violence, to assert their claim to form "Israel"? And, with the Holy Land passing into the hands of others, what scarce resource did they own and manage to take the place of that measure of value that now no longer was subjected to their rationality? Asserting a politics in which all violence was illegitimate, an economics in which nothing tangible, even real property in the Holy Land had value, the system through its counterpart categories made a single, simple, and sufficient statement. But those whom Judaism knows as "our sages of blessed memory" were not the only system builders, and theirs was not the only question about the social order framed in historical and theological, rather than analytical and philosophical terms. Their contemporary, the bishop of Hippo whom Christianity knows as Saint Augustine, set forth an account of the social order framed in the same terms and addressed to the same urgent and critical question. It is in the context of comparison that, in the end, we interpret the system that has now been described and analyzed.

5

JUDAISM AND CHRISTIANITY MEET IN THE CITY OF GOD

TRADING POWER FOR PATHOS

O ur sages of blessed memory" and Christian saints and martyrs and bishops addressed the same problem, namely, the reconciliation of this worldly power and other-worldly imperatives. The circumstance of each mirrored that of the other, but the fundamental convictions of the two coincided in their concern with sorting out the demands of Sinai: what does it mean to form a kingdom of priests and a holy people, what does it demand to be God's people.

Trading places in the end involved the movement from power to weakness, and from weakness to power. For Judaism, a new theory of the social order had to take the place of one that invoked politics and economics in this-worldly terms; for Christianity, a new theory of the social order had to take account of the remarkable shift in the situation of Christians, as they moved from catacombs to imperial court. At the same time, Rabbinic Judaism described the social order of ordinary people living everyday lives; it could not wholly abandon the social order in favor of the dominion of heaven. And Christianity had also to reconcile itself to a situation that contradicted the context in which it had begun its life, one of political weakness but moral dignity and power. So in trading places, the one gave up worldly power for an other-worldly pathos, the other abandoned the dominion of God in taking over the empire of this world. Both, then, had to work out what it meant to live in the city of God (Christianity)[1] or the dominion of heaven (Judaism) under circumstances not contemplated in the nascent stages of the respective systems.

It is only in the dialogue with Augustine, theologian of the new age, that we may take up the enchantment of Israel, its ultimate transformation from a this-worldly political and social entity into an other-worldly holy community, set down upon earth but living by the rules of heaven. Here we have the solution to the problem of change from an empowered to a disempowered Israel, in the notion that Israel forms a supernatural community intruded into time, God's stake in humanity and God's statement to humanity. Israel is then to exhibit the virtues on earth that God values in heaven, and to which God responds. And what we shall see with great clarity is that Augustine's heavenly city forms the Christian counterpart, a systematic effort to respond to the empowerment, in emperor and church order, with an explanation of power. Christian polity forms an intrusion of heaven upon earth; the heavenly city embodied in natural time and space forms God's realm.

Enchanted Judaism and *The City of God*

"Make his wishes yours, so that he will make your wishes his . . . Anyone from whom people take pleasure, God takes pleasure" (Abot 2:4). These two statements hold together the two principal elements of the conception of the relationship to God that a single word, *zekhut*, conveys. Give up, please others, do not impose your will but give way to the will of the other, and Heaven will respond by giving a lien that is not coerced but evoked. By the rationality of discipline within, we have the power to form rational relationships beyond ourselves, with Heaven; and that is how the system expands the boundaries of the social order to encompass not only the natural but also the supernatural world.

For it is the rationality of that relationship to God that governs the social order, defining the three components thereof: way of life, worldview, theory of the social order. For within that relationship we discern the model of not merely ethics but economics, not merely private morality in society but the public policy, the politics that delineates the limns of the ethnic community, and not alone the right attitude of the virtuous individual but the social philosophy of an entire nation—so the system proposes. And that is the this-worldly social order that joins with Heaven, the society that is a unique and holy family, so transformed by *zekhut* inherited and *zekhut* accomplished as to transcend the world order. That ordering of humanity in society, empowered and enriched in an enchanted political economy, links private person to the public polity through the union of a common attitude: the one of renunciation that tells me how to behave at home and in the streets, and that instructs Israel how to conduct its affairs among the nations and throughout history.

WHAT IS GODLY IN ISRAEL

✡
149
✝

Treating every deed, every gesture as capable of bringing about enchantment, the Talmuds and related Midrash-compilations imparted to the givens of everyday life—at least in their potential—remarkable power. The conviction that, by dint of special effort, I may so conduct myself as to acquire an entitlement of supernatural power turns my commonplace circumstance into an arena encompassing heaven and earth. God responds to my—and holy Israel's—virtue, filling the gap, so to speak, about myself and about my entire family that I and we leave when we forebear, withdraw, and give up what is mine and ours: our space, my self. When I do, then God responds; my sacrifice evokes memories of Abraham's readiness to sacrifice Isaac;[2] my devotion to the other calls up from Heaven what by demanding I cannot coerce. What imparts critical mass to the conception of *zekhut,* that gaining of supernatural entitlements through the surrender of what is mine, is the recasting, in the mold and model of that virtue of surrender, of the political economy of Israel in the Land of Israel. That accounts for the definition of legitimate power in politics as only weakness, economics as the rational increase of resources that are, but need not be, scarce, valued things that are capable of infinite increase.

That not only accounts for the inversion of the received categories and their reformation into mirror images of what the philosophers had made of them. In my view it also explains why a quite fresh, deeply religious system has taken the place of a compelling and well-composed philosophical one. The Mishnah's God can scarcely compete with the God of the Yerushalmi and the Midrash-compilations.[3] For the God of the philosophers, the apex of the hierarchy of all being as the framers of the Mishnah have positioned God, has made the rules and is shown by them to form the foundation of order. All things reach up to one thing, one thing contains within itself many things: these twin propositions of monotheism, which the philosophical system demonstrates in theory and proposes to realize in the facts of the social order, define a God who in an orderly way governs all the palpable relationships of nature as of supernature—but who finds a place, who comes to puissant expression, in not a single one of them. The God of the philosophers assures, sustains, supports, nourishes, guarantees, governs. But the way that God responds to what we do is all according to the rule. That is, after all, what natural philosophy proposes to uncover and discern, and what more elevated task can God perform than the nomothetic one accomplished in the daily creation of the world.

But God in the Talmuds and related Midrash-compilations gains what the philosophical God lacks, which is personality, active presence, pathos and empathy. The God of the religious system breaks the rules, accords an entitlement to this one, who has done some one remarkable deed, but not to that one, who has done nothing wrong and everything right. So a life in accord with the rules—even a life spent in the study of the Torah—in Heaven's view is outweighed by a single moment, a gesture that violates the norm, extending the outer limits of the rule, for instance, of virtue. And who but a God who, like us, feels, not only thinks, responds to impulse and sentiment, can be portrayed in such a way as this?

So I sold my ass and I gave her the proceeds, and I said to her, "Here is your money, free your husband, but do not sin [by becoming a prostitute to raise the necessary funds]."

They said to him, "You are worthy of praying and having your prayers answered."

No rule exhaustively describes a world such as this. If the God of the philosophers' Judaism makes the rules, the God of the religious Judaism breaks them. The systemic difference, of course, is readily extended outward from the personality of God: the philosophers' God thinks, the God of the religious responds, and we are in God's image, after God's likeness, not only because we through right thinking penetrate the principles of creation, but through right attitude replicate the heart of the Creator. Humanity on earth incarnates God on high, the Israelite family in particular, and, in consequence, earth and heaven join—within.

What is asked of Israel and of the Israelite individual now is Godly restraint, supernatural generosity of soul that is "in our image, after our likeness:" that is what sets aside all rules. And, since as a matter of simple fact, that appeal to transcend the norm defined not personal virtue but the sainthood of all Israel, living all together in the here and in the now, we must conclude that, within Israel's society, within what the Greco-Roman world will have called its *polis,* its political and social order, the bounds of earth have now extended to heaven. In terms of another great system composed in the same time and in response to a world-historical catastrophe of the same sort, Israel on earth dwells in the city of God. And, it must follow, God dwells with Israel, in Israel: "today, if you will it."

That insistence on the systemic centrality of the conception of *zekhut,* with all its promise for the reshaping of value, draws our attention once more to the power of a single, essentially theological conception to impart shape and structure to the social order. The Judaism set forth in the successor documents portrayed a social order in which, while taking full account of circumstance and historical context, individuals and nation alike controlled their own destiny. The circumstance of genealogy dictated whether or not the moral entity, whether the individual or the nation, would enjoy access to entitlements of supernatural favor without regard to the merit of either one. But, whether favored by a rich heritage of supernatural empowerment, as was the nation, or deprived, by reason of one's immediate ancestors, of any lien on Heaven, in the end both the nation and the individual had in hand the power to shape the future. How was this to be done? It was not alone by keeping the Torah, studying the Torah, dressing, eating, making a living, marrying, procreating, raising a family, burying and being buried, all in accord with those rules.

That life in conformity with the rule, obligatory but merely conventional, did not evoke the special interest of Heaven. Why should it? The rules describe the ordinary. But (in language used only in a later document) "God wants the heart," and that is not an ordinary thing. Nor was the power to bring rain or hold up a tottering house gained through a life of merely ordinary sanctity. Special favor responded to extraordinary actions, in the analogy of special disfavor, misfortune deemed to punish sin. And just as culpable sin, as distinct from mere error, requires an act of will, specifically, arrogance, so an act of extraordinary character requires an act of will. But, as mirror image of sin, the act would reveal in a concrete way an attitude of restraint, forbearance, gentility, and self-abnegation. A sinful act, provoking Heaven, was one that one did deliberately to defy Heaven. Then an act that would evoke Heaven's favor, so imposing on Heaven a lien that Heaven freely gave, was one that, equally deliberately and concretely, displayed humility.

But the systemic focus on the power of a single act of remarkable generosity, the surrender to the other of what is most precious to the self, whether that constituted an opinion or a possession or a feeling, in no way will have surprised the framers of the philosophical Judaism. They had laid heavy emphasis on the power of human intentionality to settle questions of the status of interstitial persons, objects, or actions, within the larger system of hierarchical classification. So in the philosophical Judaism attitude and intentionality classified what was of doubtful status, that is to say, forming the active and motivating component of the structure and

transforming the structure—a tableau of fixed and motionless figures—into a system of action and reaction. Then, in the process
of transformation, we should hardly find surprising the appeal to
the critical power of attitude and intentionality. For what we find
in the Talmuds and related Midrash-compilations is a fundamental point of connection. What was specific before, intentionality, is
now broadened and made general through extension to all aspects
of one's attitude.

Now the powerful forces coalescing in intentionality gained
very precise definition, and in their transformation from merely
concrete cases of the taxonomic power of intentionality that
worked one way here, another way there, into very broad-ranging
but quite specific and prescribed attitudes, the Talmuds and related Midrash-compilations took its leave from the initial one without a real farewell. Then what is the point of departure? It is
marked by the intense interest, in the religious Judaism, on not the
fixed given of normative intentionality,[4] but rather changing people, both individually and nationally, from what they were to
something else. And, if the change is in a single direction, it is,
nonetheless, also always personal and individual.

The change is signalled by the conception that study of the
Torah not only illuminated and educated but transformed, and,
moreover, so changed the disciple that he gained in supernatural
standing and authority. This Gnostic conception of knowledge,
however, proved only a component of a larger conception of national transformation and personal regeneration, since, as we saw,
Torah study produced *zekhut,* and all things depended on the *zekhut*
that a person, or the nation as a whole, possessed. Mastery of what
we classify as "the system's worldview" changed a person by generating *zekhut,* that is, by so affecting the person as to inculcate attitudes that would produce remarkable actions (often: acts of
omission, restraint, and forbearance) to generate *zekhut.* The change
was the end, the Torah study, the medium.

But the system's worldview was not the sole, or even the principal, component that showed how the received system was transformed by the new one. The conception of *zekhut* came to the fore
to integrate of the system's theory of the way of life of the social

order, its economics, together with its account of the social entity of the social order, its politics. The remarkable actions—perhaps those of omission more than those of commission—that produced *zekhut* yielded an increase in the scarcest of all resources, supernatural favor, and at the same time endowed a person rich in entitlements to heavenly intervention with a power to evoke that vastly outweighed the this-worldly power to coerce in the accomplishment of one's purpose.

This rapid account of the systemic structure and system, its inversion of the received categories and its formation of anticategories of its own, draws our attention to the specificity of the definition of right attitude and puissant intentionality by contrast to the generality of those same matters when represented in the philosophical system of the Mishnah. We have, therefore, to ask ourselves whether the quite concrete definition of those attitudes and correct will and proper intentionality that lead to acts that generate *zekhut* will have surprised framers of documents prior to those that attest the transformed Judaism before us. The answer is negative, and that fact alerts us to yet another fundamental continuity between the two Judaisms.

As a matter of fact, the doctrine defining the appropriate attitude persisted pretty much unchanged from the beginning. The repertoire of approved and disapproved attitude and intentionality remained constant through the half-millennium of the unfolding of the canon of Judaism from the Mishnah onward: humility, forbearance, accommodation, a spirit of conciliation. For one thing, Scripture itself is explicit that God shares and responds to the attitudes and intentionality of human beings. God cares what humanity feels—wanting love, for example—and so the conception that actions that express right attitudes of humility will evoke in Heaven a desired response will not have struck as novel the authors of the Pentateuch or the various prophetic writings, for example. The biblical record of God's feelings and God's will concerning the feelings of humanity leaves no room for doubt. What is fresh in the system before us is not the integration of the individual with the nation but the provision, for the individual, of a task and a role analogous to that of the nation.

With its interest in classifying large-scale and collective classes of things, the Mishnah's system treats matters of attitude and emotion in that same taxic context. For instance, while the Mishnah casually refers to emotions—e.g., tears of joy, tears of sorrow—where feelings matter, it always is in a public and communal context. Where there is an occasion of rejoicing, one form of joy is not to be confused with some other, or one context of sorrow with another. Accordingly, marriages are not to be held on festivals (M. M.Q. 1:7). Likewise mourning is not to take place then (M. M.Q. 1:5, 3:7–9). Where emotions play a role, it is because of the affairs of the community at large, e.g., rejoicing on a festival, mourning on a fast day (M. Suk. 5:1–4). Emotions are to be kept in hand, as in the case of the relatives of the executed felon (M. San. 6:6). If I had to specify the single underlying principle affecting all forms of emotion, for the Mishnah it is the profoundly philosophical attitude that attitudes and feelings must be kept under control, never fully expressed without reasoning about the appropriate context. Emotions must always lay down judgments.

We see in most of those cases in which emotions play a systemic and indicative, not merely an episodic and random, role, that the basic principle is the same. We can and must so frame our feelings as to accord with the appropriate rule. In only one case does emotion play a decisive role in settling an issue, and that has to do with whether or not a farmer was happy that water came upon his produce or grain. That case underlines the conclusion just now drawn. If people feel a given sentiment, it is a matter of judgment and therefore invokes the law's penalties. So in this system emotions are not treated as spontaneous, but as significant aspects of a person's judgment.

Whence then the doctrine, made so concrete and specific in the conception of *zekhut* as made systemically generative in the successor documents, that very specific attitudes, particular to persons, bear the weight of the systemic structure as a whole? It is in tractate Abot, which supplies those phrases cited at the outset to define the theology that sustains the conception of *zekhut*. Tractate Abot, conventionally attached to the Mishnah and serving as the Mishnah's advocate, turns out to form the bridge from the Mishnah to the Yerushalmi and its associated compilations of scriptural exegeses. That tractate presents the single most comprehensive account of religious affections. The reason is that, in that document above all, how we feel defines a critical aspect of virtue. The issue proves central, not peripheral. The very specific and concrete doctrine emerges fully exposed. A simple catalog of permissible feelings comprises humility, generosity, self-abnegation, love, a spirit of conciliation of the other, and eagerness to please. A list of impermissible emotions is made up of envy, ambition, jealousy, arrogance, sticking to one's opinion, self-centeredness, a grudging spirit, vengefulness, and the like. Nothing in the wonderful stories about remarkable generosity does more than render concrete the abstract doctrine of the heart's virtue that tractate Abot sets forth.

People should aim at eliciting from others acceptance and good will and should avoid confrontation, rejection, and humiliation of the other. This they do through conciliation and giving up their own claims and rights. So both catalogs form a harmonious and uniform whole, aiming at the cultivation of the humble and malleable person, one who accepts everything and resents nothing. True, these virtues, in this tractate as in the system as a whole, derive from knowledge of what really counts, which is what God wants. But God favors those who please others. The virtues appreciated by human beings prove identical to the ones to which God responds as well. And what single virtue of the heart encompasses the rest? Restraint, the source of self-abnegation, humility, serves as the anecdote for ambition, vengefulness, and, above all, for arrogance. It is restraint of our own interest that enables us to deal generously with others, humility about ourselves that generates a liberal spirit toward others. And the correspondence of heavenly and mortal attitudes is to be taken for granted—as is made explicit.

So the emotions prescribed in tractate Abot turn out to provide variations of a single feeling, which is the sentiment of the disciplined heart, whatever affective form it may take. And where does the heart learn its lessons, if not in relationship to God? So: "Make his wishes yours, so that he will make your wishes his" (Abot 2:4). Applied to relationships between human beings, this inner discipline of the emotional life will yield exactly those virtues of conciliation and self-abnegation, humility and generosity of spirit, that the framers of tractate Abot spell out in one example after another. Imputing to Heaven exactly those responses felt on earth, e.g., "Anyone from whom people take pleasure, God takes pleasure" (Abot 3:10), makes the point at the most general level.

Then what has the Talmuds contributed? Two things: (1) the conception that acts of omission or commission expressing an attitude of forbearance and self-abnegation generate *zekhut* in particular; (2) the principle that *zekhut* functions in those very specific ways that the system deems critical: as the power to attest to human transformation and regeneration, affording, in place of philosophical politics and philosophical economics, that power inhering in weakness, that wealth inhering in giving up what one has, that in the end promise the attainment of our goals. In a single sentence, the path from one system to the other is in three stages: (1) the philosophical Judaism portrayed by the Mishnah assigns to intentionality and attitude systemic centrality; (2) tractate Abot, in presenting in general terms the rationale of the Mishnah's system, defines precisely the affective attitude and intentionality that are required; (3) the religious Judaism of the Yerushalmi and associated writings joins together the systemic centrality of attitude and intentionality with the doctrine of virtue laid out in tractate Abot.

But in joining these received elements the new system emerges as distinct from the old. For when we deem the attitude of affirmation and acceptance, rather than aggression, and the intentionality of self-abnegation and forbearance, to define the means for gaining *zekhut*, what we are saying is contrary and paradoxical: if you want to have, then give up, and if you want to impose your judgment, then make the judgment of the other into your own, and if you want to coerce Heaven, then evoke in Heaven attitudes of sympathy that will lead to the actions or events that you want, whether rain, whether long life, whether the salvation of Israel and its hegemony over the nations: to rule, be ruled by Heaven; to show Heaven rules, give up what you want to the other. *Zekhut* results: the lien upon Heaven, freely given by Heaven in response to one's free surrender to the will and wish of Heaven. And by means of *zekhut,* whether one's own, whether one's ancestors', the social order finds its shape and system, and the individual his or her place within its structure.

The correspondence of the individual to the nation, both capable of gaining *zekhut* in the same way, linked the deepest personal emotions to the cosmic fate and transcendent faith of that social group of which each individual formed a part. The individual Israelite's innermost feelings, the inner heart of Israel, the microcosm, correspond to the public and historic condition of the nation, of Israel, the macrocosm. In the innermost chambers of the individual's deepest feelings, the Israelite therefore lives out the public history and destiny of the people, Israel.

JUDAISM AND CHRISTIANITY MEET IN THE CITY OF GOD

The sages who wrote the Talmud of the Land of Israel, Genesis Rabbah, Leviticus Rabbah, and Pesiqta deRab Kahana, did not stand alone in their profound reflection on how earth and heaven intersect, and how the here and the now forms a moment in history. As it happens, at the same time and, as a matter of fact, under similar circumstances of historical crisis, another system builder was at work. When we appreciate the commonalities of the task facing each party and the dimensions that turn out to take the measure of the results of each, we realize how different people, speaking each to their own world, delivering each their own statement, turn out in the same time to answer the same question in what is, as a matter of fact, pretty much the same cosmic dimensions, and, it would turn out, with the same enduring results for the formation of Western civilization.[5]

Augustine of Hippo's life, in North Africa and Italy (354–430), coincided with the period in which, to the east, the sages of the Land of Israel produced their Talmud in amplification of the Mishnah as well as their Midrash-compilations in extension of Moses's books of Genesis and Leviticus. But he comes to mind, for comparison and contrast, not merely because of temporal coincidence. Rather, the reason is that, like the sages of Judaism, he confronted the same this-worldly circumstance, one in which the old order was coming to an end—and was acknowledged to be closing. And the changes were those of power and politics. In 410 the Goths took Rome, and refugees of Alaric's conquest fled to North Africa (as well as, as a matter of fact, to the Land of Israel/Palestine, as events even early in the story of Jerome in Jerusalem tell us[6]). At the very hour of his death, some decades later, Augustine's own city, Hippo lay besieged by the Vandals. So it was at what seemed the twilight of the ancient empire of Rome that Augustine composed his account of the theology of the social order known as the *City of God.* Within his remarkable *oeuvre,* it was that work that renders of special interest here the sages' contemporary and their counterpart as a system builder.

Like the critical issue of political calamity facing sages in the aftermath of the triumph of Christianity and the failure of Julian's brief restoration of both paganism and (as to Jerusalem) Judaism, the question Augustine addressed presented a fundamental challenge to the foundations of the Christian order, coming as it did from Roman pagan aristocrats who took refuge in North Africa.[7] What caused the fall of Rome, if not the breaches in its walls made by Christianity? The first three books of the *City of God* responded, in 413, and twenty-two books in all came to a conclusion in 426: a gigantic work.[8] While the *City of God* (re)presents Christian faith "in the form of biblical history, from Genesis to Revelation," just as sages present important components of their system in the form of historical narrative, I see no important doctrinal points in common between the program of Israel's sages in the Land of Israel and that of the great Christian theologian and philosopher. Each party presented in an episodic way what can be represented as an orderly account of the social order,[9] each for the edification of its chosen audience; neither, I think, would have understood a line of the composition of the other, in writing or in concept. And that unbridgeable abyss makes all the more striking the simple fact that, from one side of the gap to the other, the distance was slight. For each party addressed questions entirely familiar, I think, to the other, and the gross and salient traits of the system of the one in some striking ways prove symmetrical to those of the other.

The relationship of the opposing cities of God and the devil, embodied in the pilgrim Church and the empirical state, presents the chief systematic problem of the *City of God*.[10] Augustine covered, in five books, "those who worshiped the gods for felicity on earth;" in five, "those who worshiped them for eternal felicity;" and twelve, the theme of the origin of "two cities, one of God, the other of the world, " "their unfolding course in the part," "their ultimate destinies."[11] True, sages reconsidered the prior disinterest in history, but they did not then produce a continuous account of everything that had ever happened, and Augustine did. Nor do the two literary monuments, Augustine's and sages', bear anything in common as to form, style, sources, mode of argument, selection of audience, or literary convention of any kind. Then why treat the system of sages and the systematic statement of Augustine as so connected as to warrant comparison? For the obvious reason that the authorship of Israel and the Christian author not only responded to the same circumstance but also framed the question deemed posed by that common circumstance in the same terms: a recasting, in historical terms, of the whole of the social order, a rethinking, in the image of Augustine, of God's city.

What then was the value of the *polis,* which throughout these pages I have rendered as "the social order," and exactly who lived in the city of the earth? It was "any group of people tainted by the Fall," any that failed to regard "the 'earthly' values they had created as transient and relative."[12] To this Augustine responds, "Away with all this arrogant bluffing: what, after all, are men but men!"[13] The rise of Rome is reduced, in Brown's words, "to a simple common denominator . . . the 'lust for domination.'" The Romans were moved by "an overweening love of praise: 'they were, therefore, "grasping for praise, open-handed with their money; honest in the pursuit of wealth, they wanted to hoard glory."'"[14] But the true glory resides not in Rome but in the city of God: "the virtues the Romans had ascribed to their heroes would be realized only in the citizens of this other city; and it is only within the walls of the Heavenly Jerusalem that Cicero's noble definition of the essence of the Roman Republic could be achieved."[15] The Judaic sages—

we now realize—assuredly concurred on whence comes glory, whence shame: the one from humility, the other, pride.

The system of Augustine addresses the crisis of change with an account of history, and it is, therefore, in the same sense as is the system of the Judaic sages, a deeply historical one: "The whole course of human history . . . could be thought of as laden with meanings which might be seized, partially by the believer, in full by the seer."[16] So Brown: "In his *City of God,* Augustine was one of the first to sense and give monumental expression to a new form of intellectual excitement." God communicates through both words and events. Specifically, history proves the presence of a division between an earthly and a heavenly city.[17] Why do I find this historical interest pertinent to my picture of a Judaism's social order? Because, in Brown's words, "there is room, in Augustine's view of the past, for the consideration of whole societies."[18] But the building block of society is relationship, and the whole of human history emerges out of the relationship of Cain and Abel, natural man after the Fall, citizen of this world, against a man who built no city, "by hoping for something else . . . he waited upon the name of the Lord."[19] Brown says:

> Augustine treats the tension between Cain and Abel as universal, because he can explain it in terms applicable to all men. All human society . . . is based on a desire to share some good. Of such goods, the most deeply felt by human beings is the need for 'peace:' that is, for a resolution of tensions, for an ordered control of unbalanced appetites in themselves, and of discordant wills in society . . . the members of the [city of earth], that is, fallen men, tend to regard their achievement of such peace in society as sufficient in itself.[20]

The city of heaven is "the consecrated commonwealth of Israel," the city of earth, everybody else.[21] Brown's summary of Augustine's main point with slight alteration serves as epitome of sages' views:

> What was at stake, in the *City of God* and in Augustine's sermons, was the capacity of men to 'long' for something different, to ex-

amine the nature of their relationship with their immediate environment; above all, to establish their identity by refusing to be engulfed in the unthinking habits of their fellows.[22]

How alien can sages, concerned as they were with the possibilities of extraordinary conduct or attitude, have found Augustine's interest in establishing identity by reflection on what others deemed routine? The obvious answer justifies juxtaposing the two systems as to not only their ineluctable questions, but also their self-evidently valid answers.

Two further rhetorical questions seem justified: if Augustine spoke of "resident aliens" when referring to the citizens of God's city,[23] then how difficult can sages have found interpreting the identity of their social entity, their Israel, in the same way: here now, but only because of tomorrow: the pilgrim people, *en route* to somewhere else. And why should we find surprising, as disciples of Israel's sages, a city of God permeated, as was Augustine's, by arguments for hope:[24]

> "'Lord, I have loved the beauty of Thy house.' From his gifts, which are scattered to good and bad alike in this, our most grim life, let us, with His help, try to express sufficiently what we have yet to experience."[25]

Two systems emerged from the catastrophes of the fifth century, Augustine's[26] for the Christian, sages' for the Judaic west. Constructed in the same age and in response to problems of the same character and quality, the systems bore nothing in common, except the fundamentally same messages about the correspondence of the individual's life to the social order, the centrality of relationship, the rule of God, and the response of God to what transcended all rules.

GOD WITH US, WE WITH GOD

By both systems, each in its own way, God is joined to the social order because it is in relationships that society takes shape and comes to expression, and all relationships, whether between one person and another or between mortals and God, are wholly consubstantial.[27] That is why, for Augustine, the relationship between the individuals, Cain and Abel, can convey and represent the relationships characteristic of societies or cities, and that is why, for sages, the relationships between one person and another can affect God's relationship to the village needing rain or the householder needing to shore up his shaky dwelling place.

True, we deal with the two utterly unrelated systems of the social order, fabricated by different people, talking about different things to different people, each meant to join the society of humanity (or a sector thereof) with the community of heaven. But both formed quite systematic and well-crafted responses to one and the same deep (and in my judgment, thoroughly merited) perception of disorder, a world that has wobbled, a universe out of line. Rome fallen, home besieged, for Augustine, corresponding to the end of autonomy and the advent of another (to be sure, *soi-disant*) "Israel," for sages, called into question orders of society of very ancient foundation. And that produced a profound sense that the rules had been broken, generating that (framing matters in contemporary psychological terms) alienation that was overcome by Augustine in his way, by sages in theirs.[28]

How, in the language of Judaism as our sages formulated it, may we express the answer to the question of the times? The shaking of the foundations of the social order shows how Israel is estranged from God. The old rules have been broken, therefore the remarkable and the exceptional succeeds. What is unnatural to the human condition of pride is humility and uncertainty, acceptance and conciliation. Those attitudes for the individual, policies for the nation, violate the rule. Then let God respond to transcending rules. And when—so the system maintains—God recognizes in Israel's heart, as much as in the nation's deliberation, the proper feelings, God will respond by ending that estrangement that marks the present age. So the single word encompassing the question addressed by the entire social system of the successor Judaism must be *alienation*. The human and shared sense of crisis—whether Augustine reflecting on the fall of Rome, or sages confronting the end of the old order—finds its response in the doctrine of God's assessment, God's response. God enters the social order imagined by sages because God in the natural order proves insufficient, a Presence inadequate to the human situation. God must dwell in the city of humanity, and Israel in the city of God. So what in secular terms we see as a historical crisis or in psychological terms as one of alienation, in religious terms we have to identify as a caesura in the bounds of eternity. The psychological theology of the system joins the human condition to the fate of the nation and the world—and links the whole to the broken heart of God.

And yet that theological observation about the incarnate God of Judaism does not point us toward the systemic center, which within my definitions of what a system is must be social and explain the order of things here and now. For in the end, a religious theory of the social order describes earth, not heaven. It simply begs the question to claim that the system in the end attended to the condition of God's heart, rather than humanity's mundane existence. For a religious system is not a theological one, and questions about the way of life, worldview, and social entity, admittedly bearing theological implications or even making theological statements, in the end find their answers in the reconstruction of the here and now. So I have not identified the central tension and the generative problematic, nor have I specified the self-evident answer to that question that the system, in every sentence and all details means to settle. It is for identifying that generative problematic of the religious Judaism of the fifth century that the comparison between the Judaism of our sages of blessed memory and the Christianity of Augustine in his *City of God* proves particularly pertinent.

THEOLOGICAL CONVERGENCE: ASKING THE QUESTION OF HISTORY IN THE SETTING OF ETERNITY

To state matters very simply, as we now realize, Augustine's personal circumstance and that of our sages correspond, so do Augustine's central question and the fundamental preoccupation of our sages. Augustine's *City of God* and the Talmud of the Land of Israel took shape in times that were changing, and both systemic statements accommodated questions of history. But we see the answer, therefore the question, when we realize that, as a matter of fact, both did so in the same way.

Specifically, Augustine, bringing to fruition the tradition of Christian historical thought commencing with Eusebius, provided for Christianity a theory of history that placed into the right perspective the events of the day. And our sages did the same, first of all affirming that events required recognition, second, then providing a theory of events that acknowledged their meaning, that is, their historicity, but that also subordinated history to considerations of eternity. The generative problematic of the Talmuds and related Midrash-compilations concerned history: vast changes in the political circumstance of Israel, perceived mutations in the tissue of social relationship, clearly an interest in revising the plain meaning of ordinary words: value, power, learning. And the systemic answer for its part addressed questions of long-term continuity, framed in genealogical terms for the now genealogically defined Israel: the past lives in us, and the system explains in very precise and specific terms just how that takes place, which is through the medium of inherited entitlement or attained entitlement. The medium was indeed the same. The message carried by *zekhut* counseled performance of actions of renunciation, in the hope that Heaven would respond. Power was weakness, value was knowledge, and knowledge was power: all things formed within the Torah.

But if that was the message by way of answer to the historical question of change and crisis, then how had the question of history come to be formulated? It was, of course, precisely what events should be deemed to constitute history, what changes matter, and what are we to do. The answer—our sages' and Augustine's alike— was that only certain happenings are eventful, bear consequence, require attention. And they are eventful because they form paradigms, Cain and Abel for Augustine, Israel's patriarchs and matriarchs for our sages.[29] Then what has happened to history as made by the barbarians at Rome and Hippo, the Byzantine Christians at Tiberias and Sepphoris? It has ceased to matter, because what happened at Rome, what happened at Tiberias, is no happening at all, but a mere happenstance. The upshot is not that history follows rules, so we can predict what will be, not at all.

Augustine did not claim to know what would happen tomorrow morning, and our sages interpreted events but did not claim to shape them, except through the Torah. The upshot is that what is going on really may be set aside in favor of what is really happening, and the story that is history has already been told in (for Augustine) the Bible and (for our sages) the Torah. But, then, that is no longer history at all, but merely, a past made into an eternal present. So, if I may specify what I conceive to be the systemic answer, it is, there are some things that matter, many that do not, and the few that matter echo from eternity to eternity, speaking in that voice, the voice of God, that is the voice of silence, still and small.

The systemic question, urgent and immediate and critical, not merely chronic, then, concerned vast historical change, comprising chains of events. The answer was that, in an exact sense, "event" has no meaning at all. Other-than-historical modes of organizing existence governed, and history in the ordinary sense did not form one of them. Without the social construction of history, there also is no need for the identification of events, that is, individual and unique happenings that bear consequence, since, within the system and structure of the successor Judaism, history forms no taxon, being replaced by *zekhut,* a historical category that was—we now realize—in the deepest sense antihistorical. So, it must follow, no happening is unique, and, on its own, no event bears consequence.

Neither Augustine nor our sages produced narrative history; both, rather, wrote reflections *on* history, a very different matter. For neither did narrative history, ordinarily a sustained paraphrastic chronicle, serve as a medium for organizing and explaining perceived experience. True, both referred to events in the past, but these were not strung together in a continuing account. They were cited because they were exemplary, not because they were unique. These events, then, were identified out of the unlimited agenda of the past as what mattered, and these occasions of consequence— as distinct from undifferentiated and unperceived happenings— were meant to explain the things that mattered in the chaos of the everyday.

In responding as they did to what we conceive to be historical events of unparalleled weight, Augustine and our sages took positions that, from our perspective, prove remarkably contemporary. For we now understand that all histories are the creation of an eternal present, that is, those moments in which histories are defined and distinguished, in which events are identified and assigned consequence, and in which sequences of events, "this particular thing happened here *and therefore* . . . ," are strung together, pearls on a string, to form ornaments of intellect. Fully recognizing that history is one of the grand fabrications of the human intellect, facts not discovered but invented, explanations that themselves form cultural indicators of how things are in the here and now, we may appreciate as far more than merely instrumental and necessary the systemic responses to the urgent questions addressed in common by our sages and by Augustine.

Shall we then represent the successor Judaism as a historical religion, in that it appeals for its worldview not to myth about gods in heaven but the history of Israel upon earth—interpreted in relationship to the acts of God in heaven to be sure? And shall we characterize that Judaism as a religion that appeals to history—that is, to events—defined in the ordinary way, important happenings, for its source of testing and establishing truth? I think not. That Judaism identifies an event through its own cognitive processes. Just as the canon that recapitulates the system, so events—things that happen given consequence—recapitulate the system. Just as the system speaks in detail through the canon, so too through its repertoire of events granted recognition the system delivers its message. But just as the canon is not the system, so the recognition of events does not classify the system as historical.

This brings me directly to the final question of systemic description: what exactly does the successor Judaism mean by events? To answer that question succinctly is simple. In the canonical literature of the successor Judaism, events find their place, within the science of learning, of *Listenwissenschaft* that characterizes this literature, along with sorts of things that, for our part, we should not characterize as events at all. Events have no autonomous standing; events are not unique, each unto itself; events have no probative value on their own. Events form cases, along with a variety of other cases, making up lists of things that, in common, point to or prove one thing. Not only so, but among the taxonomic structure at hand, events do not make up their own list at all, for what is truly eventful generates *zekhut*. It is the act of *zekhut* that unites past and present, and it is the act that gains *zekhut* that makes history for to-morrow.

Events of other kinds, even those that seem to make an enormous, and awful, difference in Israel's condition, will appear on the same list as persons, places, things. And the contrary lists—very often in the form of stories as we have seen—tell us events that in and of themselves change biography (the life and fate of an ass-driver) and make history. That means that events other than those that gain *zekhut* not only have no autonomous standing on their own, but also that events constitute no species even within a genus of a historical order. For persons, places, and things in our way of thinking do not belong on the same list as events; they are not of the same order. Within the logic of our own minds, we cannot classify the city, Paris, within the same genus as the event—the Declaration of the Rights of Man, for instance—nor is Sinai or Jerusalem of the same order of things as the Torah or the Temple, respectively. But in the logic of the Judaism before us, Jerusalem stands for sanctity and for Temple; it is of precisely the same taxic order.

What then shall we make of a list that encompasses within the same taxic composition events and things? Answering that question shows us how our sages sort out what matters from what does not, and events, by themselves, do not form a taxon and on their own bear no means and therefore do not matter. For one such list made up of events, persons, and places, is as follows: (1) Israel at the sea; (2) the ministering angels; (3) the tent of meeting; (4) the eternal house [= the Temple]; (5) Sinai. That mixes an event (Israel redeemed at the sea), a category of sensate being (angels), a location (tent of meeting, Temple), and then Sinai, which can stand for a variety of things but in context stands for the Torah. In such a list an event may or may not stand for a value or a proposition, but it does not enjoy autonomous standing; the list is not defined by the eventfulness of events and their meaning, the compilation of matters of a single genus or even a single species (tent of meeting, eternal house, are the same species here). The notion of event as autonomous, even unique, is quite absent in this taxonomy. And once events lose their autonomy, that process of selection gets under way that transforms one event into history bearing meaning and sets aside as inconsequential in the exact sense all other events.

Since this point is systemically so fundamental, let me give the case of another such list, which moves from events to other matters altogether, finding the whole subject to the same metaphor, hence homogenized. First come the events that took place at these places or with these persons: Egypt, the sea, Marah, Massah and Meribah, Horeb, the wilderness, the spies in the Land, Shittim, for Achan/Joshua and the conquest of the Land. Now that mixture of places and names clearly intends to focus on particular things that happened, and hence, were the list to which I refer to conclude at this point, we could define an event for the successor Judaism as a happening that bore consequence, taught a lesson, or exemplified a truth. In the present case, an event matters because it the mixture of rebellion and obedience. But there would then be no doubt that "event" formed a genus unto itself, and that a proper list could not encompass both events, defined conventionally as we should, and also other matters altogether.

But the literary culture at hand, this textual community proceeds, in the same literary context, to the following items: (1) the Ten Commandments; (2) the show-fringes and phylacteries; (3) the *Shema* and the Prayer; (4) the tabernacle and the cloud of the Presence of God in the world to come. Why we invoke, as our candidates for the metaphor at hand, the Ten Commandments, show-fringes and phylacteries, recitation of the *Shema* and the Prayer, the tabernacle and the cloud of the Presence of God, and the mezuzah, seems to me clear from the very catalog. These reach their climax in the analogy between the home and the tabernacle, the embrace of God and the Presence of God. So the whole is meant to list those things that draw the Israelite near God and make the Israelite cleave to God. And to this massive catalog, events are not only exemplary—which historians can concede without difficulty—but also subordinated.

They belong on the same list as actions, things, persons, places, because they form an order of being that is not to be differentiated between events (including things that stand for events) and other cultural artifacts altogether. A happening is no different from an object, in which case "event" serves no better, and no worse, than a hero, a gesture or action, recitation of a given formula, or a particular locale, to establish a truth. It is contingent, subordinate, instrumental. And why find that fact surprising, since all history comes to us in writing, and it is the culture that dictates how writing is to take place; that is why history can only paraphrase the affirmations of a system, and that is why events recapitulate in acute and concrete ways the system that classifies one thing that happens as event, but another thing is not only not an event but is not classified at all. In the present instance, an event is not at all eventful; it is merely a fact that forms part of the evidence for what is, and what is eventful is not an occasion at all, but a condition, an attitude, a perspective and a viewpoint. Then, it is clear, events are subordinated to the formation of attitudes, perspectives, viewpoints—the formative artifacts of not history in the conventional sense but culture in the framework of Sahlin's generalization, "history is culturally ordered, differently so in different societies, according to meaningful schemes of things."[30]

Events not only do not form a taxon, they also do not present a vast corpus of candidates for inclusion into some other taxon. Among the candidates, events that are selected by our documents are few indeed. They commonly encompass Israel at the sea and at Sinai, the destruction of the First Temple, the destruction of the Second Temple, events as defined by the actions of some holy men such as Abraham, Isaac, and Jacob (treated not for what they did but for who they were), Daniel, Mishael, Hananiah and Azariah, and the like. It follows that the restricted repertoire of candidates for taxonomic study encompasses remarkably few events, remarkably few for a literary culture that is commonly described as quintessentially historical!

Then what taxic indicator dictates which happenings will be deemed events and which not? What are listed throughout are not data of nature or history but of theology: the issue of history is one of relationship, just as with Augustine. Specifically, God's relationship with Israel, expressed in such facts as the three events, the first two in the past, the third in the future, namely, the three redemptions of Israel, the three patriarchs, and holy persons, actions, events, what-have-you—these are facts that are assembled and grouped. What we have is a kind of recombinant theology given narrative form through tales presented individually but not in a sustained narrative. This recombinant theology through history is accomplished when the framer ("the theologian") selects from a restricted repertoire a few items for combination. What we have is a kind of subtle restatement, through an infinite range of possibilities, of the combinations and recombinations of a few essentially simple facts (data). The net effect, then, is to exclude, rather than to include: the world is left outside. So did eternal Israel pursue its path through time, just as Rabbinic Judaism proposed, and so did the Pilgrim People, the Christian church, conceive itself in the way of Augustine.

PART 2

CHRISTIANITY

6

POLITICS AND CHRISTIANITY

ROMANS

aul's letter to the Romans was written around the year 57 C.E. to a community he had never met, although he hoped to travel there (see Rom. 15:22–25). He composed it after a period of sustained controversy, and for that reason was careful to spell out his views more fully and carefully than he had done before.

His sustained account of his own teaching includes the following passage, a classic expression of the acceptance by Christians of a world that is finally an expression of divine authority. In some of his confidence in the justice of the empire, Paul also reflects the Stoic view that the well-ordered government reflects the natural law that harmonizes all things.

TEXT: ROMANS 13:1–14

Let every person be subject to the governing authorities. For there is no authority except from God, and those that exist have been instituted by God. Therefore one who resists the authorities resists what God has appointed, and those who resist will incur judgment. For rulers are not a terror to good conduct, but to bad. Would you have no fear of him who is in authority? Then do what is good, and you will receive his approval, for he is God's servant for your good. But if you do wrong, be afraid, for he does not bear the sword in vain; he is the servant of God to execute his wrath on the wrongdoer. Therefore one must be subject, not only to avoid God's wrath but also for the sake of conscience. For the same reason you also pay taxes, for the authorities are ministers of God, attending to this very thing. Pay all of them their dues, taxes to whom taxes are due, revenue to whom revenue is due, respect to whom respect is due, honor to whom honor is due.

Owe no one anything, except to love one another; for he who loves his neighbor has fulfilled the law. The commandments, "You shall not commit adultery, You shall not kill, You shall not steal, You shall not covet," and any other commandment, are summed up in this sentence, "You shall love your neighbor as yourself." Love does no wrong to a neighbor; therefore love is the fulfilling of the law.

Besides this you know what hour it is, how it is full time now for you to awake from sleep. For salvation is nearer to us now than when we first believed; the night is far gone, the day is at hand. Let us then cast off the works of darkness and put on the armor of light; let us conduct ourselves becomingly as in the day, not in reveling and drunkenness, not in debauchery and licentiousness, not in quarreling and jealousy. But put on the Lord Jesus Christ, and make no provision for the flesh, to gratify its desires.

1 PETER

The first letter of Peter was written around the year 90 C.E., some twenty-five years after Peter's death in Rome during the Neronian persecution. Although an argument has been made that Peter was the ultimate source of some of the teaching expressed in the letter, its concerns are typical of Christianity at the close of the first century, particularly in Asia Minor (its destination, and probably its place of composition). The letter is imbued with the apocalyptic hope that the world is about to end, and that one's behavior is to be changed accordingly. Baptism is even compared to the salvation of a few people during the time of Noah. The end of all things, in other words, was taken very seriously in early Christianity.

TEXT: 1 PETER 3:8–4:19

Finally, all of you, have unity of spirit, sympathy, love of the brethren, a tender heart and a humble mind. Do not return evil for evil or reviling for reviling; but on the contrary bless, for to this you have been called, that you may obtain a blessing. For

> "He that would love life and see good days,
> let him keep his tongue from evil
> and his lips from speaking guile;
> let him turn away from evil and do right;
> let him seek peace and pursue it.
> For the eyes of the Lord are upon the righteous,
> and his ears are open to their prayer.
> But the face of the Lord is against those that do evil."

Now who is there to harm you if you are zealous for what is right? But even if you do suffer for righteousness' sake, you will be blessed. Have no fear of them, nor be troubled, but in your hearts reverence Christ as Lord. Always be prepared to make a defense to any one who calls you to account for the hope that is in you, yet do it with gentleness and reverence; and keep your conscience clear, so that, when you are abused, those who revile your good behavior in Christ may be put to shame. For it is better to suffer for doing right, if that should be God's will, than for doing wrong. For Christ also died for sins once for all, the righteous for the unrighteous, that he might bring us to God, being put to death in the flesh but made alive in the spirit; in which he went and preached to the spirits in prison, who formerly did not obey, when God's patience waited in the days of Noah, during the building of the ark, in which a few—that is, eight persons—were saved through water. Baptism, which corresponds to this, now saves you, not as a removal of dirt from the body but as an appeal to God for a clear conscience, through the Resurrection of Jesus Christ, who has gone into heaven and is at the right hand of God, with angels, authorities, and powers subject to him.

Since therefore Christ suffered in the flesh, arm yourselves with the same thought, for whoever has suffered in the flesh has ceased from sin, so as to live for the rest of the time in the flesh no longer by human passions but by the will of God. Let the time that is past suffice for doing what the Gentiles like to do, living in licentiousness, passions, drunkenness, revels, carousing, and lawless idolatry. They are surprised that you do not now join them in the same wild profligacy, and they abuse you; but they will give account to him who is ready to judge the living and the dead. For this is why the gospel was preached even to the dead, that though judged in the flesh like men, they might live in the spirit like God.

The end of all things is at hand; therefore keep sane and sober for your prayers. Above all hold unfailing your love for one another, since love covers a multitude of sins. Practice hospitality ungrudgingly to one another. As each has received a gift, employ it for one another, as good stewards of God's varied grace: whoever speaks, as one who utters oracles of God; whoever renders service, as one who renders it by the strength which God supplies; in order that in everything God may be glorified through Jesus Christ. To him belong glory and dominion for ever and ever. Amen.

Beloved, do not be surprised at the fiery ordeal which comes upon you to prove you, as though something strange were happening to you. But rejoice in so far as you share Christ's sufferings, that you may also rejoice and be glad when his glory is revealed. If you are reproached for the name of Christ, you are blessed, because the spirit of glory and of God rests upon you. But let none of you suffer as a murderer, or a thief, or a wrong-doer, or a mischief-maker; yet if one suffers as a Christian, let him not be ashamed, but under that name let him glorify God. For the time has come for judgment to begin with the household of God; and if it begins with us, what will be the end of those who do not obey the gospel of God? And

> "If the righteous man is scarcely saved,
>   where will the impious and sinner appear?"

Therefore let those who suffer according to God's will do right and entrust their souls to a faithful Creator.

PLINY

Pliny (called the Younger, to distinguish him from his uncle, a noted writer) was appointed by the Emperor Trajan as governor of the province of Bithynia and Pontus in Asia Minor. He had previously studied rhetoric and belonged to the elite of his time. His correspondence with the emperor attests the high social standing that led to his appointment. The first letter here presented conveys Trajan's agreement to grant a favor to a friend of Pliny's, and then Pliny himself sets out the problem of how to deal with Christians. In that the correspondence dates from the year 111 C.E., and relates to Asia Minor, it illuminates the circumstances in which 1 Peter was written. Nonetheless, we should bear in mind that not all emperors were as benign as Trajan, and not all governors were as cautious as Pliny.

TEXT: THE CORRESPONDENCE BETWEEN PLINY AND TRAJAN

TRAJAN TO PLINY

You are certainly well aware, my dear Pliny, that I grant these favors sparingly, seeing that I have often stated in the Senate that I have not exceeded the number which I said would meet my wishes when I first addressed its distinguished members. I have however, granted your request and issued instructions that it is to be officially recorded that I have conferred on Suetonius Tranquillus the privileges granted to parents of three children, on the usual terms.

PLINY TO THE EMPEROR TRAJAN

It is my custom to refer all my difficulties to you, Sir, for who is better able to resolve my doubts and to inform my ignorance?

I have never been present at an examination of Christians. Consequently, I do not know the nature or the extent of the punishments usually meted out to them, nor the grounds for starting an investigation and how far it should be pressed. Nor am I at all sure whether any distinction should be made between them on the grounds of age, or if young people and adults should be treated alike; whether a pardon ought to be granted to anyone retracting his beliefs, or if he has once professed Christianity, he shall gain nothing by renouncing it; and whether it is the mere name of Christian which is punishable, even if innocent of crime, or rather the crimes associated with the name.

For the moment this is the procedure I have followed with all persons brought before me on the charge of being Christians. I have asked them in person if they are Christians, and if they admit it, I repeat the question a second and third time, with a warning of the punishment awaiting them. If they persist, I order them to be led away for execution; for, whatever the nature of their admission, I am convinced that their stubbornness and unshakable obstinacy ought not to go unpunished. There have been others similarly fanatical who are Roman citizens. I have entered them on the list of persons to be sent to Rome for trial.

Now that I have begun to deal with this problem, as so often happens, the charges are becoming more widespread and increasing in variety. An anonymous pamphlet has been circulated which contains the names of a number of accused persons. Among them I considered that I should dismiss any who denied that they were or ever had been Christians when they had repeated after me a formula of invocation to the gods and had made offerings of wine and incense to your statue (which I had ordered to be brought into court for this purpose along with the images of the gods), and furthermore had reviled the name of Christ; none of which things, I understand, any genuine Christian can be induced to do.

Others, whose names were given to me by an informer, first admitted the charge and then denied it; they said that they had ceased to be Christians two or more years previously, and some of them even twenty years ago. They all did reverence to your statue and the images of the gods in the same way as the others, and reviled the name of Christ. They also declared that the sum total of their guilt or error amounted to no more than this: they had met regularly before dawn on a fixed day to chant verses alternately amongst themselves in honor of Christ as if to a god, and also to bind themselves by oath, not for any criminal purpose, but to abstain from theft, robbery, and adultery, to commit no breach of trust and not to deny a deposit when called upon to restore it. After this ceremony it had been their custom to disperse and reassemble later to take food of an ordinary, harmless kind; but they had in fact given up this practice since my edict, issued on your instructions, which banned all political societies. This made me decide it was all the more necessary to extract the truth by torture from two slave-women whom they call deaconesses. I found nothing but a degenerate sort of cult carried to extravagant lengths.

I have therefore postponed any further examination and hastened to consult you. The question seems to me to be worthy of your consideration, especially in view of the number of persons endangered; for a great many individuals of every age and class, both men and women, are being brought to trial, and this is likely to continue. It is not only the towns, but the villages and rural districts too which are infected through contact with this wretched cult. I think though that it is still possible for it to be checked and directed to better ends, for there is no doubt that people have begun to throng the temples which had been almost deserted for a long time; the sacred rites which had been allowed to lapse are being performed again, and the flesh of sacrificial victims is on sale everywhere, though up till recently scarcely anyone could be found to buy it. It is easy to infer from this that a great many people could be reformed if they were given an opportunity to repent.

181

TRAJAN TO PLINY

You have followed the right course of procedure, my dear Pliny, in your examination of the cases of persons charged with being Christians, for it is impossible to lay down a general rule or a fixed formula. These people must not be hunted out; if they are brought before you and the charge against them is proved, they must be punished, but in the case of anyone who denies that he is a Christian, and makes it clear that he is not by offering prayers to our gods, he is to be pardoned as a result of his repentance however suspect his past conduct may be. But pamphlets circulated anonymously must play no part in any accusation. They create the worst sort of precedent and are quite out of keeping with the spirit of our age.

TACITUS

Pliny the Younger wrote to another contemporary, somewhat older than himself, named Tacitus, who has been called the greatest Roman historian. His *Annals,* composed around 116 C.E., cover the period between the death of Augustus in 14 C.E. and the death of Nero in 68 C.E. His *Histories* then take the story up from 69 C.E., known as the year of the four Emperors, until the death of Domitian in 96 C.E. Tacitus's skill at characterization is evident in the excerpt, as well as his contempt for Nero's self-indulgence. Tacitus expresses no sympathy for Christianity as such, and yet he also helps us to see why a policy of overt persecution had to be tempered by the time of Trajan.

TEXT: THE *ANNALS* OF TACITUS 15.37–44

That he might gain credit for thinking himself nowhere so happy as at Rome, Nero laid out feasts in the public thoroughfares, using the whole city as if it were his own house. The most notorious and profligate of these entertainments were those given by Tigellinus, which I shall take as an example to avoid further description of such extravagances. A banquet was set out in Agrippa's basin upon a barge built for this purpose. This barge was towed about by vessels picked out with gold and ivory, and rowed by debauched youths who were assorted according to their age and their proficiency in vice. Birds and beasts had been collected from distant countries, and sea-monsters from the ocean. On the banks of the pond were brothels, filled with ladies of high rank; over against these were to be seen prostitutes, stark naked, indulging in indecent gestures and language. As night came on, the grove and booths around rang with songs, and were ablaze with lights. Nero disgraced himself by every kind of abomination, natural and unnatural, leaving no further depth of debauchery to which he could sink: a few days afterwards he even went through a regular form of marriage with one of that contaminated crew, called Pythagoras. He put on the bridal veil; witnesses were in attendance; the dowry, the marriage bed, the nuptial torch were all there, with everything exposed to view— even the things which night conceals as between man and wife.

And now came a calamitous fire—whether it was accidental or purposely contrived by the Emperor, remains uncertain: for on this point authorities are divided—more violent and destructive than any that ever befell our city. It began in that part of the Circus which adjoins the Palatine and Caelian hills. Breaking out in shops full of flammable merchandise, it took hold and gathered strength at once; and being fanned by the wind soon embraced the entire length of the Circus, where there were no mansions with protective walls, no temple-enclosures, nor anything else to arrest its course. Furiously the destroying flames swept on, first over the level ground, then up the heights, then again plunging into the hollows, with a rapidity which outstripped all efforts to cope with them, the ancient city lending itself to their progress by its narrow tortuous streets and its misshapen blocks of buildings. The shrieks of panic-stricken women; the weakness of the aged, and the helplessness of the young; the efforts of some to save themselves, of others to help their neighbors; the hurrying of those who dragged their sick along, the lingering of those who waited for them—all made the scene of inexorable confusion.

✿
183
✝

Many persons, while looking behind them, were enveloped from the front or from the side; or having escaped to the nearest place of safety, found this too in possession of the flames, and even places which they had thought beyond their reach in the same plight with the rest. At last, not knowing where to turn, or what to avoid, they poured into the streets or threw themselves down in the fields. Some, having lost their all, did not have even food for the day; others, though with means of escape open to them, preferred to perish for love of the dear ones whom they could not save. And none dared to check the flames; for there were many who threatened and forced back those who would extinguish them, while others openly flung in torches, saying that *they had their orders*—whether it really was so, or only that they wanted to plunder undisturbed.

At this moment Nero was at Antium. He did not return to the city until the flames were approaching the mansion which he had built to connect the Palatine with the Gardens of Maecenas; nor could they be stopped until the whole Palatine, including the palace and everything around it, had been consumed. Nero assigned the Campus Martius and the Agrippa monuments for the relief of people who had been driven out homeless. He threw open his own gardens also, and put up temporary buildings for the accommodation of the destitute; he brought up provisions form Ostia and the neighboring towns; and he reduced the price of corn to three sesterces the peck. But popular as these measures were, they aroused no gratitude; for a rumor had got abroad that at the moment when the city was in flames Nero had mounted upon a stage in his own house, and by way of liking modern calamities to ancient, had sung the tale of the sack of Troy.

Not until the sixth day was the fire put under control, at the foot of the Esquiline hill, by demolishing a vast extent of buildings, so as to present nothing but the ground and the open sky to its continued fury. But scarcely had the alarm subsided, or the populace recovered from their despair, when it burst out again in the more open parts of the city; and though here the loss of life was less, the destruction of temples and of porticoes devoted to enjoyment was still more complete. And the scandal attending this new fire was the greater in that it broke out in property owned by Tigellinus, in the Aemilian quarter; the general belief being that Nero had the ambition to build a new city to be called after his own name. For of the fourteen regions into which Rome was divided only four remained intact. Three were burnt to the ground; in the other seven, nothing remained save a few fragments of ruined and half-burnt houses.

To count up the number of mansions, of tenements, and of temples that were destroyed would be no easy matter. Among the oldest of the sacred buildings burnt was that dedicated by Servius Tullius to the Moon, and the Great Altar and shrine raised by Evander to the visible Hercules. The temple vowed by Romulus to Jupiter, the Stayer of Flight; the Royal Palace of Numa; the Temple of Vesta, with the Household Gods of the Roman people, were all destroyed; added to these were the treasures won in numerous battles, and masterpieces of Greek art, as well as ancient and genuine monuments of genius which were remembered by the older generation amid all the splendor of the restored city, and which could never be replaced. Some noted that the 19th of July, the day on which the fire began, was also the day on which the Senonian Gauls had taken and burnt the city; others were so curious in their calculations as to discover that the two burnings were separated from one another by exactly the same number of years, of months, and of days.

Nero profited by the ruin of his country to erect a palace in which the marvels were not to be gold and jewels, the usual and commonplace objects of luxury, so much as lawns and lakes and mock-wildernesses, with woods on one side and open glades and vistas on the other. His engineers and masters-of-works were Severus and Celer; men who had the ingenuity and the impudence to fool away the resources of the empire in the attempt to provide by art what nature had pronounced impossible.

For these men undertook to dig a navigable canal, along the rocky shore and over the hills, all the way from Lake Avernus to the mouth of the Tiber. There was no other water for supplying such a canal than that of the Pontine marshes; and even if practicable, the labor would have been prodigious, and no object would have been served. But Nero had a thirst for the incredible, and traces of his vain attempt to excavate the heights adjoining Lake Avernus are to be seen to this day.

The parts of the city unoccupied by Nero's palace were not built over without divisions, or indiscriminately, as after the Gallic fire, but in blocks of regular dimensions, with broad streets between. A limit was placed to the height of houses; open spaces were left; and colonnades were added to protect the fronts of tenements, Nero undertaking to build these at his own cost, and to hand over the building sites, cleared of rubbish, to the proprietors. He offered rewards also, in proportion to the rank and means of owners, on condition of mansions or tenements being completed within a given time; and he assigned the marshes at Ostia for the reception of the rubbish, which was taken down the Tiber in the same vessels which had brought up the corn. Certain parts of the houses were to be built without beams, and of solid stone, Gabian or Alban, those stones being impervious to fire. Then as water had often been improperly intercepted by individuals, inspectors were appointed to secure a more abundant supply, and over a larger area, for public use; owners were required to keep the means for quenching fire in some open place; common walls were forbidden, and every house had to be enclosed within walls of its own.

These useful provisions added greatly to the appearance of the new city; and yet there were not wanting persons who thought that the plan of the old city was more conducive to health, as the narrow streets and high roofs were a protection against the rays of the sun, which now beat down with double fierceness upon broad and shadeless thoroughfares.

Such were the measures suggested by human counsels; after which means were taken to propitiate the gods. The Sibylline books were consulted, and prayers were offered, as prescribed by them, to Vulcan, to Ceres, and to Proserpina. Juno was supplicated by the matrons, in the Capitol first, and afterwards at the nearest point upon the sea, from which water was drawn to sprinkle the temple and image of the goddess; banquets to the goddesses and all-night festivals were celebrated by married women.

But neither human aid, nor imperial bounty, nor atonement-offerings to the gods, could remove the sinister suspicion that the fire had been brought about by Nero's order. To put an end to this rumor, Nero shifted the charge on to others, and inflicted the most cruel tortures upon a body of men detested for their abominations and popularly known by the name of Christians. This name came from one Christus, who was put to death in the reign of Tiberius by the procurator Pontius Pilate; but though checked for the time, the detestable superstition broke out again, not in Judaea only, where the mischief began, but even in Rome, where every horrible and shameful iniquity, from every quarter of the world, pours in and finds a welcome.

First those who acknowledged themselves of this persuasion were arrested; and upon their testimony a vast number were condemned, not so much on the charge of arson as for their hatred of the human race. Their death was turned into a diversion. They were clothed in the skins of wild beasts, and torn to piece by dogs; they were fastened to crosses, or set up to be burned, so as to serve the purpose of lamps when daylight failed. Nero gave up his own gardens for this spectacle; he provided also circus games, during which he mingled with the populace, or took his stand upon a chariot, in the garb of a charioteer. But guilty as these men were and worthy of direst punishment, the fact that they were being sacrificed for no public good, but only to glut the cruelty of one man, aroused a feeling of pity on their behalf.

TERTULLIAN

Tertullian addressed his *Apology* to those who might be called upon to judge Christians, but in fact it is intended to counter the common prejudice which Christianity encountered. It is as effective an example of rhetoric as one will find, and at the same time it illustrates both the legal situation and the popular reaction to the new religion. The *Apology* was written in 197 C.E., shortly after Tertullian's conversion. It is a good example of Christianity in North Africa, coming from Carthage (which was Tertullian's birthplace). The uncompromising stance is characteristic of the climate of the movement there, and may explain why, around 207 C.E., Tertullian himself became a Montanist, attracted by the asceticism that comported with the conviction that each believer was a vessel of the holy spirit.

✿
187
✟

TEXT: TERTULLIAN'S *APOLOGY*

I. If you, the masters of the Roman Empire—you who, openly and loftily at the very head of the state, preside to do justice—if you are not allowed openly to investigate, to examine face to face, the Christian issue, to learn what it is in truth;—if, in this particular matter, and this alone, your authority either dreads or blushes to inquire in public, with all the care that justice demands;—if finally (as recently befell) the persecution of this school is so avid in the domestic tribunal as to block the way of defence;—then let truth be allowed to reach your ears at least by the hidden path of silent literature.

Truth asks no favors in her cause, since she has no surprise at her present position. Truth knows that she is a stranger on earth and easily finds enemies among men of another descent, but she knows that her descent, home, hope, recompense, honor, are in heaven. For one thing meanwhile she is eager—not to be condemned without being known. The laws are supreme in their own sphere; what loss can they suffer, if truth be heard? Why would it not enhance the glory of their supremacy to condemn truth *after* hearing her? But, if they condemn her unheard—aside from the odium of such injustice—they will merit the suspicion that they knowingly refuse to hear what, once heard, they cannot condemn.

This, then, is the first plea we lodge with you—the injustice of your hatred of the name of the Christians. The very excuse that seems to acquit it, at once aggravates and convicts that injustice—namely, ignorance. For what could be more unjust than for men to hate a thing they do not know, even if it really deserves hatred? It can only deserve hatred when it is known whether it does deserve it.

But so long as nothing at all is known of what it deserves, how can you defend the justice of the hatred? That must be established, not on the bare fact of its existence, but on knowledge. When men hate a thing simply because they do not know the character of what they hate, what prevents it being of a nature that does not deserve hate at all? Whichever alternative obtains, we maintain both points: they are ignorant as long as they hate, and their hate is unjust as long as they are ignorant. It is evidence of an ignorance which, while it is made an excuse for their injustice, really condemns it, that all who once hated Christianity because they were ignorant of the nature of what they hated, as soon as they cease to be ignorant of it, leave off hating it.

From their number come the Christians; it is on the basis of knowledge, nothing else; and they begin to hate what once they were and to profess what once they hated; and we are as many as we are alleged to be. Men proclaim aloud that the state is beset with us; in countryside, in villages, in islands—Christians; every sex, age, condition, and even rank going over to this name. They lament it as an injury; and yet even so they do not bestir their minds to reflect whether there may not be in it something good that escapes them. It is forbidden to suspect more shrewdly; it does not please them to test it at closer quarters. Here, of all places, human curiosity grows torpid. They love to be ignorant, though others rejoice to know. How much better the saying of Anacharsis about the ignorant judging the expert would have fitted them, than the unmusical who judge the musicians! They prefer not to know because they already hate. Their prejudice implies that what they do not know really is what, if they were to know, they could not hate. Because, if no just ground for hatred be found, surely it is best to leave off hating unjustly. But if the hatred prove to be deserved, so far from any of it being abated, more hatred should be added to keep it up; and justice itself would authorize that.

But, one could reply, a thing is not necessarily good because it wins many adherents; how many are predisposed to evil, how many desert to error! Who denies that? Yet a thing that is really bad, not even those who are caught by it dare to defend or to call good. Nature steeps every evil thing with either fear or shame. Evildoers are eager to escape notice; they avoid appearing; they are anxious when caught; they deny when accused; even under torture they do not easily or always confess; when condemned they always lament. They count up how often they have felt the impulses of a mind distraught; they set their deeds down to fate or to the stars; they will not admit to being what they are because they recognize it is evil. In what way is a Christian comparable? Not a man of them is ashamed of it, not a man regrets—except only that he was not a Christian earlier. If he is denounced, he glories in it; if he is accused, he does not defend himself; when he is questioned, he confesses without any pressure; when he is condemned, he renders thanks. What sort of evil is that which has none of the native marks of evil—fear, shame, evasion, regret, lament? What? Is that evil where the criminal is glad, where accusation is the thing he prays for, and punishment is his felicity? It is not for you to call it madness—*you,* a man convicted of sheer ignorance of it.

But now, if it is really certain that we are of all men the most noxious, why do you yourselves treat us otherwise than those like us, the rest of the noxious classes, when the same treatment belongs to the same fault? Whatever you charge against us, when you so charge others, they use their own eloquence, they hire the advocacy of others, to plead their innocence. There is freedom to answer, to cross-examine, since in fact it is against the law for men to be condemned, undefended and unheard. But to Christians alone it is forbidden to say anything to clear their case, to defend truth, to stop the judge from being unjust. One thing is looked for, one alone, the one thing needful for popular hatred—the confession of the name. Not investigation of the crime! Yet, if you are trying any other criminal, it does not follow at once from his confessing to the name of a murderer, or temple-robber, or sex-criminal, or enemy of the state (to touch on *our* indictments), that you are satisfied to pronounce sentence, unless you pursue all the consequent investigation, such as the character of the act, how often, where, how, when he did it, the accessories, the confederates. In our case nothing of the kind! Yet it ought just as much to be wrung out of us (whenever that false charge is made) how many murdered babies each of us had tasted, how many acts of incest he had done in the dark, what cooks were there, and what dogs. Think of the glory of that judge who had brought to light some Christian who had eaten a hundred babies!

And yet we find it is forbidden even to hunt us down. For when Pliny the Younger was governing his province and had condemned some Christians and driven others from their position, and still the sheer numbers concerned worried him as to what he ought to do thereafter, he consulted the Emperor Trajan. Pliny asserted that, apart from an obstinacy that refused to sacrifice, he had learnt nothing about the Christian mysteries—nothing beyond meetings before dawn to sing to Christ and to God, and to band themselves together in discipline, forbidding murder, adultery, fraud, treachery, and such wickedness. Trajan replied in a rescript that men of this kind were not to be sought out, but if they were brought before Pliny they must be punished.

What a decision, how inevitably confused! He says they must not be sought out, implying they are innocent; and he orders them to be punished, implying they are guilty. He spares them and rages against them, he pretends not to see and punishes. Why cheat yourself with your judgement? If you condemn them, why not hunt them down? If you do not hunt them down, why not also acquit them? To track down bandits through all the provinces is a duty assigned by lot to the garrisons. Against those answerable for treason, against public enemies, every man is a soldier; inquiry is extended to confederates, to accessories. The Christian alone may not be hunted down; but he may be summoned before the magistrate. As if hunting down led to anything but summoning to the court! So you condemn a man when summoned to court—a man whom nobody wished to be sought out, who (I suppose) really has not deserved punishment because he is guilty, but because, forbidden to be looked for, he was found!

Then, again, in that matter, you do not deal with us in accordance with your procedure in judging criminals. If the other criminals plead "Not guilty," you torture them to make them confess; the Christians alone you torture to make them deny. Yet if it were really something evil, we should deny our guilt, and you would use torture to force us to confess it. And you would not dispense with judicial investigation of our crimes on the sole ground that you were certain of their commission from the confession of the name; for to this day, though the murderer confesses, and though you know what murder is, nonetheless you wring out of him the story of his crime. How perverse, when you presume our crimes from our confession of the name and then try by torture to force us to cancel our confession, in order that, by denying the name, we may really deny the crimes too, which you had presumed from our confession of the name! I do not suppose you do not want us to be done to death—because you believe us the worst of men. For that is your way—to say to the murderer, "Deny!" and to order the temple-thief to be mangled, if he will insist on confession! If that is not your procedure with regard to us in our guilt, then it is clear you count us the most innocent of men. You will not have us (as being the most innocent of men) persist with a confession which you know you will have to condemn, not because justice requires it, but because of legal requirement.

A man shouts, "I am a Christian." He says what he is. You wish to hear what he is *not*. Presiding to extort the truth, you take infinite pains in our case, and ours alone, to hear a lie. "I am," says he, "what you ask if I am; why torture me to twist the facts? I confess, and you torture me. What would you do if I denied?" Clearly, when others deny, you do not readily believe them; if we have denied, you at once believe us. Let this perversity of yours arouse the suspicion that there may be some hidden power which makes you serve against the form, yes, against the very nature of judicial procedure, against the laws themselves. For, unless I am mistaken, those laws bid evil men to be brought to light, not hidden; they enact that those confessing be condemned, not acquitted. This is laid down by decrees of the Senate, by rescripts of the emperors.

This empire of which you are ministers is the rule of citizens, not of tyrants. With tyrants torture was also used as penalty; with you, it is moderated and used for examination only. Maintain your law by this method until the necessary confession is made. If a confession intervenes, it serves no purpose. It is the sentence that is called for then; the guilty man must cancel the penalty due by enduring it, not by being relieved of it. In the end, nobody desires to acquit him; it is not permissible to wish it; that is why no man is forced to deny his guilt. But you conceive the Christian to be a man guilty of every crime, the enemy of gods, emperors, laws, morals, of all nature together. And then you force him to deny the charge, in order to acquit him—a man you will not be able to acquit unless he has denied. You are colluding to obstruct the laws. You want him, then, to deny that he is guilty, in order to *make* him innocent—and quite against his will; and even his past is not to count against him.

What is the meaning of this perversity? this failure to reflect that more credence is to be given to a voluntary confession than to a forced denial? to reflect that, when compelled to deny, he may not honestly deny; and, once acquitted, he may again after your tribunal laugh at your exercise, once more a Christian?

So, when in every detail you treat us differently from all other criminals—as you do in concentrating on the one object of dissociating us from that name (for we are dissociated from it, if we do what non-Christians do)—you can gather that the gravamen of the case is not any crime but a name. Conscious rivalry is set up against this name, with the primary effect that men are unwilling to know for certain, what they certainly know they do not know.

So they believe things about us which are not proved, and they are unwilling for inquiry to be made, in case things they prefer to have believed should be proved untrue. The object is that the name, which is the enemy in that conscious rivalry, may, because of crimes presumed but not proven, be condemned simply on its own confession. So we are tortured when we confess; we are punished when we persist; we are acquitted when we deny; all because the battle is for a name. Finally, in reading the charge, why do you call the man a Christian, why not a murderer too, if a Christian is a murderer? Why not incestuous? Or anything else you believe us to be? Or is it that in our case and ours alone, it shames you, or vexes you, to use the actual names of our crimes? If a Christian, with no charge laid against him, is a defendant because of a name, how shocking the name must be, if the charge consists of a name and nothing more.

What does it mean, when most people shut their eyes and run so blindfold into hatred of that name, that, even if they bear favorable testimony to a man, they throw in some detestation of the name? "A good man," they say, "this Caius Seius, only that he is a Christian." Then another says: "I am surprised that that wise man, Lucius Titius, has suddenly become a Christian." Nobody reflects whether Caius is good, and Lucius sensible, just because he is a Christian, or is a Christian because he is sensible and good. They praise what they know and blame what they do not know. They spoil their knowledge with their ignorance because it is fairer to prejudge what is hidden by what is evident, than to condemn in advance what is evident because of what is hidden. Other people, persons known before they had the name to have been vagabond, worthless, and wicked, they condemn and praise in one breath. In the blindness of hate they stumble into approval. "What a woman! how wanton, how frivolous! What a young man! how wanton, how gallant! They have become Christians." So the name follows the reformation as a fresh charge. Some men even play their own advantage with this hatred, content with injustice, provided they do not have at home what they hate. The wife is chaste now; but the husband has ceased to be jealous, and has turned her out. The son is now submissive; but the father, who used to bear with his ways, has disinherited him. The slave is faithful now; but the master, once so gentle, has banished him from his sight. As soon as a man is reformed by the name, he gives offense. The improvement does not balance the hatred felt for Christians.

Now, then, if it is hatred of a name, how can a name be indicted? What charge can lie against words, unless the pronunciation of some name has a barbarous sound about it—something unlucky or scurrilous or lewd? "Christian," so far as translation goes, is derived from "anointing." Yes, and when it is mispronounced by you "Chrestian" (for you have not even certain knowledge of the mere name) it is framed from "sweetness" or "kindness." So in innocent men you hate even the innocent name.

But the school is in fact hated for the name of its founder! What novelty is it, if some way of life gives its followers a name drawn from their teacher? Are not the philosophers called after their founders—Platonists, Epicureans, Pythagoreans? And also from the places where they gathered, where they took their stand—Stoics, Academics? And physicians in the same way from Erasistratus, and grammarians from Aristarchus—cooks too from Apicius? Yet nobody is ever offended by the avowal of a name handed down with his teaching from the teacher. Clearly, if a man has proved the school a bad one and its founder as bad, he will prove the bad name also to be worthy of hate because of the guilt of the school and the founder. So before you hated the name, it would have been proper first to judge the school in the light of the founder, or the founder in the light of the school. But, as things are, inquiry as to both and knowledge of both are allowed to slide; the name is picked out; the name is the object of attack. The school is unknown; the founder is unknown; a word of itself condemns both in advance—because they bear a name, not because they are convicted of anything.

EUSEBIUS OF CAESAREA

Eusebius (260–340), bishop of Caesarea (from 314 c.e.), was deeply influenced by the martyr Pamphilus, his teacher and model. Eusebius was imprisoned in 309 at the same time Pamphilus was, although Eusebius himself was released. After Constantine embraced Christianity, Eusebius was prominent in the ecumenical church at various councils from Nicea onward, as well as a friend of the emperor's. His *History of the Church* is the starting point of ecclesiastical history. He expresses better than anyone both the pitiless quality of the persecution under Diocletian and the inexpressible relief that followed. As he explains at the end of the excerpt, by the time of Diocletian's withdrawal in 305 C.E., the empire was divided (among four rulers known as the tetrarchy, two in the east and two in the west). The mention of Constantine heralds the new day that Eusebius saw dawning in his own lifetime.

TEXT: EUSEBIUS, *HISTORY OF THE CHURCH* 8.8.1–8.13.14

One must admire those of them also that were martyred in their own land, where countless numbers, men, women, and children, despising this passing life, endured various forms of death for the sake of our Savior's teaching. Some of them were committed to the flames after being scraped and racked and grievously scourged, and suffering other manifold torments terrible to hear, while some were submerged in the sea; others with a good courage stretched forth their heads to them that cut them off, or died in the midst of their tortures, or perished of hunger; and others again were crucified, some as malefactors usually are, and some, even more brutally, were nailed in the opposite manner, head-downwards, and kept alive until they should perish of hunger on the cross.

195

But it surpasses all description what the martyrs in the Thebais endured as regards both outrages and agonies. They had the entire body torn to pieces with sharp sherds instead of claws, even until life was extinct. Women were fastened by one foot and swung through the air to a height by devices, head-downwards, their bodies completely naked with not even a covering; and thus they presented this most disgraceful, cruel and inhuman of all spectacles to the whole company of onlookers. Others, again, were fastened to trees and trunks, and so died. For they drew together by machinery the very strongest of the branches, to each of which they fastened one of the martyr's legs, and then released the branches to take up their natural position: thus they contrived to tear apart at once all of the limbs of those who were the objects of this device. And indeed all these things were done, not for a few days or for some brief space, but for a long period extending over whole years. Sometimes more than ten, at other times above twenty persons were put to death; and at others not less than thirty, now nearer sixty, and again at other times a hundred men would be slain in a single day, along with quite young children and women, being condemned to manifold punishments which followed one on the other.

And we ourselves also beheld, when we were at these places, many executed all at once in a single day, some of whom suffered decapitation, others the punishment of fire. So many were killed that the murderous axe was dulled and, worn out, was broken in pieces, while the executioners themselves grew utterly weary and took it in turns to succeed one another. It was then that we observed a most marvelous eagerness and a truly divine power and zeal in those who had placed their faith in the Christ of God. As soon as sentence was given against one group, some from one quarter and others from another would leap up to the tribunal before the judge and confess themselves Christians. They paid no heed when faced with terrors and the varied forms of tortures, but undaunted spoke boldly of piety toward the God of the universe, and with joy and laughter and gladness received the final sentence of death. They sang and sent up hymns and thanksgivings to the God of the universe even to the very last breath.

And while these indeed were marvelous, those were all the more so who were distinguished for wealth, birth and reputation, as also for learning and philosophy, and yet put everything second to true piety and faith in our Savior and Lord Jesus Christ. Such was Philoromus, who had been entrusted with an office of no small importance in the imperial administration at Alexandria, and who, in connection with the dignity and rank that he had from the Romans, used to conduct judicial inquiries every day, attended by a bodyguard of soldiers. Such also was Phileas, bishop of the church of the Thmuis, a man who was distinguished for the services he rendered to his country in public positions, and also for his skill in philosophy. And though great numbers of relatives and other friends besought them, as well as many officials of high rank, and though the judge himself exhorted them to take pity on themselves and spare their children and wives, they could not be induced by this strong pressure to decide in favor of love of life and despise the ordinances of our Savior as to confessing and denying. But with a brave and philosophic resolution, or rather with a pious and godly soul, they stood firm against all the threats and insults of the judge, and both were beheaded.

Since we said that Phileas deserved a high reputation for his accomplishment in learning, let him appear as his own witness, to show us who he was, and at the same time to relate, more accurately than we could, the martyrdoms that took place at Alexandria. Here are his words:

From the Writings of Phileas to the Thmuites

With all these examples and patterns and good models placed before us in the divine and sacred Scriptures, the blessed martyrs among us did not hesitate, but directed the eye of the soul sincerely toward the God who is over all, and with a mind resolved on death for piety they clung fast to their calling, having found that our Lord Jesus Christ became man for our sakes, that he might destroy every kind of sin, and provide us with the means of entering into eternal life. For he counted it not a prize to be on an equality with God, but emptied himself, taking the form of a servant; and being found in fashion as a man, he humbled himself unto death, even the death of the cross. So, desiring earnestly the greater gifts, the Christ-bearing martyrs endured every kind of suffering and all manner of invention of torture, not once, but even a second time in some cases. When their guards vied in all kinds of threats against them, not only in word but also in deed, they refused to give up their resolution, because perfect love casts out fear. What account would suffice to reckon up their bravery and courage under every torture? For when all who wished were given a free hand to insult them, some smote them with cudgels, others with rods, others with scourges; others, again, with straps, and others with ropes. And the spectacle of their tortures was a varied one and permeated with evil. Some with both hands bound

197

behind them were stretched upon the cross, and with the aid of devices had every limb dislocated; then, the torturers acting on orders began to lay on over their whole body, not only, as in the case of murderers, punishing their sides with the instruments of torture, but also their belly, legs, and cheeks. Others were suspended from the roof by one hand and raised aloft, and in the tension of their joints and limbs experienced unequaled agony. Others were bound with their faces toward pillars, their feet not touching the ground, and thus their bonds were drawn tight by the pressure upon them of the weight of the body. And this they would endure, not only while the warden conversed or was engaged with them, but almost throughout the entire day. For when he went away to others, he would leave the agents of his authority to keep watch in case anyone should be overcome by the tortures and seem to give in. He instructed them to add mercilessly to their bonds also, and, when they were at the last gasp after all this, to cut them down to the ground and drag them off. For he said that they were not to have the least particle of regard for us, but to be so disposed and act as if we were no longer of any account. Such was the second torture that our enemies devised in addition to the stripes. And some, even after the tortures, were placed in the stocks, and had both feet stretched out to the fourth hole, and they were compelled to lie on their back, incapacitated because of the recent wounds they had from the blows over the whole body. Others were thrown to the ground and lay there, by reason of the wholesale application of the tortures; presenting to those who saw them a sight more terrible than did the actual punishment, in that they bore on their bodies marks of the manifold and varied tortures that were devised.

In these circumstances, some died under their tortures, having shamed the adversary by their endurance; others were shut up half dead in prison, and after not many days found fulfillment afflicted in their agonies; the rest recovered under treatment, and as the result of time and their stay in prison, gained confidence. So then, when the order was given and the choice held out, either to touch the abominable sacrifice and be unmolested, receiving from them the accursed freedom; or not to sacrifice and be punished with death—without hesitation they gladly went to their death. For they knew what had been prescribed for us by the sacred Scriptures. For he says, "He that sacrifices unto other gods shall be utterly destroyed"; and, "You shall have no other gods but me."

Such are the words of the martyr, true lover both of wisdom and of God, which he sent to the brethren in his community before the final sentence, when he was still in a state of imprisonment, at one and the same time showing the conditions in which he was living, and also stirring them up to hold fast—even after his approaching fulfillment—to the worship of God in Christ.

But what need is there to make a long story and add fresh instance upon instance of the combat of the godly martyrs throughout the world, especially of those who were assailed no longer by the common law, but as if they were enemies in war? For example, armed soldiers surrounded a little town in Phrygia, of which the inhabitants were all Christians, every man of them, and setting fire to it burnt them, along with young children and women, as they were calling upon the God who is over all. The reason for this was that all the inhabitants of the town altogether, the mayor himself and the magistrates with all the officials and the whole assembly, confessed themselves Christians and refused to give the least heed to those who bade them commit idolatry.

And there was another person who had attained to a high position under the Romans, Adauctus by name, a man of distinguished Italian descent. He had advanced through every grade of honor under the emperors, so as to pass blamelessly through the general administration of what they call the magistracy and ministry of finance. And besides all this, he became prominent by his noble deeds of godliness and his confession of the Christ of God, and he was adorned with the crown of martyrdom, enduring the agony for worship while actually engaged as finance minister.

What need now to mention the rest by name, or number the multitude of the men, or picture the varied tortures inflicted upon the wonderful martyrs? Sometimes they were slain with the axe, as was the case with those in Arabia; at other times they had their legs broken, as happened to those in Cappadocia; on some occasions they were suspended on high by the feet, head-downwards, while a slow fire was kindled beneath, so that when the wood was alight they were choked by the rising smoke—a treatment meted out to those in Mesopotamia; then, too, the noses, ears and hands were severed, and the remaining limbs and parts of the body cut up, as was done at Alexandria.

Why rekindle the memory of those at Antioch, who were roasted on heated gridirons, not unto death, but with a view to lengthy torture; and of others who put their right hand into the very fire sooner than touch the accursed sacrifice? Some of them, to escape such trial, before they were caught and fell into the hands of those that plotted against them, threw themselves down from the tops of tall houses, regarding death as a prize snatched from the wickedness of evil men.

A certain holy person, admirable for excellence of soul yet in body a woman, was famed as well by all that were at Antioch for wealth, descent, and sound judgment. She had brought up in the precepts of piety her two unmarried daughters, distinguished for the full bloom of their youthful beauty. Much envy was stirred up on their account, and every effort was made to find if possible where they lay concealed. When it was discovered that they were staying in a foreign country, they were purposely recalled to Antioch. Thus they fell into the soldiers' mercy. When the woman saw that herself and her daughters were in desperate straits, she placed before them in conversation the terrible things that awaited them at human hands, and the most intolerable thing of all these terrors—the threat of rape. Neither she herself nor her girls were to submit to the least suggestion they should endure such a thing. She said that to surrender their souls to the slavery of demons was worse than all kinds of death and every form of destruction. So she maintained that to flee to the Lord was the only way to escape from it all. And when they had all agreed to the opinion, and had arranged their garments suitably around them, on coming to the middle of their journey they modestly requested the guards to allow them a little time alone, and threw themselves into the river that flowed by.

They were their own executioners. Another pair of maidens, also at Antioch, were godly in every respect and true sisters, famous by descent, distinguished for their manner of life, young in years, beautiful in body, serious in soul, pious in their deportment, admirable in their zeal. The worshipers of demons commanded them to be cast into the sea, as if the earth could not endure to bear such excellence.

So those martyrs suffered, and others in Pontus suffered things terrible to hear. Sharp reeds were driven into their fingers under the tips of the nails; in the case of others, lead was melted down by fire, and the boiling, burning stuff poured down their backs, roasting the vital parts of the body. Others endured in their private parts and bowels sufferings that were disgraceful, pitiless, unmentionable, which the noble and law-abiding judges devised with more than usual eagerness, displaying their cruelty as if it were some great stroke of wisdom; striving to outdo one another by inventing novel tortures, as if contending for prizes in a contest.

The end of these calamities came when they were at last worn out with their excessive wickedness, and were utterly weary of killing and surfeited and sated with shedding blood, and so turned to what they considered merciful and humane conduct; so that they no longer thought that they were doing any harm to us. For it was not fitting, they said, to pollute the cities with the blood of their own people, or to involve in a charge of cruelty the supreme government of the rulers, a government that was well-disposed and mild towards all. Rather that the beneficence of the humane and imperial authority should be extended to all, and the death penalty should no longer be inflicted. For they declared that this punishment of us had been stopped, thanks to the humanity of the rulers.

Then orders were given that eyes should be gouged out and one leg maimed. For this was in their opinion humanity and the lightest of punishments inflicted upon us. Because of this humanity on the part of godless men, it is now no longer possible to tell the incalculable number of those who had their right eye first cut out with a sword and then cauterized with fire, and the left foot rendered useless by the further application of branding irons to the joints, and who after this were condemned to the provincial copper mines, not so much for service as for ill treatment and

201

hardship. Various other trials also met them, which it is not possible even to recount; for their brave and good deeds surpass all reckoning.

In these conflicts the magnificent martyrs of Christ made light shine throughout all the world, and everywhere amazed the eyewitnesses of their bravery. In their own body they furnished clear proofs that the power of our Savior is truly divine and inexpressible. To mention, indeed, each by name would be a long task, not to say an impossibility.

Of those rulers of the churches who were martyred in important cities, the first name that we must record on the monuments to holy men, as a martyr of the kingdom of Christ, is that of Anthimus, bishop of the city of the Nicomedians, who was beheaded. Of the martyrs at Antioch the noblest in his entire life was Lucian, a presbyter of that community. In Nicomedia, when the emperor was there, he also proclaimed the heavenly kingdom of Christ, first by word of mouth in an Apology, and afterwards also by deeds. Of the martyrs in Phoenicia the most famous would be the pastors of the spiritual flocks of Christ, beloved of God in all things, Tyrannion, bishop of the church at Tyre; Zenobius, presbyter of the church at Sidon; and Sylvanus, bishop of the churches in the area of Emesa. Sylvanus became food for wild beasts, along with others, at Emesa itself, and so was received up into the choirs of martyrs. The other two glorified the word of God at Antioch by their endurance unto death; one of them, the bishop, was committed to the depths of the sea, while that best of physicians, Zenobius, died bravely under the tortures that were applied to his sides. Of the martyrs in Palestine, Silvanus, bishop of the churches in the region of Gaza, was beheaded at the copper mines at Phaeno, with others, in number forty save one; and two Egyptian bishops there, Peleus and Nilus (together with others), endured death by fire.

And among these we must mention the great glory of the community of Caesarea—Pamphilus, a presbyter, the most marvelous man of our day—the merit of whose brave and excellent deeds we shall record at the proper time. Of those at Alexandria and throughout all Egypt and the Thebais who were perfected gloriously, the first that must be recorded is Peter, bishop of Alexandria itself, a divine example of the teachers of godliness in Christ; and the presbyters with him Faustus, Dius and Ammonius, perfect martyrs of Christ; and Phileas, Hesychius, Pachymius, and Theodore, bishops of the churches in Egypt. There are countless other famous persons as well, who are commemorated by the communities in their own district and locality.

It is not our task to commit to writing the combat of those who fought throughout the world on behalf of divine worship, and to record in detail everything that happened to them; that would be the especial task of those who witnessed the events. Yet in another work I shall make known to those who come after us the struggles I personally witnessed. In this present book, however, I shall follow what has been said with a résumé of the things that were done against us, and with all that happened after the start of the persecution. Those are the events most instructive to my readers.

Now as concerns the state of the Roman government before the war against us, in every period that the rulers were friendly and peaceably disposed toward us, no words could sufficiently describe how bountiful and plenteous was its harvest of good things. Those who held the highest rule in the world completed the tenth and twentieth year of their reigns, and used to pass their days in festivals and public gatherings, in the most joyous feasts and banquets, possessing complete, well-established peace.

But as their authority increased without let or hindrance and day by day grew greater, all at once they departed from their peaceful attitude toward us and stirred up a relentless war. The second year of this kind of activity on their part had not fully come, when something unexpected affecting the entire government took place and turned the whole of public affairs upside down. For a fateful disease struck him who stood first among those of whom we spoke, which caused his mind to become deranged; and, together with him who had been honored with the second place after him, he resumed the ordinary life of a private citizen. And this had not yet taken place when the whole rule was split in two, a thing that had never even been recorded as having happened at any time.

Not long afterward the Emperor Constantius, who all his life long showed himself most mildly and favorably disposed toward his subjects, and most friendly toward the divine word, died according to the common law of nature, leaving his lawful son Constantine absolute ruler and Augustus in his stead. He was the first of the new tetrarchy to be proclaimed among the gods by them, being deemed worthy of every honor after death that might be due to an emperor, kindest and mildest of emperors that he was. He indeed was the only one of that time who passed the whole period of his rule in a manner worthy of his high office. In other respects he made himself most favorable and beneficent toward all; and he took no part in the war against us, but even preserved the God-fearing persons among his subjects from injury and harsh treatment. He neither pulled down the church buildings nor did he issue any new policy against us. So he has had as his reward a happy and thrice-blessed issue of his life; for he alone enjoyed a favorable and glorious end while he was still emperor, with a lawful son, in all respects most prudent and religious, to succeed him.

7

VALUES IN CHRISTIANITY

CLEMENT OF ALEXANDRIA

During the last decade of the second century, Clement of Alexandria offered instruction to Christians in that great city and intellectual center. He was active there until the persecution that broke out in 202 under Septimius Severus. Clement developed a brilliant philosophy of Christian faith, which he produced in conscious opposition to Gnostic teachings. His greatest works constitute a trilogy. The first is an introduction to Christianity as a superior philosophical teaching (the *Protreptikos*); the second, the *Paidagogos*, or "Tutor" (from which our excerpt is taken), is an account of how Christ serves as our moral guide in the quest for true knowledge and perfection. Finally, his "Miscellanies," the *Stromateis* (literally, "Carpet Bags"), is a wide-ranging and complex work. Initially, it was intended as a defense of Clement's thesis that Christian revelation surpasses the achievements of human reason, but its structure and expression are obscure. For that reason, the *Paidagogos* is probably the best introduction to Clement's innovative philosophy of Christianity.

TEXT: CLEMENT OF ALEXANDRIA, *PAIDAGOGOS*, 1.1–1.6

There are these three attributes in man: habits, deeds, and passions. Of these, habits come under the influence of the word of persuasion, the guide to godliness. This is the word that underlies and supports, like the keel of a ship, the whole structure of the faith. Under its spell, we joyfully surrender our old ideas, become young again to gain salvation, and sing in the inspired words of the psalm: "How good is God to Israel, to those who are upright of heart." As for deeds, they are affected by the word of counsel, and passions are healed by that of consolation.

This word is one in operation: the selfsame Word who forcibly draws men from their natural, worldly way of life and educates them to the only true salvation—faith in God. That is to say, the heavenly guide, the Word, once he begins to call men to salvation, takes to himself the name of persuasion. This kind of appeal, although only one part of the appeal, is properly given the name of persuasion—that is, word—since the whole worship of God has a persuasive appeal, instilling in a receptive mind the desire for life now and for the life to come. But the Word also heals and counsels, all at the same time. In fact, he follows up his own activity by encouraging the one he has already persuaded, and particularly by offering a cure for his passions.

Let us call him, then, by the one title: Paedagogue of little ones, a Paedagogue who does not simply follow behind, but who leads the way, for his aim is to improve the soul, not just to instruct it; to guide to a life of virtue, not merely to one of knowledge. Yet, that same Word does teach. It is simply that we are not now considering him in that light. As Teacher, he explains and reveals through instruction, but as Paedagogue he is practical. First he persuades men to form habits of life, then he encourages them to fulfill their duties by laying down clear-cut counsels and by exhibiting, for those who follow, examples of those who have erred in the past. Both persuasion and encouragement are most useful: the advice, that it may be obeyed; the other, given in the form of example, has a twofold object—that we may choose the good and imitate it or condemn and avoid the bad.

Healing of the passions follows as a consequence. The Paedagogue strengthens souls with the persuasion implied in these examples, and he gives the mild medicine of his loving counsels to the sick man that he may come to a full knowledge of the truth.

Health and knowledge are not the same; one is a result of study, the other of healing. In fact, if a person is sick, he cannot master any of the things taught him until he is first completely cured. We give instructions to someone who is sick for an entirely different purpose from when we instruct someone who is learning; the latter, we instruct that he may acquire knowledge, the first, that he may regain health. Just as those diseased in body require a physician, so too, those weak in soul require the Paedagogue to cure its ills. Only then does it need the Teacher to guide it and develop its capacity to know, once it is made pure and capable of retaining the revelation of the Word.

Therefore, the all-loving Word, anxious to perfect us in a way that leads progressively to salvation, observes an order well adapted to our development; at first, he persuades, then he educates, and after all this he teaches.

Our Educator, you children, resembles his Father, God, whose Son he is. He is without sin, without blame, without passion of soul, God undefiled in form of man, accomplishing his Father's will. He is God the Word, who is in the Father, and also at the right hand of the Father, with even the form of God.

He is to us the spotless image. We must try, then, to resemble him in soul as far as we are able. It is true that he himself is entirely free from human passion; that is why he alone is sinless and he alone is judge. Yet we must strive, to the best of our ability, to be as sinless as we can. There is nothing more important for us than first to be rid of sin and weakness, and then to uproot any habitually sinful inclination. The highest perfection, of course, is never to sin in any least way; but this can be said of God alone. The next highest is never deliberately to commit wrong; this is the state proper to the man who possesses wisdom. In the third place comes not sinning greatly by involuntary wrongs; this marks a man who is well educated. Finally, in the lowest degree, we must place not continuing long in sin; even this, for those who are called to recover their loss and repent, is a step on the path to salvation.

It seems to me that the Paedagogue expresses it aptly through Moses when he says: "If anyone die suddenly before the priest, the head of his consecration shall be defiled; and he shall immediately shave it." By sudden death he means an involuntary sin, and says that it defiles because it pollutes the soul. For the cure he prescribes that the head be shaved as soon as possible, meaning that the locks of ignorance that darken the reason should be shorn so that the reason (which has its seat in the head), stripped of hair, that is, wickedness, may the better continue its course to repentance.

Then a little afterwards he adds: "The former days were without reason," by which he surely means that deliberate sin is an act done contrary to reason. Involuntary sin he calls "sudden," but deliberate sin "without reason." It is precisely for this purpose that the Word, Reason itself, has taken upon himself, as the Paedagogue, the task of preventing sins against reason. Consider in this light that expression in the Scriptures: "For this reason, thus says the Lord . . ." The words that follow ("For this reason . . .") describe and condemn some sin that has been committed. The judgment contained in these words is just, for it is as if he were giving notice in the words of the prophets that, if you had not sinned, he would not have made these threats. The same is true of those other words: "For this reason, the Lord says these things . . . ," and "Because you have not heard these words, the Lord says these things . . . ," and "Behold, for this reason, the Lord says." In fact, the inspired Word exists because of both obedience and disobedience: that we may be saved by obeying it, and corrected because we have disobeyed.

Therefore, the Word is our Paedagogue who heals the unnatural passions of our soul with his counsel. The art of healing, strictly speaking, is the relief of the ills of the body, an art learned by man's wisdom. Yet the only true divine healer of human sickness, the holy relief of the soul when it is ill, is the Word of the Father. Scripture says: "Save thy servant, O my God, who puts his trust in thee. Have mercy on me, O Lord, because I have cried to thee the whole day through." In the words of Democritus, "The healer, by his art, cures the body of its diseases, but it is wisdom that rids the soul of its passions." The good Paedagogue, however, Wisdom, the Word of the Father, who created man, concerns himself with the whole creature, and as the Physician of the whole man heals both body and soul.

"Arise," he said to the paralytic, "take up the bed on which you are lying and go home." And immediately the sick man regained his health. To the man who was dead he said: "Lazarus, come forth." And the man came forth from his tomb, the same as he had been before he suffered, having experienced resurrection.

But the soul he heals in a way suitable to the nature of the soul: by his commandments and by his gifts. He is ready to heal with his counsels, but, generous with his gifts, he also says to us sinners, "Your sins are forgiven you." With this thought we have become an infant of his providence, for we share in his magnificent and unvarying order. That providence begins by ordering the world and the heavens, the course of the sun's orbit and the movements of the other heavenly bodies, all for the sake of man. Then, it concerns itself with man himself, for whom it had undertaken all these other labors. And because it considers this as its most important work, it guides man's soul on the right path by the virtues of prudence and temperance, and equips his body with beauty and harmony. Finally, into the actions of mankind it infuses uprightness and some of its own good order.

Both as God and as man, the Lord renders us every kind of service and assistance. As God, he forgives sin; as man, he educates us to avoid sin completely. Man is the work of God; he is naturally dear to him. Other things God made by a simple word of command, but man he fashioned by his own direct action and breathed into him something proper to himself. Now, a being that God himself has fashioned, and in such a way that it resembles himself closely, must have been created either because it is desirable to God in itself, or because it is useful for some other creature. If man has been created as desirable in himself, then God loves him as good since he himself is good; there is a certain affectiveness in man, which is the very quality breathed into him by God.

But, if God made man only because he considered him useful for some other creature, then he could have had no other reason for actually creating him than that with him he could become a good Creator, and then man could not attain the knowledge of God. In this case, unless man had been created, God could not have made the other creature for whose sake man was being created. So, the strength of will that God already possessed, hidden deep within himself, he actualized by this display of the external power of creating, taking this supposed other man from the man he had made. But according to this idea, he saw then what he possessed all along: the creature whom God had willed to be. It should have existed in the first place, for there is nothing that God cannot do.

Therefore, man, whom God made, is desirable in himself. But being desirable in oneself means being related to the person to whom one is desirable, and being acceptable and pleasing. But what does being pleasing to someone mean, if not being loved by him? Man is, then, an object of love; indeed, man is loved by God.

It must be so, for it was on man's account that the only begotten was sent from the bosom of the Father, as the Word of faith, faith that has a wealth of resources. The Lord clearly attests this when he says: "The Father himself loves you, because you have loved me." And again: "And you have loved them, just as you have loved me." What the Educator desires and what he proclaims, what he has in mind in his words and in his deeds, in his commands of what we are to do and what we are to avoid, is already clear. It is clear, too, that the other kind of discourse, that of the Teacher, is at once strong and spiritual, in accurate terms, but meant only for those who are initiated. But, for the present, let that be.

As for him who lovingly guides us along the way to the better life, we ought to return him love and live according to the dictate of his principles. This we should do not only by fulfilling his commandments and obeying his prohibitions, but also by turning away from the evil examples we just mentioned and imitating the good. In this way, we shall make our own actions, as far as we are able, like those of our Paedagogue, that the ancient saying, "according to his own image and likeness," may be accomplished.

For we wander in thick darkness; we need a sure and unerring guide in life. The best guide is not that blind one who, in the words of Scripture, "leads the blind into a ditch," but the Word, keen of sight, penetrating into the secret places of the heart. Just as there cannot be a light that does not give light, nor a movement that does not move nor a lover unless he loves, just so he cannot be good unless he rendered us service and led us to salvation.

Let us, then, perform the commandments through works of the Lord. Indeed, the Word himself, when he became flesh in visible form, unceasingly showed not only the theory but also the practice of virtue. Further, considering the Word as our law, let us see in his commandments and counsels direct and sure paths to eternity. For his precepts are filled, not with fear, but with persuasion. Let us welcome more and more gladly this holy obedience, and let us surrender ourselves more and more completely to the Lord, holding to the steadfast cable of his faith. Let us recognize, too, that both men and women practice the same sort of virtue. Surely, if there is but one God for both, then there is but one Paedagogue for both.

One Church, one temperance, one modesty, a common food, equality in marriage; breath, sight, hearing, knowledge, hope, obedience, love, all are alike. They who possess life in common, grace in common, and salvation in common have also love in common and education too. The Scripture says: "For in this world, they marry and are given in marriage," for this world is the only place in which the female is distinguished from the male, "but in that other world, no longer." There, the rewards of this common and holy life, based on equality, await not male or female as such, but man, removed from the lust that in this life divided man from himself.

The very name "mankind" is a name common to both males and women. Similarly, the Attic Greeks called not only the boy but also the girl by the one name of "child" if Meander, the comic poet, is to be believed in a passage of his play *Rapizomene:* "My little daughter . . . indeed, she is by nature an exceedingly loving child." Notice, too, that "sheep" is the general name used for the male and female. Yet the Lord shepherds us for ever, Amen. Now, neither sheep nor any other animal should live without a shepherd, nor should children, without a paedagogue, nor servants without a master.

That paedagogy is the training given children (*paidia*) is evident from the name itself. It remains for us to consider who the children are as explained by the Scriptures and, from the same scriptural passages, to understand the Paedagogue.

We are the children. Scripture celebrates us very often and in many different ways, and refers to us under different titles, thereby introducing variety in the simple language of the faith. For example, in the Gospel, it says: "And the Lord, standing on the shore, said to his disciples"—they were fishing—"Children, do you have no fish?" Those who already had the position of disciples he now calls "children."

Again, we read: "And they brought the children to him, that he might lay hands on them and bless them, and when the disciples tried to prevent it, Jesus said: 'Let the little children be and do not hinder them from coming to me, for of such is the kingdom of heaven.'" What such a remark means the Lord himself explains plainly later on: "Unless you turn and become like little children, you shall not enter into the kingdom of heaven." Those words are not a figure of speech for some kind of rebirth, but recommend the simplicity of childhood for our imitation.

The prophetic Spirit also describes us as children: "Plucking branches of olives," Scripture says, "or of palm, the children came out to meet the Lord, and they cried out, saying: Hosanna to the Son of David, blessed is he who comes in the name of the Lord." The word "Hosanna," translated into Greek, means "light, glory, praise, supplication to the Lord."

Incidentally, it seems to me that the Scripture, in this inspired passage, intends to accuse and condemn the careless: "Have you never read that out of the mouths of babes and sucklings, you have brought forth praise?"

In the same way again in the Gospel, the Lord shocked his companions, attempting to arouse their attention when he was about to go to his Father. To urge them to listen more intently, he tells them in advance that in a little while he will go away; so he would make them understand that while the Word has not yet ascended into heaven, they must gather in the fruits of truth with greater care. So it is that once more he calls them children: "Children," he says, "yet a little while and I am with you." Again, he likens the kingdom of heaven to children sitting in the marketplace and saying, "We piped for you, and you did not dance, we mourned and you did not grieve." And the Gospel adds other such usages.

✡
212
✝

But it is not only the Gospel that speaks in this way. Prophecy agrees with it. David, for example, says: "Praise the Lord, O children, praise the name of the Lord." And Isaiah: "Behold, I and my children whom God has given me."

Does it surprise you to hear that full-grown men of all nations are children in God's eyes? Then you do not know much about the Attic language, where we can see that beautiful and attractive young women who are moreover free-born, are called "children," and slaves are called "little children," although they are young women. They are complimented by such flattering names because of the flower of their youth.

Whenever he says: "Let my lambs stand on my right," he means the simple: children, not men, are in the category of sheep. He considers the lambs as deserving to be mentioned first, thereby praising, before all other qualities men can possess, gentleness and simplicity of mind and guilelessness.

Again, whenever he speaks of "young suckling calves," and of "the guileless and meek dove," he means us. Through Moses he orders that two young birds, a pair of pigeons or of turtle doves, be offered for sin; this means that the sinlessness of such gentle birds and their guilelessness and forgetfulness of injury is very acceptable to God. So he is instructing us to offer a sacrifice bearing the character of that which we have offended against. The plight of the poor doves, moreover, will instil into us a beginning of abhorrence for sin.

There is a passage in Scripture that shows that he refers to us also as young birds: "As the hen gathers her chicks under her wings." In that sense we are the Lord's young birds, a name that graphically and mystically describes the simplicity of soul belonging to childhood. At times, he calls us children, at other times, chicks, sometimes, infants, here and there sons, and very often offspring, a new people, a young people. "A new name," he says, "will be given my servants"—by new name he means one that is different and everlasting, pure and simple, suggestive of childhood and of candor—"which will be blessed upon the earth."

At another time, he speaks allegorically of us as colts. He means by that that we are unyoked to evil, unsubdued by wickedness, unaffected, high-spirited only with our Father. We are colts, not stallions "who whinny lustfully for their neighbor's wife, beasts of burden unrestrained in their lust." Rather, we are free and newly born, joyous in our faith, holding fast to the course of truth, swift in seeking salvation, spurning and trampling upon worldliness. "Rejoice greatly, O daughter of Sion. Shout for joy, O daughter of Jerusalem. Behold, your King comes to you, just and saving, and he is poor and riding upon an ass and upon a young colt." He is not satisfied to say "colt"; he adds "young," to emphasize mankind's rejuvenation in Christ and its unending, eternal youth and simplicity. Such young colts as we infants are reared by our divine Tamer. Although the passage speaks of the new man as a young ass, it, too, is a colt.

Again, it is said: "He tethers his colt to the vine." This means he united the simple, infant people to the Word, whom the vine signifies. For the vine produces wine; the Word produces blood. Both are saving potions: one, for the health of the body; the other, for the spirit.

But that he calls us lambs, too, the Spirit gives unmistakable evidence through Isaiah: "He shall feed his flock like a shepherd; he shall gather together the lambs with his arm." Once again, he uses the more innocent class of sheep, lambs, as a figure for simplicity.

There can be no doubt that we also call the most excellent and perfect possessions in life by names derived from the word "child" (*pais*), that is, training (*paideia*) and paedagogy. We define paedagogy as a sound training from childhood in the path of virtue. Be that as it may, the Lord once very clearly revealed what he means by the name "children." A dispute having arisen among the apostles as to which of them was greater, Jesus made a child stand among them, saying: "If anyone will humble himself as this little child, he is greater in the kingdom of heaven." Therefore, he does not mean by "child" one who has not yet reached the use of reason because of his immaturity, as some have thought. When he says: "Unless you become as these children, you shall not enter the kingdom of heaven," he is not commending a lack of learning. We are not little ones in the sense that we roll on the floor or crawl on the ground as snakes do. That is to grovel in unreasoning desires with our whole body prostrate. We strain upward with our minds, we have given up sin and the world, we tread the earth, although with light foot, only to the degree that we are in the world. We, indeed, cultivate holy wisdom, which seems foolishness to those bent on evil.

Really, then, those people are children who know God alone as their Father, who are simple, infants, guileless, who are lovers of the horns of the unicorns. To those, surely, who have progressed in the Word, he has proclaimed his message, bidding them to be unconcerned with the affairs of this life and encouraging them to imitate children and depend upon the Father alone. So it is that he says in what follows: "Do not be anxious about the morrow; for tomorrow will have anxieties of its own." Here his command is to lay aside the cares of life and devote oneself to the Father alone. Whoever fulfills this command is an infant, indeed, and a child, both before God and the world: to the world, in the sense of one who is aberrant; to God, in the sense of one dearly beloved.

Now if there is, as the Scripture says, but "one teacher, in heaven," then, surely all who are on earth can with good reason be called disciples. The plain truth is that what is perfect belongs to the Lord, who is ever teaching, while the role of child and little one belongs to us, who are ever learning. In fact, the inspired word reserves the name "man" to what is complete; David, for example, says of the devil: "The Lord abominates the man of blood," man in the sense that he is complete in wickedness. Scripture calls the Lord man, too, in the sense that he is complete in righteousness. The apostle, writing to the Corinthians, says: "For I have betrothed you to one man, that I might present you a chaste virgin to Christ," whether as infants or saints, at any rate, to the Lord alone. And in writing to the Ephesians he reveals clearly what is at issue, saying: "Until we all attain to the unity of the faith and of the deep knowledge of God, to perfect man, to the mature measure of the fullness of Christ; that we may be no longer children, tossed to and fro and carried about by every wind of doctrine devised in the wickedness of man, in craftiness, according to the wiles of error. Rather speaking the truth in love, we are to grow up in all things in him." He says these things to build up the body of Christ, "who is the head," and man because he alone is perfect in righteousness. If we, the children, protect ourselves from the winds that blow us off course into the pride of heresy and refuse to listen to those who set up other fathers for us, we are made perfect by accepting Christ as our head and becoming ourselves the Church.

From all this it is plain to see that the name "infant" is not used in the sense of being foolish. Childishness means that, but "infant" (*nēpios*) really means "one newly become gentle" (*neēpios*), just as the word "gentle" means being mild-mannered. So, "infant" means one just recently become gentle and meek of disposition. The blessed Paul obviously shows this when he says, "Although as the apostles of Christ we could have been a burden among you, still while in your midst we were infants, as if a nurse were cherishing her own children." An infant is gentle and for that reason decidedly amenable, mild and simple, without deceit or pretense, direct and upright of mind. Childlikeness is the foundation for simplicity and truthfulness. "For upon whom shall I look," it is said in Scripture, "if not the meek and the peaceful?" Of such sort is the virginal Word, gentle and unaffected. This is why, too, we speak of a virgin as a tender woman, and of a child as tender-minded. We are tender, too, in the sense that we have become amenable to persuasion, and we are ready to practice goodness, with anger under control and unhampered by malice or dishonesty.

The old people were perverse and hard of heart, but we, the new people, the assembly of infants, are as amenable as a child. In the Epistle to the Romans, the apostle declares that he rejoices in "the hearts of the innocent." But he goes on to set limits to this childlikeness: "I would have you wise as to what is good, and guileless as to what is evil." Indeed, for neither is the Greek word *nēpios*, "infant," meant in a negative sense, even though the grammarians have decided that the prefix *nē* is a privative.

Indeed, if they who decry childlikeness call us foolish, you see they are really speaking evil of the Lord. They imply that those who seek the protection of God are fools. But if they will accept the term "infants" in the sense of the simple—and it must be taken in this sense—then we glory in the name. The new minds are indeed infants, they who have newly become wise despite their former folly, who have risen up according to the new covenant. Only recently, in fact, has God become known, because of the coming of Christ. "For no one has known God, but the Son, and him to whom the Son has revealed him."

Then the new people, in contrast to the older people, are young, because they have heard the new good things. This unaging youth of ours is fruitful; we are ever at the prime of intelligence, ever young, ever childlike, ever new. For those who have partaken of the new Word must themselves be new. But whatever partakes of eternity assumes, by that very fact, the qualities of the incorruptible; therefore, the name "childhood" is for us a lifelong springtime, because the truth abiding in us is ageless and our being, made to overflow with that truth, is ageless, too. Surely, wisdom is ever fruitful, ever fixed unchangeably on the same truths, never varying.

"The children," it is said, "shall be put upon the shoulders, and they shall be comforted on the knees, as one whom the mother comforts, so will I comfort you." A mother draws her children near her; we seek our mother, the Church. Whatever is weak and tender has an appeal and sweetness and lovableness of its own, deflecting anger, just because in its weakness it does stand in need of help. Just as the male and female parent regard their young tenderly—whether it be horses their colts, or cows their calves, or lions their cubs, or deer their fawn, or men their children—so, too, does the Father of all receive those who seek his aid, giving them a new birth by the Spirit into sonship. He recognizes them as gentle, he loves only them, and he comes to the aid of such as these and defends them. That is why he calls them his children.

I turn to Isaac as an illustration of this sort of childhood. Isaac means "rejoicing." The inquisitive king saw him playing with his wife and helpmate, Rebecca. The king (his name was Abimelek) represents, I believe, a wisdom above this world, looking down upon the mystery signified by such childlike playing. Rebecca means "endurance." What prudent playing! Rejoicing joined to endurance, with the king as spectator. The Spirit exults in such children in Christ, attended with endurance. This is godly, childlike play.

Heraclitus tells us that his Zeus, too, indulges in play. Indeed, what occupation is more becoming a wise and perfect man than to play and rejoice in the beautiful with endurance and to manage the beautiful by celebrating God?

It is possible to take the meaning of the prophetic word in still another sense: that it refers to our rejoicing and making merry because of our salvation, like Isaac's. He rejoiced because he had been saved from death; that is why he played and rejoiced with his spouse, as we with our helpmate in salvation, the Church. The Church, too, has been given the reassuring name "steadfast endurance," either because she continues for all eternity always rejoicing, or because she is formed of the endurance of those who believe, of us who are the members of Christ. The testimony given by those who have endured until the end, and their thanksgiving as well, is a mystical playing; salvation supports this holy gladness of heart. The king is Christ, looking down from above on our rejoicing, and "peering through the door," as Scripture says, on our gratitude and blessing that produces in us joy and cheerfulness with endurance. He views the assembly of such as these, his own Church, showing only his face—which was wanting to the Church— a Church completed with its kingly head. What is the door by which the Lord shows himself? It is his flesh by which he becomes manifest.

Isaac is another type, too (he can easily be taken in this other sense), this time of the Lord. He was a son, just as is the Son, for he is the son of Abraham as Christ is of God. He was a sacrifice, as was the Lord, but he was not offered, while the Lord was. All he did was to carry the wood of his sacrifice, just as the Lord bore the wood of the Cross. Isaac rejoiced for a mystical reason, to prefigure the joy with which the Lord has filled us, in redeeming us from corruption through the blood of the Lord. Isaac did not actually suffer, not only to concede the primacy of suffering to the Word, but also to suggest, by not being slain, the divinity of the Lord; Jesus rose again after his burial, without having suffered, like Isaac delivered from the altar of sacrifice.

But there is another and even greater support for this argument, which I shall now explain. The Spirit inspired Isaiah to call the Lord a child: "Behold, a child is born to us, and a son is given us, and the government is upon his shoulders: and his name shall be called Angel of the great council." What is this child, this infant, that the government is upon his shoulders? It is he after whose image we are also little ones. Through the same prophet his greatness is described: "Wonderful, Counselor, mighty God, everlasting Father, Prince of peace;" because he fulfills his childhood, "of his peace there shall be no end." The great God: the perfect Child! Son, in Father; Father, in Son. Is not the childhood of this child perfect, embracing, leading us children, who are his infants? This is he who stretches out his hands to us, hands so clearly to be trusted.

Again, John, "the prophet greatest among those born of woman," also testified to his childhood: "Behold the Lamb of God." Scripture speaks of children and infants as "lambs"; thus in this passage, in calling God the Word, become man for us, "the Lamb of God," because of his desire to be like us in all things, he is speaking of him as the Son of God, the infant of the Father.

It is possible, too, for us to make a completely adequate answer to any carping critics. We are children and infants, but certainly not because the learning we acquire is puerile or rudimentary, as those puffed up in their own knowledge falsely charge. On the contrary, when we were reborn, we straightway received the perfection for which we strive. For we were enlightened, that is, we came to the knowledge of God. Certainly, he who possesses knowledge of the Perfect Being is not imperfect.

But do not find fault with me for claiming that I have such knowledge of God. This claim was made appropriate by the Word, and he is free to do so. When the Lord was baptized, a voice sounded from heaven, as a witness to him who was beloved: "you are my beloved son; this day have I begotten you."

Now let us ask the wise: on that day when Christ was reborn, was he already perfect, or—a silly suggestion—was he defective? If the latter, then he needed to add to his knowledge. But, since he is God, it is not likely that he learned even one thing more. No one can be greater than the Word, nor can anyone be the teacher of him who is the one only Teacher. Are they unwilling, then, to admit that the Word, perfect son born of a perfect Father, was perfectly reborn, according to the working of the divine plan? But, if he is perfect, then why was one already perfect baptized?

It was necessary, they tell us, that the commandment given to men might be fulfilled.

Very good, I reply. But was he, by that baptism conferred through John, made perfect?

It is clear that he was.

But not by learning anything more?

No, indeed.

Is it, then, that he was made perfect only in the sense of being washed, and that he was consecrated by the descent of the Holy Spirit?

Yes, that is the true explanation.

This is what happens with us, whose model the Lord became. When we are baptized, we are enlightened; being enlightened, we become sons; becoming sons, we are made perfect; and becoming perfect, we are made divine. "I have said," it is written, "you are gods and all of you the sons of the Most High."

This is often called "free gift," "enlightenment," "perfection," and "cleansing"—"cleansing," because through it we are completely purified of our sins; "free gift," because by it the punishments due to our sins are remitted; "enlightenment," since by it we behold the wonderful holy light of salvation, that is, it enables us to see God clearly; finally, we call it "perfection" as needing nothing further, for what more does he need who possesses the knowledge of God? It would indeed be absurd to call something that was not fully perfect a gift of God. He is perfect; therefore, the gifts he bestows are also perfect. Just as at his command all things came into existence, so, on his mere desire to give, grace is fulfilled. What is yet to come, his will alone has already anticipated.

Moreover, release from evil is only the beginning of salvation. Only those who have first begun the end of life are already perfect. But we live, we who have even now been freed from death. Salvation is the following of Christ. "What was made in him is life." "Amen, amen," he tells us, "I say to you, he who hears my word and believes him who sent me has life everlasting and does not come to judgment, but has passed from death to life." The very fact that we believe in him and are reborn is perfection of life. For

God is by no means weak. As his will is creation, and is called the universe, so his desire is the salvation of men, and is called the Church. He knows whom he has called; and whom he has called he has saved; he has called and at the same time saved. "Now you yourselves," the apostle says, "are taught of God." It is not right, then, for us to consider imperfect the teaching that is given by him. That instruction is the eternal salvation that comes through the eternal Savior, to whom be thanksgiving for ever. Amen.

Even though a man receive nothing more than this rebirth, still, because he is by that fact enlightened, he is immediately rid of darkness, as the name itself suggests, and automatically receives light. It is just like men who shake off sleep and then are wide awake interiorly; or, better, like those suffering from some blinding disease of the eyes and receive no light from the outside and have none themselves, but must first remove the impediment from their eyes before they can have a free pupil. In the same way, those who are baptized wipe off the sins that cloud over the divine spirit and then acquire a vision of Spirit that is clear and unimpeded and full of light, the sort of sight that alone enables us to behold divinity, with the help of the Holy Spirit who is poured forth from heaven upon us. This is a donation of eternal radiance, giving the power to see the eternal light. Like indeed attracts like; so what is holy attracts him who is the source of holiness, who properly speaking is called Light. "For you once were darkness, but now light in the Lord." That is why, I believe, the ancients once called man by a name that means light.

221

But, they object, man has not yet received the gift of perfection. I agree with them, except that he is already in the light and darkness does not overtake him. There is nothing at all in between light and darkness. Perfection lies ahead, in the resurrection of the faithful, but it consists in obtaining the promise that has already been given to us. We say emphatically that both of these things cannot coexist at the same time: arrival at the goal and the anticipation of that arrival by the mind. Eternity and time are not the same thing, nor are the beginning and the completion. They cannot be. But both are concerned with the same thing, and there is only one person involved in both. Faith, then, generated in time, is the starting point, if we may use the term, while the completion is the possession of the promise, made enduring for all eternity.

The Lord has himself revealed clearly that salvation will be bestowed impartially, when he said: "This is the will of my Father . . . that whoever beholds the Son, and believes in him, has life everlasting, and I will raise him up on the last day." Certainly, as far as is possible in this world (which is the reference of the expression "last day"), we believe that, while we wait for the time when it will come to an end, we have already been made perfect. For the perfection of instruction is faith. That is why he says: "He who believes in the Son has life everlasting." Assuredly, if we who believe already have life everlasting, what more remains but the enjoyment of that life everlasting? Nothing is lacking in faith, for of its nature it is perfect and entirely complete. If there is anything lacking in it, it is not wholly perfect, nor is it truly faith, if defective in any way. After our departure from here, there is not a different sort of thing awaiting us who have believed in this life, and who have already received a pledge and foretaste. In believing, we already anticipate in advance what we will receive as an actuality after the resurrection, that the words may be accomplished: "Be it done unto you according to your faith." Here, where faith is, there is promise; but the fulfillment of promise is enjoyment. Therefore, while our knowledge consists in enlightenment, the goal of knowledge is enjoyment, which is the last thing to be obtained.

In the same way that inexperience yields to experience, and impossibility to possibility, so darkness is completely dispelled by light. Darkness is ignorance, for it makes us fall into sin and lose the ability to see the truth clearly. But knowledge brings light, for it dispels the darkness of ignorance and endows us with keenness of vision. The very act of expelling things that are bad reveals what is good. For the things that ignorance restricts, to our harm, knowledge sets free, for our good. The quickest way to loose those bonds is to make use of man's faith, and God's grace, for sins are forgiven through the one divine remedy, baptism in the Word. All our sins, in fact, are washed away; instantaneously we are no longer beset by evil. This is one grace of enlightenment, that we no longer are in the same state as before we were cleansed. Even before this teaching was given us, we who were uninstructed, but were learning, heard that instruction is engendered together with enlightenment, bathing the mind in light. Yet, no one could say just when. Instruction is given to engender faith, but faith is trained by the Holy Spirit in baptism.

The Apostle states very clearly that faith is salvation reaching the whole of mankind, and that it is an impartial share of union with the just and loving God, given to all. He says: "But before the faith came, we were kept imprisoned under the law, shut up for the faith that was to be revealed. Therefore, the law has been our paedagogue in Christ, that we might be justified by faith. But now that faith has come, we are no longer under a paedagogue."

Do you not hear those words: "that we are no longer under the law," which was accompanied by fear, but under the Word, the Paedagogue of our free will? Then, he adds these words, without making any distinction of persons: "For you are all the children of God through faith in Christ Jesus. For all you who have been baptized into Christ have put on Christ. There is neither Jew nor Greek; there is neither slave nor freeman; there is neither male nor female. You are all one in Christ Jesus." It is not, then, that some are enlightened and others are only less perfect souls in the same Word, but all, putting aside their carnal desires, are equal and spiritual before the Lord. He writes again, in another passage: "For in one Spirit we were all baptized into one body, whether Jews or Greeks, whether slaves or free; and we all drank one drink."

It will not be improper to adopt the words of those who teach that the remembrance of higher things is a refinement of the spirit and who hold that the process of refinement is a withdrawal from inferior things by recalling higher things. Recalling higher things necessarily leads to repentance for the lower. That is to say, these people maintain that the spirit retraces its steps when it repents. In the same way, after we have repented of our sins, renounced our wickedness and been purified by baptism, we turn back to the eternal light, as children to their father. Rejoicing in the spirit, Jesus said: "I praise you, Father, God of heaven and earth, that you hid these things from the wise and prudent, and revealed them to infants." The Paedagogue and Teacher is there naming us infants, meaning that we are more ready for salvation than the worldly wise who, believing themselves wise, have blinded their own eyes. And he cries out in joy and in great delight, as if attuning himself to the spirit of the infants: "Yes, Father, for such was your good pleasure." That is why he has revealed to infants what has been hid from the wise and prudent of this world.

It is with good reason, then, that we consider ourselves as the children of God, who, having put off the old man and the cloak of wickedness, have put on the incorruption of Christ, so that, being renewed, a holy people, reborn, we might keep the man unstained, and he might be an infant in the sense of a newborn child of God, purified of uncleanness and vice. The blessed Paul, at any rate, settles the matter for us in unmistakable words, when he writes in the First Epistle to the Corinthians: "Brethren, do not become children in mind, but in malice be children and in mind mature."

That other passage of his: "When I was a child, I thought as a child, I spoke as a child," is a figure of speech for his manner of living under the law, when he persecuted the Word, not as one become simple, but as one still senseless, because he thought childish things, and spoke childish things, blaspheming Him. The word "childish" can signify these two different things, one good and one bad.

"Now that I have become a man," Paul continues, "I have put away childish things." He is not referring to the growing stature that comes with age, nor yet to any definite period of time, nor even to any secret teaching reserved only for men and the more mature when he claims that he left and put away all childishness. Rather, he means to say that those who live by the law are childish in the sense that they are subject to fear, like children afraid of monsters, while those who are obedient to the Word and are completely free are in his opinion, men: we who have believed, who are saved by our own voluntary choice and who are not subject to unreasonable fear, but only sensible concern. We will find proof of this in the Apostle himself, for he says that the Jews were heirs according to the first covenant, but according to the promise, we are: "Now I say, as long as the heir is a child, he differs in no way from a slave, though he is the master of all; but he is under guardians and stewards until the time set by his father. So we, too, when we were children, were enslaved under the elements of the world. But when the fullness of time came, God sent his son, born of a woman, born under the law, that he might redeem those who were under the law, that we might receive the sonship," through him. Notice that he admits that those who are subject to fear and to sin are infants, but considers those who are subject to faith mature, and calls them sons, in contrast with those infants who live by the law. "For you are no longer a slave," he says, "but a son; and if a son, an heir also through God." But what is lacking to the son after he has obtained the inheritance?

But it is well to expound that first passage. "When I was a child," that is, when I was a Jew (he was a Hebrew from the first), "I thought as a child," since I followed the law. "Now that I have become a man," no longer thinking the things of a child—that is, of the law—but those of a man—that is, of Christ who is, as I re- marked before, the only one Scripture considers a man—"I put away the things of a child." Yet there is a childhood in Christ, which is perfection, in contrast to that of the law.

Now that we have reached this point, let us defend this child- likeness of ours by interpreting the passage from the Apostle in which he says: "I fed you with milk, as infants in Christ, not solid food, for you were not yet ready for it. Nor are you now ready for it." Now, it does not seem to me that these words should be taken in the Jewish sense. I will set beside it another passage from Scrip- ture: "I will bring you forth to a good land that flows with milk and honey." A considerable difficulty arises from the figure used in these passages; what do they mean to convey? If the childhood implied by the reference to milk is only the beginning of faith in Christ, and is minimized as puerile and imperfect, then how can the repose enjoyed by the perfect and the knowledgeable (*gnostic*), implied by the expression "strong meat," be spoken of in any fa- vorable way as the milk of children? Can it not be that the parti- cle "as," which shows that a metaphor is being used, really indicates some such thing as this: "I have fed you milk in Christ," and then,

225

after a short pause, adding "as infants"? If we break up the reading in this way, we shall convey this meaning: "I have instructed you in Christ, who is the simple and true and real spiritual nourishment." That is what life-giving milk really is by nature, flowing from breasts of tender love. Therefore, understand the whole passage in this way: "Just as nurses nourish newborn children with milk, so also I have nourished you with Christ the Word who is milk, feeding you, bit by bit, a spiritual nourishment."

Therefore, milk is perfection because it is the perfect food, and leads those who are without rest to perfection. So it is that even for their place of rest this same milk, with honey, is promised them. With reason, then, is milk promised the just in the other passage, that the Word may be revealed unmistakably as both Alpha and Omega, the beginning and the end: the Word, symbolized by milk. Even Homer unwittingly foreshadowed some such thing when he called the just among men "milk-fed."

We can also interpret the Scripture in another sense: "And I, brethren, could not speak to you as to spiritual men, but only as carnal, as to infants in Christ." So, it is possible to consider those who are just recently instructed in the faith and are still little ones in Christ as carnal, for he calls those who have already believed by the Holy Spirit, spiritual, and those newly taught and not yet purified, carnal. He speaks of these last as carnal with good reason, for, like the Gentiles, they still "mind the things of the flesh." "For since there are jealousy and strife among you, are you not carnal and walking as mere men?" For the same reason he says: "I gave you milk to drink": I have poured out upon you knowledge in instruction as nourishment for life everlasting. Even the word "drink" is a figurative sign for perfection, since it is only the completely mature who are said to drink, while infants suck.

The Lord says: "My blood is true drink." Do not, then, the words "I gave you milk to drink" signify perfect happiness in the Word who is milk, that is, knowledge of the truth? The rest of the passage, "not solid food, for you were not yet ready for it," can signify the full revelation, face to face, in the world to come, likened to solid food. "We see now through a mirror," the same Apostle says, "but then, face to face." That is why he adds to the first sentence: "but you are not yet ready for it, for you are still carnal." He refers to thinking, loving, desiring, jealously seeking—being angry and envious over—the things of the flesh. No longer being in the flesh, seeing does not mean what some have thought. For then, in the flesh, possessing an appearance like the angels', we should see face to face what we have been promised. But if, after our departure from this life, the promise really is that "which eye has not seen, nor has it entered into the mind of man," how can we be said to see, if the meaning is not that we contemplate it in Spirit, but that we receive in instruction, "what ear has never heard"? Only Paul was taken to the third heaven, and even he was commanded to hold his peace.

But if it is human wisdom that is the crowning boast of knowledge, as we are now to consider, listen to the command laid down in the Scripture: "Let not the wise man boast in his wisdom, and let not the strong man boast in his strength. Let him that boasts, boast in the Lord." We, however, are they who are "taught of God," and who boast in the name of Christ. Is there any reason, then, that we should not understand the Apostle to be referring to this when he speaks of the "milk of infants"? Whether we are the shepherds who preside over the churches in imitation of the Good Shepherd, or you the sheep, should we not understand that in speaking of the Lord as the milk of the flock, he is safeguarding the unity of his thought by a metaphor? Certainly, the passage, "I gave you milk to drink, not solid food, for you were not yet ready for it," can be adapted to this sense, too, if we only take "solid food" as substantially the same thing as milk, not something different from it. Either way, it is the same Word, whether light and mild as milk or become firm and solid as food.

Still, taking it in this sense, we can also consider preaching as milk, poured out far and wide, and faith as food, made solid by instruction as the foundation. Faith is more substantial, in fact, than hearing, and is assimilated into the very soul and is, therefore, likened to solid food. The Lord presents the same foods elsewhere as symbols of another sort, when he says in the Gospel according to John: "You shall eat my flesh and drink my blood." Here he uses food and drink, as a striking figure for faith and for the promise. Through these, the Church, made up of many members, as man is, takes her nourishment and grows; she is welded together and formed into a unit out of both body, which is faith, and soul, which is hope; just as the Lord, out of flesh and blood. Hope, indeed, which holds faith together as its soul, is the blood of faith. Once hope is extinguished, then the life-principle of faith expires, as when blood is drawn from the veins.

If there are any contentious objectors who think to rise to a higher knowledge, and insist that milk means primary instructions in the sense of primary food, and that meat means spiritual knowledge, let them understand this: when they claim that solid food, meat, is the Body and Blood of Jesus, they are being carried away by their boastful wisdom, contrary to the simple truth. For blood is the first substance produced in a man; some go so far as to call it the very substance of the soul. It is blood that is changed by the heat of the body once the mother has conceived, and in a maternal response develops and matures, for the well-being of the child. Blood is more liquid than flesh—in fact, it is a sort of liquid flesh— yet milk is more nourishing than blood and more finely broken down. Then, whether it is a question of the blood supplied to the embryo, flowing directly through the umbilical cord from the mother, or of the menstrual flow which by the command of the all-nourishing God, Author of life, is prevented from following its normal course and made to course to the already swelling breasts by a process of physical diffusion, and there, changed by the heat of the spirit, is provided the infant as his eagerly desired nourishment, in either case, what is changing is blood.

Of all the organs of the body, the breasts are the most sensitive to the condition of the womb. After childbirth, when the vein through which the blood was carried to the embryo has been cut off, then, with the passage obstructed, the blood is forced up into the breasts. As the blood accumulates, the breasts begin to distend and the blood begins to turn into milk, like its change in an infected wound into pus. Or perhaps the blood is drawn out in the natural hollows of the breasts from the veins located there and dilated by the natural effects of pregnancy, or, mixed with air absorbed from the lungs near by, it becomes white as it is cast off, and though remaining blood in substance, turns into something different, much like foam spumed off from the sea, which "spits forth foam" when mixed with air, as the poets tell us. Regardless of which explanation is true, milk retains its underlying substance of blood. In this way it is like rivers that are churned into froth as they rush along, swallowing air and letting out its roar, or like saliva in our mouth, which turns white from contact with air. What is unreasonable, then, in saying that blood, united with air, is transformed into the lightest and whitest of all substances? It goes through change in attributes, but not in its substance. There can be no doubt that we can find nothing more nourishing, more palatable, or whiter than milk. But heavenly food is similar to milk in every way: by its nature it is palatable through grace; nourishing, for it is life; and dazzling white, for it is the light of Christ. Therefore, it is more than evident that the blood of Christ is milk.

Thus is milk supplied to the infant, and suited to its purpose from its production in childbirth. The breasts, which up to then had been pointing out, straight toward the husband, now begin to incline in the direction of the child, indicating that the nourishment produced by nature to sustain health is easy to obtain. The breasts, unlike springs, are not always full of milk ready to be drawn off, but manufacture milk by changing the nourishment stored up in them, and then they discharge it. There is a nourishment corresponding to this food, a food satisfying the needs of the re-created, reborn child; it also is prepared by God, the nourisher and Father not only of those who are born, but also of those who are born again. This food is of the same kind as the manna that he made to rain down from heaven upon the ancient Hebrews, the celestial food of angels. In fact, even to this day, nurses still call the first flow of milk by the name manna, but, even though women continue to give a flow of milk after they have conceived and given birth, it was not the breasts of women that were blessed by the Lord, the fruit of a virgin, or named as the true nourishment. No, because now that the loving and kind Father has rained down the Word, it is he himself who has become the spiritual nourishment of the good.

O mystic wonder! The Father of all is one, the Word who belongs to all is one, the Holy Spirit is one and the same for all. And one alone, too, is the Virgin Mother. I like to call her the Church. She alone, although a mother, had no milk because she alone never became a wife. She is at once virgin and mother: as virgin, undefiled; as mother, beloved. Calling her children about her, she nourishes them with milk that is holy: the infant Word. That is why she has no milk, because this Son of hers, beautiful and all hers, the body of Christ, is milk. The new people she nurtures on the Word, for he himself begot them in throes of his flesh and wrapped them in the swaddling clothes of his precious blood. What a holy begetting! What holy swaddling clothes! The Word is everything to his little ones, both father and mother, paedagogue and nurse. "You shall eat my flesh," he says, "and drink my blood." These homely foods the Lord provides. He delivers up his own flesh and pours out his own blood. There is nothing lacking his children, that they may grow. What a mysterious paradox! He bids us put off the former mortality of the flesh and, with it, the former nourishment, and receive instead this other new mode of Christ, to find place in ourselves for him as far as we can, and to enshrine the Savior in our hearts that we may be rid of the passions of the flesh.

Yet, possibly you do not relish this turn of thought, but prefer to be more down to earth. Then listen to this interpretation: the flesh is a figure of speech for the Holy Spirit, for by it flesh was produced; the blood corresponds to the Word, for he has been poured forth as precious blood for life; the union of the two is the Lord, nourishment of infants: the Lord, both Spirit and Word. Our nourishment, that is, the Lord Jesus, the Word of God, is Spirit become flesh, sanctified flesh from heaven. This is our nourishment, the milk flowing from the Father by which alone we infants are fed. The Word himself, the "well-beloved," our provider, has saved mankind by shedding his blood for us. Therefore, we fly trustfully to the "care-banishing breast" of God the Father; the breast that is the Word, who is the only one who can truly provide us the milk of love. Only those who nurse at the breast are blessed. Peter tells us: "Lay aside therefore all malice and all deceit and all pretense, and envy and slander. Crave, as newborn babes, spiritual milk, that by it you may grow to salvation; if indeed, you have tasted that the Lord is sweet."

Yet if we concede to our critics that "solid food" is something more than milk, then we are creating confusion for ourselves and we prove that we have little understanding of nature. The truth is that, when the atmosphere becomes heavier during the winter, and heat is retained within the body without its passing off, then food is more readily digested by natural heat and changed into blood, which flows through the veins. The veins, which had not been full before, now begin to pulse and to enlarge, and those who are nursing yield a greater abundance of milk precisely during this season. We have already shown that it is blood that during pregnancy changes into milk, but not in its substance, very much like light hair which, as we know, turns gray with the passing of the years. During the summer, however, the body is more porous, so that food is passed off much more quickly in perspiration; for that reason, since less food is retained, there is less blood and less milk. But, if food that is retained turns into blood, and the blood into milk, then blood is the source of milk, just as blood is of man, and the grape is of the vine.

We are nursed with milk, the Lord's own nourishment, as soon as we leave our mother's womb; and as soon as we are born anew we are favored with the good tidings of hope of rest, that heavenly Jerusalem in which, as it is written, "milk and honey rain down." In this material figure, we are given a pledge of the food of holiness, for, though solid food must be put away sooner or later, as the Apostle says, the nourishment that we derive from milk leads us directly to heaven, since it educates us to be citizens of heaven and companions of the angels. Since the Word is an overflowing fountain of life, and is also called a river of oil, then certainly Paul can use a similar figure of speech and call Him "milk," adding: "I gave you to drink." The Word is for drinking, nourishment of truth. Drink is called liquid food, for the same thing can possess the qualities of both solid food and of drink if we consider it from different aspects, as cheese, which may be considered either a solid made from milk, or milk become solid. Now, I am not interested in chasing words; I am only trying to show that the one substance can serve as both kinds of nourishment. For instance, infants at the breast find in milk alone all the food and drink they need.

The Lord said: "I have a food to eat of which you do not know. My food is to do the will of him who sent me." Here is another food, a figure very similar to that of milk: it is the will of God. And he—unusually—called the accomplishment of his sufferings a "cup," in the sense that he had to drain it entirely by himself. Just as the fulfillment of his Father's will was food for Christ, so, for us infants who draw milk from the breast, that is, the Word of Heaven, it is Christ himself who is our food. Again, the Greek word for "seeking" also means "craving," implying that to infants who seek the Word the craved-for milk is given from the Father's breasts of love for man.

There was another time that the Word proclaimed himself bread from heaven: "Moses did not give you the bread from heaven," he said, "but my Father gives you the true bread from heaven. For the bread of God is that which comes down from heaven and gives life to the world. And the bread which I will give is my flesh for the life of the world." In this passage, we must read a mystic meaning for bread. He says that he is flesh, and that means flesh that has risen; bread rises from the decay of the sown seed—and it has risen through fire for the joy of the Church, as baked bread. But we will treat this more clearly and in greater detail in a treatise *On the Resurrection.*

"And the bread which I will give you," the Lord said, "is my flesh." But flesh is nourished by blood, and blood is spoken of under the figure of wine. Therefore, we must understand him to mean that just as bread dipped in a mixture of water and wine absorbs the wine and leaves the water, so the flesh of the Lord, bread of heaven, drinks up the blood, that is, it nurtures to immortality those among men who are heavenly minded, and leaves for corruption only the desires of the flesh.

In all these various ways and figures of speech is the Word spoken of: solid food, flesh, nourishment, bread, blood and milk. The Lord is all these things for the refreshment of us who believe in him. Let no one think it strange, then, that we speak of the blood of the Lord also under the figure of milk. Is it not named wine, figuratively? "He washes his garment in wine," it says, "and his robe in the blood of the grape." In his Spirit he says he will attire the body of the Word with his own blood, just as he will nurture those who hunger for the Word in his own Spirit.

The blood of just Abel, too, pleading before the throne of God, gives evidence that the Word is blood, because blood, of itself, could never plead, unless it were considered a word. The just man of ancient times is, indeed, a type of the new just Man, and the blood that once made its plea, in reality, was pleading as a symbol of the new blood. The blood, as the Word, sent up its cry, foreshadowing that the Word would suffer.

This flesh and the blood it contains, fostering one another mutually, are fed and made to increase by milk. And the development of a seed after it has been conceived comes about by contact with the pure blood left from the monthly purification; just as the first-drawn milk of the cow causes its milk to coagulate, so, by congealing the blood, the power contained in the seed accomplishes the substance of that development. The blending of the two thrives, but an excess of either is likely to end in barrenness. Certainly, a seed planted in the ground will be swept away by a heavy downpour of rain, while, even during a drought when moisture dries up, a viscous sap holds the seed together and makes it grow. There are those who hold that the animal semen is substantially foam of its blood, violently agitated in the act of intercourse by the natural heat of the male, and in its agitation, turned into foam and then deposited in the spermatic ducts. According to Diogenes Apolloniates, this is the derivation of the Greek word for sexual pleasure, *aphrodisia*.

233

From all these arguments it becomes clear that blood is the fundamental principle of the human body. Recall that the first substance in the womb is a milky liquid that gathers there and turns into blood and then into flesh and finally, when the heat of the spirit which forms the embryo solidifies this composite, develops into a living being. Even after birth, the infant is still nurtured on the same blood, for the flow of milk is the product of blood.

Milk is the spring that gives nourishment. By its presence, a woman is known to have given birth and become a mother, and therefore, it bestows on her a certain lovableness that arouses reverence. That is the reason the Holy Spirit mystically puts these words of the Apostle on the lips of the Lord: "I have given you milk to drink." For, if we have been reborn to become members of Christ, then he who gives us this new birth nurtures us with milk flowing from himself, the Word. Anyone who begets naturally provides sustenance for him whom he has begotten; in the case of his rebirth, man's nourishment must be spiritual. Doubtless, then, we belong entirely to Christ as his property from every point of view: by reason of relationship, because his blood has redeemed us; by our resemblance to him, through the upbringing we receive from the Word, and in immortality, because of the guidance he imparts. "Raising children, for mortals, is often the cause of greater affection than begetting them." So, too, the blood and the milk of the Lord are a symbol of his sufferings and of his teachings. Accordingly, each of us little ones may make our boast in the Lord, crying out: "From out a noble father and noble blood, I make my claim to be."

Surely, it is clear by now that milk is developed from blood by some sort of change. But that is not to say that we cannot learn something more, from sheep and oxen. During the time of year called spring, when the climate has a higher degree of humidity and when the grass and the meadows become green and filled with the sap of life, then the sheep and the oxen right away take on a greater abundance of blood, as the distension of their veins proves, and so, because of more blood, they yield milk in more copious supply. But in summertime, their blood is warmed and dried up by the scorching heat, and so does not form into milk, so that these animals yield much less milk.

Milk has an affinity with water, just as the spiritual water of cleansing has with spiritual nourishment. This may be proved by the fact that one who swallows a bit of cold water, along with the milk we are talking about, immediately feels the good effects; actually, the water keeps milk from turning sour, not because it reacts on it adversely, but because it is so much akin to what is being consumed with it. In fact, milk has the same intimate relationship with water that the Word has with baptism. For, milk is the only liquid that absorbs water into itself, and is used as a cathartic when so mixed, just as baptism purifies us from sin.

On the other hand, milk is mixed with honey, too, with good results, again as a cathartic that is also a sweet-tasting food. In the same way, the Word, penetrated with love for man, heals sicknesses and purifies from sin. The expression, "the word flows sweeter than honey," is said, I believe, of the Word who is also honey, for the inspired word so often praises him "above honey and the honeycomb."

Again, we find that milk is mixed with sweet wine. Such a mixture is very beneficial, just as suffering tempers men to gain immortality. The reason is that milk is curdled by wine and separated into its component parts, so that the whey can then be drawn off as a less essential part of the milk. In the same way, the spiritual intermingling of faith with the passions of men curdles their carnal lusts and raises them to eternity, making them divine with the qualities of divinity.

Then there are many people who use the fat part of milk, the part called butter, for light. This is an unmistakable analogy for the rich oil of the Word who is the only one who can give to infants both nourishment and growth and light. And so, Scripture says of the Lord: "He fed them with the fruits of the fields, and he suckled them with honey from rocks and oil from out of the hardest rocks, butter of the herd and milk of the sheep, with the fat of lambs," and he gave them, too, all the other things it mentions. The prophet, too, used the same words when he referred to the birth of the Child: "And he will eat butter and honey."

235

It is a matter for wonder to me that some people dare to call themselves perfect and Gnostics, laying claim in their inflated pride to a loftier state than the Apostle. Paul himself made only this claim: "Not that I have already obtained this, or already have been made perfect, but I press on hoping that I may lay hold of that for which Christ Jesus has laid hold of me. But one thing I do: forgetting what is behind, I strain forward to what is before, I press on toward the goal, to the prize of God's heavenly call in Christ Jesus." He considers himself perfect in the sense that he has changed his old way of life and follows a better one, but not in the sense that he is perfect in knowledge. He only desires what is perfect. That is why he adds: "Let us then, as many as are perfect, be of this mind," meaning simply that perfection is turning away from sin and being reborn, after we have forgotten the sins that are behind, to faith in the only Perfect One.

GREGORY OF NYSSA

Gregory of Nyssa inhabited a very different world from Clement's. By his time, Christianity was in fashion within the empire. He was the brother of Basil of Caesarea in the Cappadocian region of Asia Minor, and Gregory himself was bishop of Nyssa (between 371 and 394). Together with their friend Gregory, son of the bishop of Nazianzus, they are known as the "Cappadocian Fathers." They were champions of the emerging Trinitarian doctrine of their day, and Gregory especially represents the interpenetration of the Hellenistic literary tradition with the orientation of Christianity. Deeply influenced by Origen, he also remained married long into his episcopate, and took monastic vows only after his wife's death.

TEXT: GREGORY OF NYSSA, *ON WHAT IS MEANT BY THE PROFESSION "CHRISTIAN"*

In now sending this letter to your Reverence, I am behaving like those debtors who happen upon some good fortune and pay the entire amount owed at one fell swoop. For after being constantly in your debt (because among Christians a promise is a debt), I now wish to fill in the past lapse of letters, which I contracted unwillingly, by extending this letter to such a length that it will count as many when it is judged by the customary length of letters. But, in order that I may not go on idly writing at length, I think that it will be good for me to imitate in my epistolary style the conversations we used to have when we were face to face. Indeed, I remember very well that the occasion of our discussions every time was a concern for virtue and exercise related to the service of God. You always reacted attentively to what was said, although you did not accept it without examining it, and we, advancing in time, solved everything we sought by following our discussion. If it were possible, even now, for the impetus of discussion to be derived from your presence, it would be better in every way. There would be a mutual benefit from our seeing each other (what in life is sweeter to me than this?) and, under the plectrum of your intelligence, our old lyre would reawaken. But, since the necessity of life causes us to be separated in body, even if our souls are always united, it is necessary to assume your role also, if some logical conclusion is to develop for us. First of all, however, it would be best to propose a hypothesis profitable to the soul for the scope of our letter, and, then, to direct our argument to what lies before us. Therefore, let us ask as in a logical problem: What is meant by the profession "Christian"?

For surely, a consideration of this issue will not be without profit, since, if what is indicated by this name is determined accurately, we shall have much assistance for a life in accordance with virtue, provided, as our name implies, that we are eager for a lofty discipline. A person who wants to be called a doctor or an orator or a geometrician is not worthy of a title until he has some training in the subject and until he discovers from experience what he is being called, and the person wishing to be thus addressed in accordance with truth, so that the form of address will not be a misnomer, will want the use of the title to depend on the practice itself. In the same way, if we seek the true meaning of the word "Christian" and find it, we will not choose not to conform to what the name implies when it is used of us, in order that the popular story about the monkey may not also be applicable to us.

They say that a certain showman in the city of Alexandria trained a monkey to dance with some grace, and dressed him in a dancer's mask and a suitable costume. He put him in a chorus and gained fame by the monkey's twisting himself in time with the music and concealing his nature in every way by what he was doing and what he appeared to be. While the audience was enthralled by the novelty of the spectacle, one of the clever persons present, by means of a trick, showed those watching the performance that the dancer was a monkey. When everyone was crying out and applauding the gesticulations of the monkey, who was moving rhythmically with the music, they say that he threw onto the dancing place some of the sweets that arouse the greediness of such animals. The monkey, without a moment's delay, when he saw the almonds scattered in front of the chorus, forgetting the dancing and the applause and the elaborate costume, ran after them and grabbed what he found in the palms of his hands. And in order that the mask would not get in the way of his mouth, he energetically thrust aside the disguise with his nails and shredded the clever workmanship; he immediately evoked a laugh from the spectators in place of their praise and admiration, as he emerged ugly and ridiculous from the mask. Therefore, just as the clever device was not sufficient for that creature to be considered a man, once his nature was disclosed in greediness for the sweets, so those individuals not truly shaping their own natures by faith will easily be disclosed in the kinds of greediness that come from the devil as being something other than what they are called. For, instead of a fig or an almond or some such thing, conceit and love of honor and love of gain and love of pleasure, and whatever else the evil assembly of the devil places before greedy men instead of sweets, easily bring to light the apelike souls who, through pretense of imitation play the role of the Christian and then remove the mask of moderation or meekness or some other virtue in a moment of personal crisis. It is necessary, therefore, for us to understand what the profession of Christianity means, for then, perhaps, we will become what the term means to say and not be seen through by the One who perceives what is hidden. It must not be found that we have disguised ourselves by a bare confession and by the pretense of the name alone, when we are actually something contrary to what we appear to be.

Let us, then, consider, first of all, from the term itself what Christianity means. From those who are wiser it is, of course, possible for us to discover a significance more profound and more noble in every way, more in keeping with the dignity of the word. However, what we begin with is this: the word "Christ," exchanged for a clearer and more familiar word, means "the king," and Holy Scripture, in accordance with proper usage, indicates royal dignity with such a word. But since, as Scripture says, the divine is inexpressible, incomprehensible, exceeding all comprehensible thought, the Holy Spirit must inspire prophets and apostles, and they contribute with many words and insights to our understanding of the incorruptible nature, one setting us right about one divine idea and another about another. His dominion over all is suggested by the name of Kingdom, and his purity and freedom from every passion and every evil is indicated by the names of the virtues, each being understood as referring to higher signification. Such expressions are used as "justice itself" and "wisdom and power" and "truth" and "goodness" and "life" and "salvation" and "incorruptibility" and "permanence" and "lack of change" and whatever elevated concept there is, and Christ is and is said to be all of them. If, therefore, the comprehension of every lofty idea is conceived of in the name of Christ (for the other qualities mentioned are included under the higher designation, each of them being implied in the notion of kingdom), perhaps some understanding of the interpretation of Christianity will follow. If we, who are joined to him by faith in him, are called by his name whose incorruptible nature is beyond verbal interpretation, it is altogether necessary for us to become what is contemplated in connection with that incorruptible nature and to achieve an identity that follows along with it. For just as by participating in Christ we are given the title "Christian," so also are we drawn into a share in the lofty ideas that it implies. Just as in a chain, what draws the loop at the top also draws the next loops, in like manner, since the rest of the words interpreting his ineffable and multiform blessedness are joined to the word "Christ," it is necessary for the person drawn along with him to share these qualities with him.

If, therefore, someone puts on the name of Christ, but does not exhibit in his life what is indicated by the term, such a person belies the name and puts on a lifeless mask in accordance with the model proposed to us (of humanly formed features put on a monkey). For it is not possible for Christ not to be justice and purity and truth and estrangement from all evil, nor is it possible to be a Christian (that is, truly a Christian) without displaying in oneself a participation in these qualities. If one can give a definition of the meaning of Christianity, we shall define it as follows: Christianity is an imitation of the divine nature. Now, let no one object to the definition as being immoderate and exceeding the lowliness of our nature; it does not go beyond our nature. Indeed, if anyone considers the first condition of man, he will find through the scriptural teachings that the definition does not exceed the measure of our nature. The first constitution of man was as an imitation of the likeness of God. So Moses, in philosophizing about man, where he says that God made man, states that: "He created him in the image of God," and the profession "Christianity, " therefore, brings man back to his original good fortune.

But, if man was originally a likeness of God, perhaps we have not gone beyond the limit in declaring that Christianity is an imitation of the divine nature. Great, indeed, is the promise of this title. Perhaps it would be fitting to investigate also whether not conforming to the definition in one's life is dangerous for one who makes use of the word. What is meant here might become clear from examples. Let it be supposed that a professional painter is given a commission to paint a picture of the king for those living far away. If he draws an ugly and ill-formed shape on the wood and calls this unseemly figure an image of the king, would it not be likely that authority as a whole would be annoyed, on the grounds that the handsome original had been insulted through this bad painting among those who had never seen the king? For people will necessarily think that the original is what the form on the icon shows him to be. If, then, the definition says that Christianity is an imitation of God, the person who has never been given an explanation of this mystery will think that the divine is such as he sees life among us to be, accepting it as a valid imitation of God. So that, if he sees models of complete good, he will believe that the divine revered by us is good. But if someone is emotional and brutal, changing from one passion to another, and reflecting forms of beasts in his character (for it is easily possible to see how the changes in our nature correspond to beasts), when such a person calls himself a Christian and it is clear to all that the promise of the name professes an imitation of God, then, that person makes the divine, which is believed to be reflected in our private life, an object of censure among unbelievers. Scripture, therefore, utters a kind of fearful threat to such persons, crying: "Woe to those on ac-

count of whom my name is blasphemed among the nations." And
our Lord seems to me to be guiding our thoughts in this direction
when he says to those able to hear: "You are to be perfect, even as
your heavenly Father is perfect." For, in naming the true Father as
Father of the faithful, he wishes those born through him to have
the same perfection of the good things seen in the Father.

Then you will ask me: "How could it come about that human
lowliness could be extended to the blessedness seen in God, since
the impossibility of the command is immediately evident? How
could it be possible for the earthly to be like the One in heaven, the
very difference in nature proving that the imitation is out of reach?
For it is as hopeless to make oneself equal in appearance to the
heavenly greatness and the beauties in it as it is for man on earth
to make himself like the God of heaven." But the explanation of
this is clear. The Gospel does not order human nature to be com-
pounded with divine nature, but it does order good actions to be
imitated in life as much as possible. But what actions of ours are
like the actions of God? Those that are alien from all evil, purify-
ing themselves as far as possible in deed and word and thought
from all vileness. This is truly the imitation of the divine and the
perfection connected with the God of heaven.

It does not seem to me that the Gospel is speaking of the fir-
mament of heaven as some remote habitation of God when it ad-
vises us to be perfect as our heavenly Father is perfect. The divine
is equally present in all things, and, in like manner, it pervades all
creation and it does not exist separated from being, but the divine
nature touches each element of being with equal honor, encompassing all things within its own comprehensive power. And the
prophet provides this instruction, "even if I am in heaven in my
thought, even if I examine what is below the earth in my calcula-
tion, even if I extend the intellectual part of my soul to the boundaries of being, I see all things in the power of your right hand," for
the text is as follows: "If I go up to the heavens, you are there; if I
sink to the nether world, you are present there. If I take the wings
of the dawn, or settle at the farthest limits of the sea, even there
your hand shall guide me, and your right hand hold me fast." It is
taught from these words that not being separated by choice from

God is the heavenly habitation. Since the world above is known to
be pure from evil (Holy Scripture often mentions this to us sym-
bolically), and since experiences connected with evil take place in
this more material life below, here the inventor of evil, the serpent,
crawls and creeps through life on earth, as is said of it in the symbolic statement: "On your belly shall you crawl and dust shall you
eat, all the days of your life."

This kind of movement and this type of food explain to us that
this refers to the life on earth that accepts the serpent of manifold
evil and nurtures this creature that creeps upon it. Therefore, the
one who orders us to imitate our heavenly Father orders us to purify ourselves from earthly passions. This is a separation that does
not come about through a change of place, but is achieved only
through the operation of choice. If, then, alienation from evil is accomplished only by the impetus of thought, the evangelical word
enjoins nothing impossible upon us. There is no trouble connected
with the impetus of thought, since it is possible for us without ex-
ertion to be present through thought wherever we wish to be, so
that a heavenly sojourn is easy for anyone who wants it, even on
earth. As the Gospel suggests, by our thinking heavenly thoughts
and depositing in its treasury there is a wealth of virtue: "Do not
lay up for yourselves treasures on earth," it says, "but lay up for
yourselves treasures in heaven, where neither moth nor rust con-
sumes nor thieves break in and steal." By these words, he indicates
the incorruptible power that governs blessedness above. For in the
midst of the ruin of life here, one produces many different kinds
of evil for oneself in the course of human encounters. Either one
begets through thought a moth, which, because of its corroding
and destroying power, renders useless anything it grows upon unless
it is shaken off, and creeps toward whatever is lying about, sug-
gesting through its movement a path of destruction for those it
comes near; or, if all is secure within, there is a conspiracy of external circumstances. Either the treasure of the heart is shut off
through pleasure or the receptacle of the soul is rendered empty
of virtue through some other experience, being distracted by desire or grief or some such emotion. But since the Lord says that
in the treasures above neither moth nor rust is present, nor evil

from theft, which teaches us to be suspicious, we must transfer our activities to a region where what is stored is not only safe and undiminished forever, but where it also produces many kinds of interest. Because of the nature of the one receiving the deposit, it is altogether necessary that the return be amplified. For just as we, in accordance with our nature, accomplish little in making our deposit because we are what we are, so, also, it follows that the One who is rich in every way will give to the depositor a return that reflects his nature. So let no one be discouraged when he brings into the divine treasury what is in keeping with his own power, assuming that he will go off with what corresponds to the amount he has given, but let him anticipate, according to the Gospel, which says he will receive in exchange large for small, the heavenly for the earthly, the eternal for the temporal, such things as are not able to be grasped by thought or explained by word, concerning which the inspired Scripture teaches: "Eye has not seen, ear has not heard, nor has it entered into the heart of man, what things God has prepared for those who love him."

So, esteemed head, we have given you payment in full, not only for the letters not sent before, but also in advance for the ones that may not be written hereafter. May you fare well in the Lord and may what is pleasing to God be always in your mind and heart and in ours.

8

CHRISTIAN TELEOLOGIES

THE SHEPHERD OF HERMAS

T he *Shepherd of Hermas* is said by the Muratorian list, the earliest statement of the authoritative writings of the New Testament, to have been recently composed. For that reason, public reading of *The Shepherd* is not authorized by the Muratorian list, although private reading is permitted. The implication is that the work was produced around the year 150, although it contains reference to Clement, the bishop of Rome who died around 96 C.E. A popular work consumed with the problem of the reality of sin after baptism, *The Shepherd of Hermas* was probably produced over decades as Christians attempted to frame their lives according to the visions of their vivid faith.

TEXT: *THE SHEPHERD OF HERMAS* I.1–II.4

He who brought me up sold me to a certain Rhoda at Rome. After many years I knew her very well, and began to love her as a sister. After some time I saw her bathing in the river Tiber and gave her my hand and helped her out of the river. When I saw her beauty I reflected in my heart and said: "I should be happy if I had a wife of such beauty and manner." This alone I considered, and nothing else, no, not one thing. After some time, I was going to Cumae, and glorifying the creations of God, for they are great and remarkable and powerful, and as I walked along I became sleepy. And a spirit took me and led me away through some terrain without a path, through which a man could not walk, but the ground was precipitous and broken up by the streams of water. Then I crossed the river, and came to the level ground and knelt down and began to pray to the Lord and to confess my sins. Now while I was praying heaven opened, and I saw that woman whom I had desired greeting me out of heaven and saying: "Hail, Hermas." And I looked at her, and said to her: "Lady, what are you doing here?" and she answered me: "I was taken up to censure your sins to the Lord." I said to her: "Are you now my accusation?" "No," she said, "but listen to the words that I am going to say to you. God who dwells in heaven and created that which is out of that which is not, and increased and multiplied it for the sake of his holy Church, is angry with you because you sinned against me." I answered and said to her: "Did I sin against you? In what way, or when did I say a shameful word to you? Did I not always regard you as a goddess? Did I not always respect you as a sister? Why do you charge me falsely, woman, with these wicked and impure things?" She laughed and said to me: "The desire of wickedness came up in your heart. Or do you not think that it is a wicked deed for a righteous man if a wicked desire come up in his heart? Yes, it is a sin," said she, "and a great one. For the righteous considers righteous things. As long as his designs are righteous his repute stands fast in heaven, and he finds the Lord favorable in his every concern. But they who consider wicked things in their hearts bring upon themselves death and captivity, especially those who obtain this world for themselves, and take pride in their wealth, and do not lay hold of the good things that are to come. Their souls will repent; yet have they no hope, but they have abandoned themselves and their life. But pray to God, and He shall heal the sins of yourself and of all your house and of all the saints."

After she had spoken these words heaven was shut, and I was all trembling and grieving. And I was saying to myself: "If this sin is recorded against me, how shall I be saved? Or how shall I propitiate God for my fully formed sins? Or with what words shall I beseech the Lord so that he will be placated for me?" While I was

considering and hesitating over these things in my heart I saw before me a white chair of great size made of snow-white wool; and
there came a woman, old and clothed in shining garments with a
book in her hands, and she sat down alone and greeted me: "Hail,
Hermas!" And I, grieving and weeping, said: "Hail, Lady!" And she
said to me: "Why are you gloomy, Hermas? You who are patient
and without bile, who are always laughing, why are you so down-
cast in appearance and unhappy?" And I said to her: "Because of
a most excellent lady, who says that I sinned against her." And she
said: "By no means let this thing happen to the servant of God; but
for all that the thought did arise in your heart concerning her. It
is such a design as this that brings sin on the servants of God. For
it is an evil and mad purpose against a revered spirit and one already approved, if a man desire an evil deed, and especially if it be
Hermas the temperate, who abstains from every evil desire and is
full of all simplicity and great innocence.

"But it is not for this that God is angry with you, but in order
that you should convert your family, which has done wrong against
the Lord, and against you, their parents. But you are indulgent,
and do not correct your family, but have allowed them to become
corrupt. For this reason the Lord is angry with you, but he will
heal all the past evils in your family, for because of their sins and
wrong you have been corrupted by the things of daily life. But the
great mercy of the Lord has had pity on you and on your family,
and will make you strong and will establish you in his glory. Only
do not be idle, but have courage and strengthen your family. For
as the smith, by hammering his work, prevails in the task that he
desires, so also the daily righteous word prevails over wickedness.
Do not cease, then, correcting your children, for I know that if
they repent with all their heart, they will be inscribed in the books
of life with the saints." After she had ceased these words she said
to me: "Would you like to hear me read aloud?" and I said: "I
should like it, Lady." She said to me: "Listen then, and hear the
glories of God." I heard great and wonderful things that I have not
the strength to remember; for all the words were frightful, such as
a man cannot bear. Then I remembered the last words, for they
were useful to us and gentle: "Lo, the God of the powers, whom I

✡
247
☦

love, by his mighty power, and by his great understanding created the world, and by his glorious counsel surrounded his creation with beauty, and by his mighty word fixed heaven and founded the earth upon the waters, and by his own wisdom and forethought created his holy Church, which he also blessed—Lo, he changes heaven, and the mountains and the hills and the seas, and all things are becoming smooth for his chosen ones, so he might give them the promise which he made with great glory and joy, if they keep the ordinances of God, which they received with great faith."

So, when she had finished reading, and rose from the chair, there came four young men, and took up the chair and went away towards the east. And she called me and touched my chest and said to me; "Did my reading please you?" and I said to her: "Lady, this last part pleases me, but the first part was hard and difficult." And she said to me: "This last part is for the righteous, but the first part was for the nations and the apostates." While she was speaking with me two men appeared, and took her by the arms and they went away toward the east, where the chair had gone. But she went away cheerfully, and as she went said to me, "Courage, Hermas."

While I was going to Cumae, at about the same time as the year before, as I walked along I remembered the vision of the previous year, and the spirit again took me up and brought me away to the same place, where I had been the previous year. So when I came to the place, I knelt down and began to pray to the Lord and to glorify his name, because he had thought me worthy, and had made known to me my former sins. But after I rose from prayer I saw before me the elder lady, whom I had seen the year before, walking and reading out from a little book. And she said to me: "Can you take this as a message to God's elect ones?" I said to her: "Lady, I cannot remember so much; but give me the little book to copy." "Take it," she said, "and give it me back." I took it and went away to a certain place in the country, and copied it all, letter by letter, for I could not distinguish the syllables. Then when I had finished the letters of the little book it was suddenly taken out of my hand; but I did not see by whom.

But after fifteen days, when I had fasted and besought the Lord greatly, knowledge of the writing was revealed to me. And these things were written: "Your seed, Hermas, have disregarded God, and have blasphemed the Lord, and have betrayed their parents in great wickedness, and they are called the betrayers of parents, and their betrayal has not profited them, but they have added to their sins wanton deeds and evil matings, and so their crimes have been completed. But make these words known to all your children and to your wife, who shall in future be to you as a sister. For she also does not refrain her tongue, with which she does evil; but when she has heard these words she will refrain it, and will obtain mercy. After you have made known these words to them, which the master commanded me to be revealed to you, all the sins which they have formerly committed shall be forgiven them, and they shall be forgiven to all the saints who have sinned up to this day, if they repent with their whole heart, and put aside double-mindedness from their heart. For the master has sworn to his elect by his glory that if there be still sin after this day has been fixed, they shall have no salvation; for repentance for the just has a limit; the days of repentance have been fulfilled for all the saints, but for the nations repentance is open until the last day. You shall speak, then, to the leaders of the Church, that they reform their ways in righteousness, to receive in full the promises with great glory. You, therefore, who work righteousness, must remain steadfast and be not double-minded, that your company may be with the holy angels. Blessed are you, as many as endure the great persecution which is coming, and as many as shall not deny their life. For the Lord has sworn by his Son that those who have denied their Christ have been rejected from their life, that is, those who deny him in the days to come. But those who denied him formerly have obtained forgiveness through his great mercy.

"But, Hermas, no longer bear a grudge against your children, nor neglect your sister, that they may be cleansed from their former sins. For they will be corrected with righteous correction, if you bear no grudge against them. The bearing of grudges works death. But you, Hermas, had great troubles of your own because of the transgressions of your family, because you did not pay attention to them. But you neglected them and became entangled in their evil deeds. But you are saved by not having broken away from the living God, and by your simplicity and great temperance. These things have saved you, if you remain in them, and they save all whose deeds are such, and who walk in innocence and simplicity. These shall overcome all wickedness and remain steadfast to eternal life. Blessed are all they who do righteousness; they shall not perish forever. But you shall say to Maximus: Behold, persecution is coming, if it seems good to you deny again. The Lord is near those that turn to him, as it is written in the Book of Eldad and Modat, who prophesied to the people in the wilderness."

And a revelation was made to me, brethren, while I slept, by a very beautiful young man who said to me, "Who do you think that the elder lady was from whom you received the little book?" I said, "The Sibyl." "You are wrong," he said. "She is not." "Who is she, then?" I said. "The Church," he said. I said to him, "Why then is she old?" "Because," he said, "she was created the first of all things. For this reason is she old; and for her sake was the world established." And afterwards I saw a vision in my house. The elder lady came and asked me if I had already given the book to the elders. I said that I had not given it. "You have done well," she said, "for I have words to add. When, therefore, I have finished all the words they shall be made known by you to all the elect. You shall therefore write two little books and send one to Clement and one to Grapte. Clement then shall send it to the cities abroad, for that is his duty; and Grapte shall exhort the widows and orphans; but in this city you shall read it yourself with the elders who are in charge of the church."

ORIGEN

Born in 185, Origen knew the consequences that faith could have in the Roman world: his father died in the persecution of Septimius Severus in 202. Origen accepted the sort of renunciation demanded of apostles in the Gospels, putting aside his possessions to develop what Eusebius calls the philosophical life demanded by Jesus (see Eusebius, *History of the Church,* 6.3). Eusebius also reports that Origen castrated himself (*History of the Church,* 6.8), inspired by Jesus' teaching in Matthew 19:12. His learning resulted in his appointment to the Catechetical School in Alexandria, following the great examples of Pantaenus and Clement. Origen later moved to Caesarea in Palestine, as a result of a bitter dispute with Demetrius, the bishop of Alexandria. During the Decian persecution (250 C.E.) Origen was tortured, and he died of ill health in 254. Origen was the most powerful Christian thinker of his time. His *Hexapla* pioneered the comparative study of texts of the Old Testament, while his commentaries and sermons illustrate the development of a conscious method of interpretation. His most characteristic work, *On First Principles,* is the first comprehensive Christian philosophy. It offers a systematic account of God, the world, free will, and Scripture. His *Against Celsus* is a classic work of apologetics, and his contribution to the theory and practice of prayer is unparalleled.

Throughout, Origen remains a creative and challenging thinker. Condemned by councils of the Church for his daring assertion that even the devil could one day repent and be saved, Origen is perhaps the most fascinating theologian in the Christian tradition.

TEXT: ORIGEN *ON FIRST PRINCIPLES,* 2.10–11

Since our discourse has reminded us of the judgment to come and of retribution and the punishment of sinners, in accordance with the warnings of the Holy Scriptures and the contents of the Church's teaching to the effect that at the time of the judgment "eternal fire" and "outer darkness" and a "prison" and a "furnace" and other similar things have been prepared for sinners, let us see what we ought to think about these matters also.

Now to approach them in the requisite order we must first, it seems to me, move to a discussion of the resurrection, in order to learn what it is that shall come either to punishment or to rest and blessedness. On this matter we have already argued more fully in the other books that we have written on the resurrection and have shown what were our views about it. Now, however, for the sake of logical continuity in this treatise, it seems not unreasonable to repeat a few of the arguments from our former works, particularly because some make this objection to the faith of the Church, that our beliefs about the resurrection are altogether foolish and silly.

The chief objectors are the heretics, who must, I think, be answered in this way. If they admit themselves that there is a resurrection of the dead, let them answer us this question: "What was it that died? Was it not a body?" If so, there will be a resurrection of the body. Then again, let them say whether they believe that we are to be possessed of bodies, or not. I submit that, seeing that the apostle Paul says, "It is sown an animate body, it will rise again a spiritual body," these men cannot deny that a body rises or that in the resurrection we are to be possessed of bodies. What then? If it is certain that we are to be possessed of bodies, and if those bodies that have fallen are declared to rise again—and the expression "rise again" could not properly be used except of that which had previously fallen—then there can be doubt that these bodies rise again in order that at the resurrection we may once more be clothed with them. The one thing, therefore, is bound up with the other. For if bodies rise again, undoubtedly they rise again as a clothing for us, and if it is necessary, as it certainly is, for us to live in bodies, we ought to live in no other bodies but our own. And if it is true that they rise again and do so as "spiritual," there is no doubt that this means that they rise again from the dead with corruption banished and mortality laid aside. Otherwise it would seem vain and useless to rise from the dead only in order to die all over again. Finally, this can be the more clearly understood by carefully observing what is the quality of the "animate body" which, when sown in the earth, can reproduce the quality of a "spiritual body." For from the animate body the very power and grace of the resurrection evokes the spiritual body, when it transforms it from dishonor to glory.

Since the heretics, however, think themselves most learned and wise, we shall ask them whether every body has some form, that is, whether it is fashioned in some shape. If they say there is a body that is not fashioned in some shape, they will show themselves the most ignorant and foolish of men; for no one, except an utter stranger to all learning, will deny that a body has a shape. But if they give the logical answer and say that every body is fashioned in some definite shape, we shall inquire of them whether they can explain and describe to us the shape of a "spiritual body"; which they certainly will in no way be able to do. Further, we shall ask them for an explanation of the differences among those who rise again. How will they prove the truth of the saying, "There is one flesh of birds, another of fish; there are also bodies celestial and bodies terrestrial; but there is one glory of the celestial, another of the terrestrial, one glory of the sun, another glory of the moon, another glory of the stars, one star differs from another star in glory; so also is the resurrection of the dead"? According to this gradation, then, let them explain the differences of glory among those who rise again. And if by any means they have tried to think out some reasoning along the lines of the differences among the heavenly bodies, we shall request them also to mark the differences in the resurrection by a comparison drawn from earthly bodies.

We indeed understand the matter in the following way. The Apostle, when he wished to describe how great were the differences among those who rise in glory, that is, the saints, drew a comparison from the heavenly bodies, saying, "One glory of the sun, another glory of the moon, another glory of the stars." When, on the other hand, he wished to teach us the differences among those who shall come to the resurrection without being purified in this life, that is, as sinners, he draws an illustration from earthly creatures and says, "One flesh of birds, another of fishes." For heavenly things are worthy of being compared with the saints, and earthly with sinners. Let this be said in opposition to those who deny the resurrection of the dead, that is, the resurrection of bodies.

253

We now direct the discussion to some of our own people, who either from want of intellect or from lack of instruction introduce an exceedingly low and mean idea of the resurrection of the body. We ask these men in what manner they think that the "animate body" will, by the grace of the resurrection, be changed and become "spiritual"; and in what manner they think that what is sown "in dishonor" is to "rise in glory," and what is sown "in corruption" is to be transformed into "incorruption." Certainly if they believe the Apostle, who says that the body, when it rises in glory and in power and in incorruptibility, has already become spiritual, it seems absurd and contrary to the meaning of the Apostle to say that it is still entangled in the passions of flesh and blood. After all, he says plainly, "Flesh and blood shall not inherit the kingdom of God, neither shall corruption inherit incorruption." Further, how do they take the passage in which the Apostle says, "We shall all be changed"? This change, the order of which we have spoken of above, is to be eagerly anticipated, and we are undoubtedly right in expecting it to consist in some act that is worthy of the divine grace. For we believe that it will be a change of like order to that in which, as the Apostle describes it, "a bare grain of wheat or of some other kind" is sown in the earth, but "God gives it a body as it pleases him," after the grain of wheat itself has first died.

So our bodies should be supposed to fall like a grain of wheat into the earth, but implanted in them is the cause that maintains the essence of the body. Although the bodies die and are corrupted and scattered, nevertheless by the Word of God that same cause that has all along been safe in the essence of the body raises them up from the earth and restores and refashions them, just as the power that exists in a grain of wheat refashions and restores the grain, after its corruption and death, into a body with stalk and ear. And so in the case of those who shall be counted worthy of obtaining an inheritance in the kingdom of heaven, the cause before mentioned, by which the body is refashioned, at the order of God refashions out of the earthly and animate body a spiritual body, which can dwell in heaven. To those who have proved of inferior merit, or of something still meaner than this, or even of the lowest and most insignificant grade, will be given a body of glory and dignity corresponding to the dignity of each one's life and soul. Nevertheless, even for those who are to be destined to eternal fire or to punishments, the body that rises is so incorruptible, through the transformation wrought by the resurrection, that it cannot be corrupted and dissolved even by these punishments.

If, then, this is the character of the body that rises from the dead, let us now see what is the meaning of the threat of eternal fire. Now we find in the prophet Isaiah that the fire by which each man is punished is described as belonging to himself. For it says, "Walk in the light of your fire and in the flame which you have kindled for yourselves." These words seem to indicate that every sinner kindles for himself the flame of his own fire, and is not plunged into a fire that has been previously kindled by someone else or that existed before him. Of this fire the food and material are our sins, which are called by the apostle Paul wood and hay and stubble. And I think that just as in the body an abundance of food or nourishment that disagrees either by its quality or its quantity gives rise to fevers differing in kind and duration according to the degree in which the combination of noxious elements supplies fuel for them—the quality of which material, made up of the diverse noxious elements, being the cause that renders the attack sharper or more protracted—so when the soul has gathered within itself a multitude of evil deeds and an abundance of sins, at the appropriate time the whole mass of evil boils up into punishment and is kindled into penalties. Then the mind itself, or conscience, by divine power keeping everything in memory, having pressed into itself signs and forms of things done at the moment of sinning, will display before its own eyes a kind of history of its evil deeds, of every foul and disgraceful act and all unholy conduct it committed. Then the conscience is harried and pierced by its own jabs, and becomes an accuser and witness against itself.

This, I think, was what the apostle Paul felt when he said, "Their thoughts one with another accusing or else excusing them, in the day when God shall judge the secrets of men, according to my gospel, by Jesus Christ." From which it is understood that in the very essence of the soul certain torments are produced from the harmful impulses of sins.

So that the explanation of the matter does not seem difficult to grasp to you, it is possible to consider the damages of passion that usually afflict souls. So, the soul is burnt up with the flames of love, or tormented by the fires of jealousy or envy, or harried with furious anger, or consumed with insanity or intense sadness. Remember how some men, finding the excess of these ills too heavy to bear, have deemed it more tolerable to submit to death than to endure such tortures. You will reasonably ask whether for men who have been entangled in the ills that arise from the abovementioned faults and have been unable all the time they were in this life to secure for themselves any amelioration and have so departed from this world, it might be a sufficient punishment that they should be tortured by the long continuance in them of those harmful desires. Anger, rage, insanity, sorrow produced a deadly poison, which was in this life assuaged by no healing remedy; when these desires have been changed must they be tormented by the jabs of general punishment?

Now I think that another species of punishment may be understood to exist. Just as, when the limbs of the body are broken and torn away from their respective connections, we feel an intense and excruciating pain, so when the soul is found apart from that order and connection and harmony in which it was created by God for good action and useful experience and not at concord with itself in the connection of its rational movements, it must be supposed to bear the penalty and torture of its own want of cohesion and to experience the punishment due to its unstable and disordered condition. But when the soul, thus torn and rent asunder, has been tried by the application of fire, it is undoubtedly wrought into a condition of stronger inward connection and renewal.

There are many other matters, too, that are hidden from us, and are known only to Him who is the physician of our souls. For bodily health we occasionally find it necessary to take some very unpleasant and bitter medicine as a cure for the ills we have brought on through eating and drinking, and sometimes, if the character of the illness demands it, we need the severe treatment of the knife and a painful operation. And should the disease have extended beyond the reach even of these remedies, in the last resort the illness is burnt out by fire. How much more should we realize that God our physician, in his desire to wash away the ills of our souls, which they have brought on themselves through a variety of sins and crimes, makes use of this sort of penal cure, even of the infliction of a punishment of fire on those who have lost their soul's health.

Representations of this are found also in the Holy Scriptures. For instance, in Deuteronomy the divine word threatens that sinners are to be punished with "fevers and cold and pallor," and tortured with "feebleness of eyes and insanity and paralysis and blindness and weakness of the kidneys." And so if anyone will gather at his leisure from the whole of Scripture all the references to diseases that in threats against sinners are enumerated by the names of bodily sicknesses, he will find that through them allusion is being made to ills or punishments of souls. And to help us understand that as physicians supply aids to the diseased with the object of restoring them to health through careful treatment, so with the same motive God acts toward those who have lapsed and fallen into sin, there is proof. Through the prophet Jeremiah, God's "cup of fury" is commanded "to be set before all nations" that "they may drink it and become mad and spew it out." In this passage there is a threat that says, "If anyone refuse to drink, he shall not be cleansed"; from which certainly we understand that the fury of God's vengeance ministers to the purification of souls.

Isaiah teaches that even the punishments that are said to be inflicted by fire are meant to be applied as a help, when he speaks thus about Israel: "The Lord will wash away the filth of the sons and daughters of Sion, and will purge away the blood from the midst of them by the spirit of judgment and the spirit of burning." And of the Chaldeans he speaks thus: "You have coals of fire, sit upon them; they shall be to you for a help." In other places he says: "The Lord shall sanctify in burning fire"; and in the prophet Malachi God speaks as follows: "The Lord shall sift and refine his people as gold and silver; he shall refine and purify and pour forth purified the sons of Judah."

257

Moreover, the saying in the Gospel about unfaithful stewards, who must be "cut asunder" and "their portion placed with the unbelievers," as if the portion that was not their own were to be sent somewhere else, undoubtedly alludes to some sort of punishment, as it seems to me, which falls on those whose spirit has to be separated from their soul. Now if this spirit is understood as belonging to the divine nature, that is, as being the Holy Spirit, we perceive that the passage relates to the gift of the Holy Spirit. It tells us that when, whether through baptism or the grace of the Spirit, the "word of wisdom" or the "word of knowledge" or any other endowment has been given to a man as a gift and is not rightly used—that is to say, either "hidden in the earth" or "bound up in a napkin"—the gift of the Spirit will surely be withdrawn from his soul, and the portion that remains, namely the essence of the soul, will be placed with the unbelievers, cut asunder and separated from that Spirit with whom, by joining itself to the Lord, it ought to have been "one spirit."

If the spirit is not the Spirit of God but is to be understood as the nature of the soul itself, then that portion of it will be called the better, which was made in the "image and likeness" of God, whereas the other portion will be that which, after the misuse of free will, was taken up contrary to the nature of its first condition and purity. This portion, as being the friend and beloved companion of the material body, is visited with the fate of the unbelievers. But the cutting asunder may also be understood in a third sense. Each of the faithful, though he be the least in the Church, is we are told attended by an angel who is declared by the Savior always to "behold the face of God the Father"; this angel of God, who was certainly one with him over whom he was set, is to be withdrawn from him by God if by disobedience he becomes unworthy. In that case "his portion," that is, the portion consisting of his human nature, being torn asunder from the divine part, is to be numbered with the unbelievers, seeing that he did not faithfully observe the warnings of the angel allotted to him by God.

The "outer darkness," too, is in my opinion not to be understood as a place with a murky atmosphere and no light at all, but rather as a description of those who through their immersion in the darkness of deep ignorance have become separated from every light of intelligence. It is also to be seen whether possibly this expression does not mean that just as the saints will receive back the very bodies in which they have lived in holiness and purity during their stay in the habitations of this life, but bright and glorious as a result of the resurrection, so, too, the impious, who in this life have loved the darkness of error and the night of ignorance, will after the resurrection be clothed with murky and black bodies, in order that this very gloom of ignorance, which in the present world has taken possession of the inner parts of their mind, may in the world to come be revealed through the garment of their outward body. The "prison" is to be viewed in a similar way. Let these remarks, which we have made at this point, to preserve the order of our discourse in the fewest possible words, suffice for the present.

Let us now consider briefly what we should think about the promises. It is certain that no living creature can be altogether inactive and immovable, but that it is eager for every kind of movement and for continual action and volition; and it is clear, I think, that this nature resides in all living beings. Much more then must a rational being such as man be always engaged in some movement or activity. And if a man forgets himself and is unaware of what befits him, his whole purpose centers on bodily experiences and in all his movements he is occupied with the pleasures and lusts of the body. If, however, he is one who strives to care or provide for the common good, he applies himself either to serving the state or obeying the magistrates or to whatever else may seem to be clearly of common advantage. But if there be a man who can discern something better than these activities, which appear to be connected with the body, and can give diligent attention to wisdom and knowledge, he will undoubtedly direct all his efforts toward studies of another sort, with the object of learning, through inquiry into truth, what are the causes and reason of things. As therefore in this life one man decides that the highest good is the pleasure of the body, another the service of the state, and another devotion to studies and learning, so we seek to know whether in that life that is the true one, the life that is said to be "hid with Christ in God," that is, in the eternal life, there will be for us some order or condition of existence.

Now some men, who reject the labor of thinking and seek after the outward and literal meaning of the law, or rather give way to their own desires and lusts, disciples of the mere letter, consider that the promises of the future are to be looked for in the form of pleasure and bodily luxury. And chiefly on this account they desire after the resurrection to have flesh of such a sort that they will never lack the power to eat and drink and to do all things that pertain to flesh and blood, not following the teaching of the apostle Paul about the resurrection of a "spiritual body." Consequently, they go on to say that even after the resurrection there will be engagements to marry and the procreation of children, for they picture to themselves the earthly city of Jerusalem about to be rebuilt with precious stones laid down for its foundations and its walls erected of jasper and its battlements adorned with crystal; it will also have an outer wall composed of different precious stones, namely, jasper, sapphire, chalcedony, emerald, sardius, onyx, chrysolite, chrysoprase, hyacinth and amethyst. Then, too, they suppose that "aliens" are to be given them to minister to their pleasures, and that they will have these for "plowmen" or "vine-dressers" or "wall-builders," so that by them their ruined and fallen city may be raised up again; and they consider that they are to receive the "wealth of nations" to live on and that they will have control over their riches, so that even the camels of Midian and Ephah will come and bring them "gold, incense and precious stones."

All this they try to prove on prophetic authority from those passages that describe the promises made to Jerusalem; where it is also said that "they who serve God shall eat and drink, but sinners shall hunger and thirst," and that "the righteous shall enjoy gladness, but confusion shall possess the wicked." From the New Testament, too, they quote the Savior's saying, in which he makes a promise to his disciples of the gladness that wine brings; "I will not drink of this cup until the day that I drink it new with you in my Father's kingdom." They add also the following, that the Savior calls those blessed, who now hunger and thirst, and promises them that they shall be filled; and they quote from the Scriptures many other illustrations, the force of which they do not perceive must be figurative. Then, too, after the fashion of what happens in this life, and of this world's gradations of dignity or rank or supreme power, they consider that they will be kings and princes, just like the corresponding earthly rulers, relying on the saying in the Gospel, "You shall have authority over five cities." And, to speak briefly, they desire that all things that they look for in the promises should correspond in every detail with the course of this life, that is, that what exists now should exist again. Such are the thoughts of men who believe indeed in Christ, but because they understand the divine Scriptures in a Judaic sense, they extract from them nothing that is worthy of the divine promises.

Those, however, who accept the theory of the Scriptures that accords with the meaning of the apostles, do indeed hope that the saints will eat; but that they will eat the "bread of life," which is to nourish the soul with the food of truth and wisdom, and enlighten the mind and to cause it to drink from the cup of divine wisdom, as the divine Scripture says: "Wisdom has prepared her table, she has slain her victims, she has mingled her wine in the bowl and cries with a loud voice, 'Turn in to me and eat the bread which I have prepared for you, and drink the wine which I have mingled for you.'" The mind, when nourished by this food of wisdom to a whole and perfect state, as man was made in the beginning, will be restored to the "image and likeness" of God; so that, even though a man may have departed out of this life insufficiently instructed, but with a record of acceptable works, he can be instructed in that Jerusalem, the city of the saints, that is, he can be taught and informed and fashioned into a "living stone," a "stone precious and elect," because he has borne with courage and endurance the trials of life and the struggles after piety. There, too, he will come to a truer and clearer knowledge of what is already proclaimed here, that "man does not live by bread alone, but by every word that proceeds out of the mouth of God." So the principalities must be understood to be those who both rule over those of lower condition and instruct and teach them and initiate them into things divine.

✿
261
✝

But if these considerations seem to fall short to minds that hope for what is worthy of desire, let us back up a little, and although an immature longing for the reality of things is natural to us and implanted in our soul, let us inquire so that we may at last be able, by a consistent theory, to describe the true forms of the "bread of life" and the quality of that "wine" and the property of the "principalities." As, then, in those arts, which are accomplished by hand, the design, the why or how or for what uses a thing is made, is a matter of judgment, but its practical efficacy is unfolded through the help of the work of the hands, so in the case of God's works, which have been made by him, we see them, but their design and meaning must remain a secret. Now when our eye sees the works of the craftsman, if an article has been made with unusual skill, immediately the heart burns to discover of what sort it is and how and for what uses it was made. Much more, and beyond all comparison, does the heart burn with unspeakable longing to learn the reason of those things that we perceive to have been done by God. This longing, this love has, we believe, undoubtedly been implanted in us by God; and as the eye naturally demands light and vision and our body by its nature desires food and drink, so our mind cherishes a natural and appropriate longing to know God's truth and to learn the causes of things.

Now we have not received this longing from God on the condition that it should not or could not ever be satisfied; for in that case the love of truth would appear to have been implanted in our mind by God the author to no purpose, if its gratification were never to be accomplished. So when even in this life men devote themselves with great labor to sacred and religious studies, although they obtain only some small fragments out of the immense treasures of divine knowledge, yet they gain this advantage, that they occupy their mind and understanding with these questions and press onward in their eager desire. Moreover, they derive much assistance from the fact that by turning their mind to the study and love of truth they render themselves more capable of receiving instruction in the future. For when a man wishes to paint a picture, if he first sketches with the faint touch of a light stylus the outlines of the proposed figure and inserts suitable marks to indicate features afterwards to be added, this preliminary drawing with its faint outline undoubtedly renders the canvas more susceptible to receive the true colors. So it will be with us, if only that faint form and outline is inscribed on the tablets of our heart by the stylus of our Lord Jesus Christ. This is perhaps the reason why it is said, "To every one that hath shall be given and added." It is established, then, that to those who have now in this life a kind of outline of truth and knowledge there shall be added in the future the beauty of the perfect image.

Such was, I think, the desire indicated by him who said, "I am hard pressed between the two, having a desire to depart and be with Christ; for this is far better." Paul knew that when he went back to Christ he would learn more clearly the reasons for all things that happen on earth, that is, the reasons that account for man, for man's soul or the mind, or whichever of these constitutes spirit, and what is the "living spirit," and what is the grace of the Holy

Spirit, which is given to the faithful. Then indeed he will also understand the significance of the name Israel, and of the diversity of nations; and also of the twelve tribes contained in Israel, and of the people of each individual tribe. He will also understand the reason for the priests and Levites and for the different priestly orders, and whose type it was that was seen by Moses; and he will learn, too, what is the true meaning in God's sight of the jubilees and the weeks of years. Further, he will see the reason of the feast days and the holidays and will perceive the causes of all the sacrifices and purifications. He will observe the reason for the cleansing from leprosy and for the different kinds of leprosy, and the meaning of the purification of those who have an emission of seed. He will learn about the good powers, what they are, and their greatness and qualities, and likewise about the opposite kind, and the explanation of the love that the former bear toward mankind and of the contentious jealousy of the latter. He will perceive what is the reason of souls and the meaning of the diversity among animals, those that live in water, and birds, and beasts; and for what cause each genus is divided into so many species; and what purpose of the Creator or what indication of his wisdom is concealed in each individual thing. Further, he will learn the reason why certain powers are attached to certain roots and herbs, and why they are repelled by other roots and herbs; and what is the rationale for the fallen angels, and for what cause they are allowed to flatter in some respects those who do not despise them with complete faith and to exist for the purpose of deceiving and leading astray. He will learn the judgment of divine providence upon each individual thing; about things that happen to men, that they happen not by chance or accident, but by a reason so carefully thought out, and inaccessible, that it does not overlook even the number of the hairs, not only of the saints but indeed of all men; the scope of which providence extends even to the "two sparrows" which are sold for a denarius, whether "sparrows" is to be understood spiritually or literally. For now in this present life we seek, but there we shall see plainly.

All this leads us to suppose that no small interval of time may pass before the reason merely of things on earth can be shown to worthy and deserving men after their departure from life, in order that through their acquaintance with it all and the grace of full knowledge they may enjoy an indescribable gladness. Then, the air between heaven and earth is not devoid of animate and even rational beings, as the Apostle said, "Wherein in times past you walked according to the course of this world, according to the prince of the power of this air, the spirit who now works in the children of disobedience," and again, "We shall be caught up in the clouds to meet Christ in the air, and so shall we ever be with the Lord." It is to be supposed that the saints will remain there for some time, until they learn the reason of the twin ordering of what goes on in the air. By twin ordering I mean, for example, when we were on earth we saw animals or trees and we perceived the differences among them and also the very great diversity among men. But when we saw these things we did not understand the *reason* for them; but this was suggested to us only by the very diversity of what we saw, that we should search out and inquire for what reason all these were created diverse and arranged in such variety. And if we have cherished on earth a zeal and love for this kind of knowledge, there will given to us after death an acquaintance with and understanding of that reason, if indeed the matter turns out as should be wished. When therefore we have comprehended that wholly, we shall comprehend in twin ordering the things we saw on earth.

Such a view is to be developed of the abode in the air. I think that the saints when they depart from this life will remain in some place situated on the earth, which the divine Scripture calls "paradise." This will be a place of learning and, so to speak, a lecture room or school for souls, in which they may be taught about all that they had seen on earth and may also receive some indications of what is to follow in the future. Just as when placed in this life they had obtained certain indications of the future, seen indeed "through a glass darkly," and yet truly seen "in part," they are revealed more openly and clearly to the saints in the proper places and times. If anyone is of truly pure heart and of clean mind and well-trained understanding he will make swifter progress and quickly ascend to the region of the air, until he reaches the Kingdom of heaven, passing through the series of those "mansions," if I may so call them, which the Greeks have termed spheres—that is, globes—but which the divine Scripture calls heavens. In each of these he will first observe all that happens there, and then learn the reason why it happens; and thus he will proceed in order through each stage, following him who has "entered into the heavens, Jesus the Son of God," who has said, "I will that, where I am, they also may be with me." Further, he alludes to this diversity of places when he says, "In my Father's house are many mansions." He himself, however, is everywhere and runs through all things; nor are we any longer to think of him as being confined within those narrow limits in which he once lived for our sakes, that is, not as being in that circumscribed condition which was his when he dwelt on earth among men in a body like ours, so that it was then possible to think of him as being enclosed in some one place.

When the saints have reached the heavenly places, then they will see clearly the nature of the stars, one by one, and will understand whether they are living creatures or whatever else is the case. They will also perceive the other reasons for God's works, which he himself shall reveal to them. For now he will show to them, as to sons, the causes of things and the power of his creation, teaching them why one star is placed in its particular position in the sky and why it is separated from another by so great an interval of space; what would happen, for example, if it were nearer or farther away; or if this star had been greater than that, how the entire universe would not be the same but everything would be changed into another form. And when they have gone through everything connected with the reason of the stars and with those patterns contained in heaven, then they will come to the things which are not seen, to those whose very names we have as yet not heard, and to the things invisible. That there are many of these Paul the apostle taught, but what they are or what differences exist among them we cannot even guess with our feeble intellect.

And so the mind increases in its single nature through the reasons, not as it increased when in this life—in the flesh or body and in the soul—but developed in mind and intelligence, it advances as a mind already perfect to perfect knowledge. It is no longer hindered by its former carnal senses, but developing in intellectual growth, ever approaching the pure, it gazes "face to face," if I may so speak, on the causes of things. And it attains perfection, first that perfection by which it rises to this condition, and secondly that by which it remains therein, while it has for the food on which it feeds the theorems of the meaning of things and the nature of their causes. For in this life our bodies grew at first into that which we now are bodily, the increase being supplied in our early years merely by a sufficiency of food. After our full height has been reached by the measure of growth, we use food not in order to grow but as a means of surviving and preserving life within us. So, too, I think that the mind, when it has come to perfection, still feeds on appropriate and suitable food in a measure that can admit neither of want nor of superfluity. But in all respects this food must be understood to be the contemplation and understanding of God, and its measures to be those that are appropriate and suitable to this nature that has been made and created. These measures will rightly be observed by every one of those who are beginning to see God, that is, to understand him through purity of heart.

9

HISTORY IN CHRIST

AUGUSTINE

Augustine was born in 354 in Tagaste in North Africa, the son of a petty administrator and his Christian wife. A benefactor from Tagaste enabled him to continue his studies in rhetoric in Carthage, where he was deeply influenced by his reading of Cicero, and then accepted the popular philosophy of Manicheanism. Its conception of the struggle between good and evil as two masses opposed to one another appealed to him deeply.

Further study in Rome and Milan led to Augustine's conversion to Christianity. Rome brought him into contact with thinkers who showed him that Manicheanism was based on unproved dogma, while in Milan he heard the sermons of Bishop Ambrose. Ambrose demonstrated to Augustine that the authority of faith did not contradict reason. At the same time, a reading of Neoplatonism enabled Augustine to conceive of God as immaterial, beyond time and space.

Philosophy was the first expression of Augustine's faith. Even while he was preparing for baptism, he wrote treatises, and he continued doing so in Rome afterwards. Then he returned to Tagaste, living and writing with a few friends. A visit to Hippo Regius proved fateful, however. He was made a priest, and later became bishop of the small town. He continued to write extensively, but in a more pointed way against those who attacked the church. He particularly concerned himself with Manicheanism. But in addition, he criticized two viewpoints that demanded perfection of Christians. The Donatists attempted to force from the church those who had cooperated with Roman authorities during the period of persecution, while the Pelagians argued that human effort was sufficient to attain redemption. In those controversies, Augustine's mastery of the concept of grace was brilliantly articulated.

In addition, Augustine wrote on how to instruct new members of the church, and he composed the homilies that were the basis of his popular fame. Three profoundly innovative works have influenced the world of letters and Christian doctrine ever since. His *Confessions* (finished in 400) are the epitome of his introspective method: the analysis of his own life enables him to lay out the forces at work in the human soul. The *City of God* (413–425), occasioned by the sack of Rome in 410, sets out the pattern of redemption within the patterns of global history. *On the Trinity*—his great synthetic work, begun in 400—is a meditation on the imprint of God's image within us and around us. Augustine died in 430, while Hippo was under siege by the Vandals.

TEXT: SAINT AUGUSTINE, *CITY OF GOD*, 22.12–22.22

Some question us very closely, and in their questioning ridicule our belief in the resurrected flesh. They ask whether abortive fetuses will rise again; they quote the words of the Lord: "Truly I say unto you, not a hair of your head shall perish," then ask whether all will have equal height and strength, or will have different bodily sizes. For if the size of all bodies is to be equal, how will those abortive births (if they, too, are to rise again) have a bodily size that they did not have before? Or, if they are not to rise, since they were not properly born, but discharged, the same question is raised of infants—when they die in infancy, how will they acquire the stature that we now see is lacking? For we will not deny the resurrection of any who are capable both of being born, and of being born again in baptism. Then they ask how that equality is to be accommodated. For if all are to be as large and as tall as the largest and tallest have been here, the problem concerns not only infants, but also the majority of men: from what source will come the portion that was lacking here, if each one is to receive what he had here?

The Apostle says that we shall all come "to the measure of the age of the fullness of Christ," and again, that we are those "whom he predestined to be conformed to the image of his Son." If this means that the stature and measure of Christ's body are to be those of the human bodies of all in his Kingdom, they argue: It will be necessary in many cases to subtract something from the size or height of the body. Then where will the promise be, "Not a hair of your head shall perish," if so much will perish, even of the body's mass? And on the subject of the hair itself the question can be raised whether what has fallen by cutting is to come back. If so, who would not shudder at the deformity? For the same rule would evidently apply to fingernails and toenails, that everything must be restored which was trimmed in grooming the body. And where will grace be—grace which surely ought to be greater in that immortal state than was possible in this state of corruption? But if they are not restored, they perish; then how is it, they say, that not a hair of the head will perish? A similar argument is made about thinness and fatness, for if all will be equal, certainly some will not be thin while others are fat. Hence, some will put on flesh while others lose it, and there is not to be a restoration of what once existed, but in one case the addition of what did not exist, in another the loss of what did.

Objections are also made concerning the decay and dissolution of dead bodies. One is changed into dust, another evaporates into the air; some are consumed by beasts, some by fire; some perish by shipwreck, or drown by accident, so that their flesh rots and dissolves into liquid. The objectors are to no small extent disturbed by this, and will not believe that all these materials can be gathered up and renewed as human flesh. They also follow up every kind of monstrosity and defect, whether accidental or congenital; with mingled horror and ridicule they mention monstrous births, and ask what will be the state of each deformity in the resurrection. For, if we say that no such thing will belong to the resurrected body, they think that they will refute us by the marks of the wounds with which we preach the Lord Christ arose. But among all these objections the most difficult question proposed is: Into whose flesh will the flesh return when under pressure of famine a man is kept alive by eating human flesh? For that flesh was changed into the flesh of the person who lived on that strange diet, and replaced a loss that was evident in his leanness. Will the flesh return to the man to whom it first belonged, or to the one who acquired it afterwards? They ask the question in order to mock at our belief in the resurrection, and in order either (like Plato) to promise the human soul a change from real griefs to false joys, or else (like Porphyry) to admit that after many cycles of living again and again in different bodies the soul at last ends its miseries, and never returns to them, not, however, that it has now an immortal body, but that it escapes having any kind of body.

To these objections on their side I will reply in the order in which I have arranged them, as God's mercy grants help to my efforts. I do not dare either to affirm or to deny that abortive fetuses, who lived and died in the womb, will rise from the dead. Yet I do not see how they fail to share in the resurrection of the dead unless they are not counted in the number of the dead. For then, not all the dead will rise, leaving some human souls without bodies forever (that had once had human bodies, though only in their mother's womb). But if all human souls are to receive in rising again the bodies that they had, wherever they had them while living and wherever they left them when dying, I find no reason to say that such dead have no part in the resurrection, even those who died in their mother's uterus. But each may choose whichever of these views he likes. Then, if they are to rise, one must understand as referring to abortive fetuses whatever we shall say concerning infants already born.

What are we to say about infants, except that they will not be raised with the small body in which they died, but by a miracle of God will receive in a moment what would have accrued to them at a later time? For in the saying of the Lord: "A hair of your head will not perish," it is stated that nothing that once was will be lacking, but it is not denied that there may be something more that once was lacking. But the dead infant lacked the full size of his body. Though a perfect infant he certainly lacks the perfection of bodily extent, beyond which, when it has accrued, his stature could not increase. All men have this limit of perfection; they are conceived and born with it, but they have it in principle, not in actual mass, just as all the members already exist latently in the seed, and even after birth some things are still lacking, such as teeth and the like. In this principle, which is impressed on the corporeal substance of each one, the parts that as yet do not exist—or rather (if I may say so) are not seen—are already latent and with the passage of time they will come into being, or better, into view. So by this principle the infant who is going to be short or tall is already short or tall. In accordance with this principle we assuredly do not fear any diminution of the body in the resurrection. For even if the equality of all required all to reach gigantic extent, so that those who were largest need lose nothing in stature (and so contradict the saying of Christ that not even a hair of the head would perish), how could the creator who created all things from nothing lack material to add whatever as marvelous designer he knows should be added?

But since Christ rose with the same bodily extent as that with which he died, it is wrong to say that when the time of the general resurrection comes his bodily size will increase, so that he will be equal to the tallest, though he had no such size in the body when he appeared to his disciples with the size in which he was known to them. But if we say that all larger bodies must be reduced to the standard of the Lord's body, much will waste away from the bodies of many, though he promised that not a hair would perish. Hence it follows that each one is to receive his own measure, whether the actual size that he had at death (in youth or when old) or if he died beforehand, the size that he would have reached. And we must understand that what the Apostle says about "the measure of the age of the fullness of Christ" was spoken for another purpose, that is, to say that the measure of his age will be completed when to him as head all among Christian people are added enough to perfect his members. Or, if this had reference to the resurrection of bodies, we should understand that the bodies of the dead do not rise with shape either older or younger than the

271

state of youth, but have bodies of the age and strength that we know Christ reached here. For even the learned of this world have defined youth as reaching to thirty years, stating that when that limit is reached, then man begins to decline into the worse conditions of a burdensome and senile age. Hence it was not said "into the measure of the body," or "into the measure of the height," but "into the measure of the age of the fullness of Christ."

The passage also which says that the elect are conformed to the image of the Son of God can be understood of the inner man. On this point another passage says: "Be not conformed to this world, but be reformed in the renewing of your mind." So that we are reformed in order not to be conformed to this world, and we are conformed to the Son of God. It can also be taken to mean that as he was conformed to us in his mortality, so we should be to him in his immortality, and this refers to the time of the bodily resurrection. But if by these words we are advised in what form bodies will rise, as in the case of the "measure," so in this "conformation," not size, but age, must be understood. And so all will arise with bodies as large as they were or they would have been in full-grown youth. Yet no harm will be done if the form be that of a little child or old man, where no weakness of mind or body obtains. So if any one maintains that each one will rise with the same size of body with which he died, there is no need to engage in laborious controversy with him.

The Scriptures say: "Till we all come to the perfect man, to the measure of the age of the fullness of Christ," and: "Conformed to the image of the Son of God." On account of these sayings some believe that women will not rise in female sex, but that all will be males, since God made only man from clay, and the woman from the man. But they seem wiser to me who do not doubt that both sexes will rise. For there will be no lust there, which is the cause of shame. For before they sinned they were naked, and the man and woman were not ashamed. So all defects will be taken away from those bodies, but their nature will be preserved. The female sex is not a defect, but a natural state, which will then be free from intercourse and childbirth. There will be female parts, not suited to their old use, but to a new beauty, and this will not arouse the greed of the beholder, for there will be no greed, but it will inspire praise of the wisdom and goodness of God, who both created what was not, and freed from corruption what he made.

For as in the beginning of the human race a woman was made from a rib taken from the side of the sleeping man, it was fitting that by such a deed even then Christ and the church should be prophesied. For that sleep of the man was the death of Christ, and when he was hanging lifeless on the cross, his side was pierced with a spear, and from it flowed blood and water, which we know are the sacraments through which the church is built. For the Scripture used this very word, saying not that he "formed" or "fashioned," but that "he built it into a woman." Hence the Apostle also speaks of the building of the body of Christ, which is the church. So woman is a creature of God, just as man is; by her being made from the man, unity was commended, while by her being made in that manner, as we have said, Christ and the church were symbolized. Therefore, he who created both sexes will restore both.

Finally, Jesus himself was asked by the Sadducees, who denied the resurrection, whose wife the woman would be of seven brothers who had each had her, inasmuch as each of them wished to raise up seed to his deceased brother, as the law had enjoined. "You are deceived," he said, "not knowing the Scriptures nor the power of God." And though here was an occasion to say: "Concerning the woman you ask me about, she will be a man herself, not a woman," he did not say this, but said: "In the resurrection they will neither marry nor take wives, but they will be as the angels of God in heaven." They will be equal to angels in immortality and happiness, not in flesh, nor indeed in resurrection, which the angels had no need of, since they could not die. So the Lord denied that there would be marriage in the resurrection, not that there would be women. And at the time a question was under consideration that he could have settled more quickly and easily by denying the female sex, if he had foreknown that there was to be none. Instead, he proved that there would be when he said: "They will not marry," which is said of women, "nor take wives," which is said of men. So those who either marry husbands or take wives here will be present there, but will not do those things there.

Then, as for the Apostle's saying that we shall all attain "to the perfect man," we must consider the whole context of the passage, which is as follows: "He who descended is also the one who ascended above all the heavens, that he might fulfill all things. And he himself gave some men as apostles, some as prophets, some indeed as evangelists, and some as pastors and teachers, in order to perfect the saints for the work of ministering and for building up the body of Christ, until we all attain to the unity of the faith and the full knowledge of the Son of God, to the perfect man, to the measure of the age of the fullness of Christ, so that we may no longer be young children, tossed about and carried around by every wind of doctrine through the cunning of men and their cleverness in inventing error. Rather practicing the truth in love we are to grow up in every way in him who is the head, Christ, from whom the whole body, being connected and united by each influence of support, each part in its due measure makes its bodily growth in its building up in love."

Here is the perfect man, head and the body, which consists of all the members to be made up at the proper time. Now, however, members are daily being added to that body, and thus the church is being built, to which the Scripture says: "But you are the body and members of Christ"; and in another passage: "For his body, which is the church," and again likewise: "We, being many, are one bread, one body." Concerning the building of this body the passage we have quoted also says: "In order to perfect the saints for the work of ministering and for building up the body of Christ." Then follow the words we are discussing: "Until we all attain to the unity of the faith and the full knowledge of the Son of God, to the perfect man, to the measure of the age of the fullness of Christ," and so on, till he shows to what body that measure should be understood to belong by saying: "We are to grow up in every way in him who is the head, Christ, from whom the whole body, being connected and united by each influence of support, each part in its due measure." Hence, just as there is a due measure of each part, so there is a measure of the fullness of the whole body, which consists of all its members, and of this it is said, "to the measure of the age of the fullness of Christ." This fullness is mentioned also in the place where he says of Christ: "And him he gave as head over all things to the church, which is his body, the fullness of him who fills all in all."

But even if this should be taken as a reference to the shape each one will have in the resurrection, what would prevent us from understanding the woman also when the man is named, taking "man" to mean "human being," as in the passage, "Blessed is the man who fears the Lord," which surely includes also women who fear the Lord?

Now what answer shall I make about hair and nails? Once it is understood that in order to prevent any deformity in the body nothing will be allowed to perish from the body, it is at the same time understood that those things that might cause a deformed shape will be restored, not to the places where they would cause an ugly disproportion, but to the total mass of the body. For example, if a vase were made of clay, then the whole reduced to the original lump of clay and formed into a vase a second time, it would not be necessary for that part of the clay that was in the handle to return to the new handle, or what was in the base to form a base again, but only for all to be turned into all, that is, all the clay into all the vase with no part lost. Accordingly, if the hair that was shorn time after time, and the nails that are trimmed off, produce ugliness by returning to their old place, they will not return. Yet those who are raised will not perish, because they will be turned into the same flesh, so that whatever their circumstances in the body, the proportion of parts is retained by the change of material.

When the Lord says, "A hair of your head shall not perish," that can be understood much more aptly, not of the length, but of the number of hairs. Hence he says elsewhere, "The hairs of your head are all numbered." I do not say this to imply that anything that naturally belongs to the body will perish for anyone. But when some ugliness is innate—and this certainly could happen for no other reason than to show from this also how this present state of mortals is one of punishment—the restoration will be such that the deformity will disappear while the substance will be preserved intact. A human artist can melt down a statue that for some reason he had made with a deformity, and recast it most beautifully, so that none of its substance is lost, but only its deformity. If anything in the first figure stood out unbecomingly and did not suit the equality of the parts, he need not cut it off from the whole that he formed and separate it, but he can so scatter it and mix it with the whole that he neither creates an ugly thing nor does he lessen the amount of substance. What is to be thought of the almighty Artist? Will he not be able to remove and destroy all the deformities of human bodies, not only the common ones, but also the rare and monstrous? These have their place in this wretched life, but are inconsistent with that future happiness of the saints. Any of these deformities caused by the natural but unseemly growth of bodily substance are removed without diminishing the body.

Therefore those who are too gaunt or too fat need not fear to find themselves there too in a condition that they would not have chosen here, if they had had a choice. For all bodily beauty is a harmony of parts, with an attractive appearance. But when there is no harmony of parts a thing offends either because it is misshapen, or too small or too large. Accordingly, there will be no deformity caused by disharmony of the parts there where even misshapen parts will be straightened, and where the lack of what is fitting will be supplied from a source known to the Creator, and the excess beyond the seemly will be taken away while material integrity is preserved. And how attractive will the appearance be when the righteous shall shine like the sun in the kingdom of their Father!

This brightness, in the case of Christ's risen body after his resurrection, was hidden from the eyes of the disciples, rather than nonexistent. For the weak sight of men would not have endured it, when he came to be observed by his disciples with such attention that they could recognize him. So also he showed the scars of his wounds which they handled, and he took food and drink, not because he needed sustenance but because of that power that made this possible for him as well. When something present is not visible to those who see other equally present objects, as was the case with that brightness we speak of, unseen by those who saw other objects, it is called in Greek *aorasis*. Our translators could not find a Latin equivalent, and in the Book of Genesis translated it *caecitas,* or "blindness." For this is what the men of Sodom suffered when they were looking for the door of the righteous man and could not find it. If it had been the blindness in which nothing can be seen, they would not have been looking for the door to enter, but for guides to take them away from there.

Our love for the blessed martyrs somehow makes us to wish in that Kingdom to see in their bodies the scars of the wounds that they have suffered for the name of Christ, and perhaps we shall see them. For it will not be a deformity in them, but an honor, and in their body will shine a certain beauty, not of the body, but of virtue. Still, if limbs have been cut off or torn away from the martyrs, they will not for this reason be without those limbs in the resurrection. For it was said to them, "A hair of your head shall not perish." But if in that new age it is fitting that the marks of their glorious wounds be seen in that immortal flesh, then in the place where the limbs were struck off or cut away that they might be separated, there will be seen scars, but the limbs will nevertheless be restored, not destroyed. And so though all the defects that may have befallen the body will then be gone, the marks of virtue are not to be considered or spoken of as defects.

Moreover, let it never be said that the almighty Creator, in his purpose of raising up bodies and restoring them to life, is unable to recall all the substance that beasts or fire have consumed, or that has crumbled to dust or ashes, or has been dissolved in water or gone with the winds. Let it never be said that there is any recess or hidden place in nature where anything, though removed from our perceptions, can hide from the knowledge or escape the power of the Creator of all. When Cicero, the renowned writer of the pagans, wished to define God precisely, as well as he could, he said, "He is a kind of mind, unfettered and free, severed from all perishable matter, conscious of all and moving all things, and self-endowed with unending motion." This definition he found in the teachings of the great philosophers. Then, to speak in their language, how is anything hid from him who perceives all things, or how does it escape beyond recall from him who moves all things?

This leads me also to answer the question that seems still more difficult than the others, that is, when the flesh of a dead man becomes also the flesh of another living man, to which of them will it return in the resurrection? For if a man, exhausted and driven by hunger, should eat the bodies of men—an evil that has sometimes happened both as attested in ancient history and the unhappy experiences of our times have taught—will anyone by honest reasoning contend that the whole is digested and passes out through the rear, and nothing of it is changed and converted into the flesh of the eater? The very change from his former emaciation shows well enough what were the losses made up by such food. I have already set down a little while ago some arguments that should duly serve to solve this problem as well. For whatever flesh is lost in hunger is undoubtedly gone out into the air, and we have said that almighty God can summon from the air what has escaped. So that flesh will be restored to the man in whom it first took shape as human flesh. For it must be reckoned as borrowed, so to speak, by the second man, and like any debt, must be repaid to the one from whom it was borrowed. And to the man who was emptied with hunger, his own flesh will be restored by him who can recall even what vanished into the air. Even if it had utterly perished, and no substance of his remained in any of nature's hiding places, the Almighty would restore it from any source he might choose. But since we have the statement of the trust where it says, "A hair of your head shall not perish," it is absurd to think that while a man's hair cannot perish, so much flesh wasted and consumed by hunger could perish.

Now that all these objections have been considered and dealt with according to our small ability, the conclusion is reached that in the resurrection of the flesh for eternity the bodies will have those dimensions that the body of each one was attaining, or reached, in full-grown youth, with harmony and beauty preserved in the proportions of all the members. If, to preserve this beauty something is taken from the unseemly size of one part, to be spread over the whole, so as not to perish but keep the harmony of the parts everywhere, it is not unreasonable for us to think that some of this matter should be added also to the height of the body. For to preserve beauty the flesh, which would certainly be unseemly if abnormally concentrated in one part, is distributed over all. But if someone contends that every man will rise with the same height of body with which he died, there is no need to oppose him contentiously. Only let every deformity be excluded, every weakness, impediment or decay, and whatever else is not suited to a Kingdom in which the sons of the resurrection and the promise will be equal to the angels of God—if not in body, or age, at least in happiness.

Whatever, therefore, has perished from living bodies or corpses after death will be restored, and, along with that which has remained in the tombs, will rise changed from the old animal body into a new spiritual body, clothed with incorruption and immortality. Even if by some grievous accident or by the inhumanity of enemies the whole should be utterly ground to dust and scattered in the air or water so that, as far as possible, it is left no existence at all, it can by no means be removed from the omnipotence of the Creator. Not a hair of its head will perish. Hence the spiritual flesh will be subject to spirit, but it will still be flesh, not spirit; just as the carnal spirit was subject to the flesh, but was still spirit, not flesh. Of this we have an example in the deformity of our penal state. For those men to whom the Apostle says: "I could not speak to you as unto spiritual, but as unto carnal," were carnal not in flesh but in spirit. And the man who is called spiritual in this life is still carnal in respect to his body, and sees another law in his members fighting against the law of his mind. But he will be spiritual in respect to his body as well when the same flesh is raised so as to fulfil the Scripture, "It is sown an animate body, it will rise a spiritual body."

But since we have had no experience as yet to tell us what this spiritual body is, or how great its beauty is, I suspect that all utterance published concerning it is rash. Nevertheless, the joy of our hope is not to be silenced for the glory of God, and from the inmost midst of burning, holy love come the words: "Lord, I have loved the beauty of Thy house." From the gifts that he bestows on the good and the evil in this most troubled life, with his help let us estimate, as best we can, how great is that which we have not yet experienced, and surely are not able worthily to express. I lay aside when God made man upright. I lay aside that happy life of the two in fruitful Paradise, since it was so brief that it did not last even till their offspring should have any sense of it. But in *this life* which we know, in which we still live, whose trials—or rather the trial that is the whole—we are ever in, no matter what we achieve, never ceasing: who can explain the marks of the goodness of God towards the human race?

This very life, if life it can be called, full of so many sorts of evil, bears witness that from its very beginning all the progeny of mortals was damned. For what else is the meaning of the dreadful depth of ignorance, from which all error arises, which has taken in to its dark embrace all the sons of Adam so that man cannot be freed without toil, pain, and fear? What is this love of so many vain and harmful things, from which come gnawing cares, disturbances, griefs, fears, mad joys, discords, strifes, wars, plots, wraths, enmities, deceits, flattery, fraud, theft, robbery, falsehood, pride, ambition, envy, murder, parricide, cruelty, ferocity, vileness, indulgence, wantonness, impudence, shamelessness, fornication, adultery, incest, and so many outrageous and foul forms of unnatural vice in each sex, which it is indecent even to mention: sacrilege, heresies, blasphemies, perjuries, oppressions of the innocent, calumnies, deceptions, duplicities, false witness, unjust verdicts, violence, brigandage, and all the other evils that do not come to mind now, but still do not retire from the life of men? These are misdeeds of bad men, for they spring from that root of error and perverse love with which every son of Adam is born. Indeed, who does not know with what ignorance of truth, obvious already in infancy, and with what wealth of vain desire, which begins to appear in childhood, man comes into this life, so that if he is allowed to live and do as he likes, he falls into all, or many, of these crimes and disgraces that I have rehearsed, and others that I was unable to rehearse?

But since divine governance does not entirely forsake the condemned, and since God does not in anger shut up his mercies, even in the experience of humankind prohibition and instruction keep watch against those dark evils with which we are born, and oppose their attacks. Still, even they are filled with toil and pain. For what is the meaning of the manifold threats that are employed to restrain the foolishness of children? What of the paedagogues, the masters, the cane, the thongs, the rods and that discipline whereby Holy Scripture says the sides of the beloved son should be beaten, lest he grow up unbroken? For when he is once hardened, he can be tamed only with difficulty, or perhaps not at all. What is the purpose of all these punishments, except to overcome inexperience and restrain base desire, which are evils with which we come into this world? Why is it that we remember with effort but forget without effort? That we learn with effort but stay ignorant without effort? That we are active with effort, and useless without effort? Is it not clear from this how the defective nature is inclined and prone to decline, and how great the help it needs in order to escape from this predicament? Idleness, sluggishness, laziness, carelessness are certainly vices by which work is avoided, yet work, even useful work, is itself a punishment.

But beside the punishments of children, without which they will not learn what their elders wish—and they rarely wish effectively—how many and how great are the penalties that trouble humankind—penalties that appertain, not to the wickedness and worthlessness of the perverse, but to the common condition and misery of all! Who can sum them up in any discourse? Or who can grasp them in any act of thought? How great is the fear and the disaster of bereavement and mourning, of injuries and condemnations, of men's deceptions and lies, of false suspicions, of all violent crimes and profanations of other men! For from them come plundering and captivity, chains and prison, exile and torture, the severing of limbs and destruction of the means of sensation, the seizure of the body to gratify the obscene lust of the rapist and many other shocking deeds often done.

What fear there is of the countless accidents that threaten the body from without—of heat and cold, storms, rain, floods, shattering thunder, hail, lightning, earthquakes and chasms in the earth; of being crushed by falling buildings, or run down by frightened or vicious domestic animals; of the numerous poisons in plants, springs, currents of air, and animals; of the simply painful or even deadly bites of wild beasts; of the madness that is contracted from a mad dog, when even an animal that fawns and is friendly to its owner is sometimes feared more strongly and more bitterly than

lions and snakes, and the man who happens to be infected with
the vile contagion is driven so mad that he is feared by parents,
wife, and children more than any wild beast! What ills sailors endure, and those who travel by land! Who goes anywhere and is not
liable to unexpected accidents? A man returning home from the
forum with sound limbs fell, broke his leg and finished this life
from the wound. Who seems safer than a man seated? Yet Eli the
priest fell from the chair in which he was sitting, and died. Farm-
ers, or rather, all men fear danger to their crops from sky and earth
and hurtful animals, but they commonly feel safe when the grain
is finally gathered and stored. Yet we know men who have lost an
excellent crop of grain, when it was suddenly expelled from the
granaries and carried away by a flood, while men fled in horror.

Who can rely on his innocence for protection against the manifold attacks of demons? No one is confident, when they sometimes harass baptized infants (and nothing is more innocent than
they!) so that in them above all it appears, with God's permission,
what a lamentable misfortune this life is and how much the felicity of another life is to be desired. In fact, from the body itself arise
so many diseases that not even the books of the doctors contain
them all, and in the case of most of them, or almost all of them,
the treatments and drugs themselves are painful. Thus men are
taken from a penal destruction by a penal remedy. Has not fierce
heat brought thirsty men to the point where they would drink
human urine, even their own? Has not hunger brought them to
the point where they could not refrain from eating human flesh?
And not merely dead bodies that they found, but human beings
slain for this purpose; not merely strangers, but sons eaten by their
mothers with an incredible barbarity caused by ravening hunger.
Finally, there is sleep itself, which has as its own name, a word
meaning "rest"—who can tell in words how restless it often is because of what is seen in dreams, and with what terrible things it
alarms the miserable soul and senses? The terrible things are deceits, but they appear so vividly and clearly that we cannot distinguish them from realities. In certain diseases and under the
influence of certain drugs men even when awake are afflicted with
such false appearances, and sometimes malignant demons by their

many different frauds deceive even well men by such appearances. Even if they are unable by these means to bring men into subjection, they nevertheless abuse their sense with longing alone and make them believe what is false.

From the hell of this miserable life no one is freed except by the grace of our Savior Christ, our God and Lord (for his very name "Jesus" means "Savior"), and not to begin something worse, an eternal state that is not life, but death. For though in this life there are great consolations when cures are wrought by holy objects and holy saints, still even these benefits are not always granted to those who ask, lest religion be sought for their sake. Religion is rather to be sought for the sake of another life, where there will be no evils at all, and to that end even in the midst of these present evils all good men are helped by grace, so that, as they endure them with greater faith, they may be sustained with a stronger heart. The learned of this world say that philosophy also helps to achieve truth. The gods have given the true philosophy, as Cicero says, to a select few, nor have they given, nor could they have given, says he, any greater gift to men. To this extent even our opponents are compelled somehow to admit the need of divine grace in finding, not just any philosophy, but the true philosophy. But if the divine gives only to a few the true philosophy, which is the one help against the miseries of this life, it is clear enough from this too that humankind has been condemned to endure those miseries as a penalty. Moreover, just as by their admission there is no greater divine gift than this, so it is to be believed that it is the gift of no other God than he who is declared the greatest of all, even by the worshipers of many gods.

283

Notes

1. Sages' Empowered Israel

1. The polemic against Esau/Rome is simple. Rome claims to be Israel in that it adheres to the Old Testament, that is, the written Torah of Sinai. Specifically, Rome is represented as only Christian Rome can have been represented: it superficially *looks* kosher but it is unkosher. Pagan Rome cannot ever have looked kosher, but Christian Rome, with its appeal to continuity with ancient Israel, could and did and, moreover, claimed to. It bore some traits that validate, but lacked others that validate.

2. That these symbols concede nothing to Christian monotheism and veneration of the Torah of Moses (in its written medium) is obvious, but not the point of analysis here. Rome in the fourth century became Christian. Sages responded by facing that fact quite squarely and saying, "Indeed, it is as you say, a kind of Israel, an heir of Abraham as your texts explicitly claim. But we remain the sole legitimate Israel, the bearer of the birthright—we and not you. So you are our brother: Esau, Ishmael, Edom." And the rest follows.

3. Trans. T. Zahavy, *The Talmud of the Land of Israel*. I. *Tractate Berakhot* (Chicago: University of Chicago Press, 1990).

4. In these paragraphs are summarized the results of J. Neusner, *Judaism in Society: The Evidence of the Yerushalmi: Toward the Natural History of a Religion* (Chicago: University of Chicago Press, 1983).

5. That both are Israelites proves that the differentiating criterion is not gentile versus Israelite, but virtue within Israel. Gentile power is a fact of life, not a systemically consequential consideration.

6. But not as an identifiable economic class or genealogical caste.

7. That acknowledgment forms the counterpart to the one that tacitly admits there were gentile authorities over Jews, and recusant Jews.

8. Omitting reference to the competition runs parallel to ignoring forces that affect the Jews but fall outside sages' control, and Jews who do not keep the law or acknowledge sages' authority.

9. Of course, there is no conception of a budget. But that concept, in political economy, would be long in coming, and if there is a counterpart to a budget in Plato's *Republic,* or even in the great Aristotle's *Politics,* I do not know what it was.

10. The formal traits of the matched sets of six items are clear as indicated. The interpolated materials, M. 2:1G–J, K–O, M. 2:2E–J, M. 2:3B–E, present three disputes between Judah and Meir or sages, the point of which is clear as given. Judah obviously has generated the conceptions of the disputes. K–O differ. They simply introduce extraneous material, outside both the frame of the disciplined construction and the equally disciplined dispute materials.

11. A–D present miscellaneous rules; A refers to the rule at M. 1:5. M. 2:4E–N, M. 2:5 provide a systematic exegesis of Deut. 17:15–19.

12. I find puzzling the claim that the Gospels' representation of the trial of Jesus in any way finds explanation in details of the Mishnah and its continuator writings. It is hard to imagine the high priest, as the Mishnah portrays him, in charge of such a proceeding, and I cannot point to a single passage in the Mishnah that suggests the high priest would conduct a political (or any other kind of) trial of this kind. And yet not a few explanations of the trial of Jesus appeal to the Mishnah and still later writings to account for one detail or another. It is hard for me to see how, in general, these writings pertain in any way whatsoever, hence, on what basis any detail in them can serve to explain any detail of the trial as it is portrayed. We have already noticed that "the kingdom of heaven" has no political connotation whatsoever in the passages in which it occurs. Yet accounts of "the kingdom of heaven" in the sayings of Jesus also appeal to the politics of Judaism as set forth in the Mishnah, contrasting "Judaism's" political, with "Christianity's" otherworldly and more spiritual conception of the kingdom of heaven. That may well be so in general, but the passages of the Mishnah that know "the kingdom of heaven" are not the ones that speak of politics at all.

2. THE RABBINIC POLEMIC AGAINST WEALTH

1. Genesis Rabbah XLI:III.1.A–B.
2. Genesis Rabbah LXXIII:XI.1.D.

3. Genesis Rabbah XLII:I.1.

4. In a well-crafted system, of course, principal parts prove inter-changeable or closely aligned, and that is surely the case here. But I have already observed that the successor system is far more tightly con-structed than the initial one, in that the politics and the economics flow into one another, in a way in which, in the initial, philosophical system, they do not. The disembedded character of the Mishnah's economics has already impressed us.

5. Pesiqta deRab Kahana VI:III.3.B.

4. ZEKHUT AND THE RABBINIC THEOLOGY OF HISTORY

1. Note the fine perception of S. Levy, who translates, "original virtue." See his *Original Virtue and Other Studies,* (London, 1900). But that rendition does not encompass the genealogical aspect of matters and emphasizes the contrast with "original sin," which I think Levy quite per- spicaciously proposed to address in just this setting.

2. The commonly used single word, "merit," used in translating *zekhut,* does not apply, for "merit" bears the sense of reward for carrying out an obligation, e.g., by doing such and such, he merited so and so. *Zekhut,* by contrast, commonly refers to acts of supererogatory free will, and therefore while such acts are meritorious in the sense of being vir-tuous (by definition), they are not acts that one owes but that one gives. And the rewards that accumulate in response to such actions are always miraculous or supernatural or signs of divine grace, e.g., an unusually long life, the power to prevent a dilapidated building from collapsing. *Zekhut* speaks of unearned merit, which is not merited; a better transla-tion is "original grace," that is, "grace originating elsewhere." The point of origination may be personal, an act done not to gain zekhut but capable of provoking divine grace; or genealogical, a grace bestowed upon us in honor of our ancestors.

3. Marcus Jastrow, *A Dictionary of the Targumim, the Talmud Babli and Yerushalmi, and the Midrashic Literature* (repr. N.Y., 1950: Pardes Publishing House, Inc.), 398.

4. That of course is not the whole story, and one of the subtleties of *zekhut* emerges when we realize that it is a basically antihistorical reading of history, as chapter 5, on the City of God, will show.

5. God's "remembering" is the principal point in the scriptural sit-uations adduced as evidence for the ancient origins of the concept of

zekhut. Then the other part of the same concept, that there are deeds I may do that gain *zekhut* for myself, is excluded, and hence *zekhut* as it is revealed in the systemic sources is not represented in the scriptural ones.

6. Indeed, the conception of merit is so alien to the concept of *zekhut,* which one enjoys whether or not one personally has done something to merit it, that I am puzzled on how "merit" ever seemed to anyone to serve as a translation of the word *zekhut.* If I can inherit the entitlements accrued by my ancestors, then these entitlements not only cannot be classed as merit(ed by me), they must be classed as a heritage bestowed by others and not merited by me at all. And, along these same lines, the *zekhut* that I gain for myself may entitle me to certain benefits, but it may also accrue to the advantage of the community in which I live (as is made explicit by Abot for Moses's *zekhut*) and also of my descendants. The transitive character of *zekhut,* the power we have of receiving it from others and handing it on to others, serves as the distinctive trait of this particular entitlement, and, it must follow from that definitive characteristic, *zekhut* is the opposite of merit, as I said, and its character is obscured by the confusion created through that long-standing and conventional, but wrong translation of the word.

7. And that political definition of the systemic role and function of *zekhut* is strengthened by the polemical power of the concept vis-à-vis the Christian critique of Israel after the flesh. The doctrine of the *zekhut* of the ancestors served as a component of the powerful polemic concerning Israel. Specifically, that concrete, historical Israel, meaning for Christian theologians "Israel after the flesh," in the literature before us manifestly and explicitly claimed fleshly origin in Abraham and Sarah. The extended family indeed constituted precisely what the Christian theologians said: an Israel after the flesh, a family linked by genealogy. The heritage then became an inheritance, and what was inherited from the ancestors was a heavenly store, a treasure of *zekhut,* which protected the descendants when their own *zekhut* proved insufficient. The conflict is a political one, involving the legitimacy of the power of the now-Christian empire, denied by this "Israel," affirmed by the other one.

8. And it is by no means an accident, therefore, that Genesis was one of the two Pentateuchal books selected by the system builders for their Midrash-exegesis. The systemic centrality of *zekhut* accounts for their selection.

9. Freedman, *Genesis Rabbah* (London, 1948), 684, n. 2: It introduces a plea for or affirmation of protection received for the sake of the patriarchs.

10. The philosophical system, by contrast, had regarded as important principally the issue of classifying persons, e.g., by castes or by other indicators; the Mishnah's paramount system of hierarchical classification had treated the individual in the way it treated all other matters, and so, we now see, does the system of *zekhut*: now to be broadened into the definition, accomplishing a lien upon Heaven.

11. Freedman, *Genesis Rabbah* (London, 1948: Soncino), 992, n. 6.

12. Freedman, *Genesis Rabbah,* 684, n. 2: It introduces a plea for or affirmation of protection received for the sake of the patriarchs.

5. JUDAISM AND CHRISTIANITY MEET IN THE CITY OF GOD

1. I owe to William Scott Green the idea of comparing the theology of history of Rabbinic Judaism with that of Augustine.

2. Note the fine perception of S. Levy, *Original Virtue and Other Studies,* 2–3: "Some act of obedience, constituting the Ascent of man, is the origin of virtue and the cause of reward for virtue. . . . What is the conspicuous act of obedience which, in Judaism, forms the striking contrast to Adam's act of disobedience, in Christianity? The submission of Isaac in being bound on the altar . . . is regarded in Jewish theology as the historic cause of the imputation of virtue to his descendants." It is not an accident, then, as we shall see, that Augustine selected as his paradigmatic historical exemplar the conflict of Cain and Abel, the city of God being inhabited by Abel and his descendants; he required a virtue pertinent to all of humanity, not to Israel alone, for his argument, so it seems to me as an outsider to the subject.

3. My initial comments on that matter are in *The Incarnation of God: The Character of Divinity in Formative Judaism* (Philadelphia: Fortress Press, 1988).

4. That is, an assessment of what people will ordinarily think or propose or wish to have happen. The rule is set by that norm, not by exceptions, and on that basis, in the initial system, we are able to determine what (an ordinary person's) intentionality will dictate in a given interstitial case.

5. One need not exaggerate the influence of either St. Augustine or our sages of blessed memory to claim that the Christianity and the Judaism framed by each, respectively, defined norms and set the course for the two great religions of the West.

6. I refer to J. N. D. Kelly, *Jerome: His Life, Writings, and Controversies* (New York: Harper & Row, 1975).

7. The bibliography for this chapter lists the books I have consulted. In no way claiming to know the scholarship on Augustine, even in the English language, I chose to rely mostly on a single work, consulting others mostly for my own illumination. It is the up-to-date and, I think, universally respected account by Peter Brown, *Augustine of Hippo* (Berkeley and Los Angeles: University of California Press, 1967). The pertinent passage is on p. 302. All otherwise unidentified page references to follow are to this work. My modest generalizations about the intersection of the two systems on some points important to each rests, for Augustine, entirely on Brown. I found very helpful the outline of the work presented by John Neville Figgis, *The Political Aspects of S. Augustine's 'City of God'* (London: Longmans Green and Co., 1921), 1–31, and the characterization of Augustine's thought by Herbert A. Deane, *The Political and Social Ideas of St. Augustine* (New York & London: Columbia University Press, 1963). In Deane's lucid account, anyone in search of specific doctrinal parallels between sages' system and that of Augustine will find ample evidence that there is none of consequence. As will become clear, what I find heuristically suggestive are structural and functional parallels, not points of doctrinal coincidence of any material importance. My sense is that the success of Brown's book overshadowed the important contribution of Gerald Bonner, *St. Augustine of Hippo. Life and Controversies* (London: SCM Press, Ltd., 1963), a less dazzling, but more systematic and (it seems to me) useful presentation. A brief and clear account of the two cities is in Eugene Teselle, *Augustine the Theologian* (New York: Herder and Herder, 1970), 268–78, who outlines the variety of approaches taken to the description and interpretation of the work: polemical, apologetic; philosophy or theology of history; analysis of political ideology; source of principles of political and moral theory; and of ecclesiastical policy; and the like. The achievement of F. Van der Meer, *Augustine the Bishop: Religion and Society at the Dawn of the Middle Ages* (New York: Harper & Row, 1961), translated by Brian Battershaw and G. R. Lamp, is not to be missed: a fine example of the narrative-reading of religion by a historian of religion of one useful kind. Precisely what Augustine méans by "the city of God" is worked out by John O'Meara, *The Charter of Christendom: The Significance of the City of God* (New York: Macmillan, 1961), who says (p. 43) that "the city of God exists already in heaven and, apart from certain pilgrim men who are on their way to it while they are on this earth, in heaven only." When I speak of sages' having extended the boundaries of the social system from earth

to heaven, I mean to suggest something roughly parallel, in that, when women and men on earth conform to the Torah, they find themselves in the image and after the likeness of heaven. The sense of the concept "history," then, is "the story of two cities," so Hardy, 267 ff. (cf. Edward R. Hardy Jr., "The City of God," in Roy W. Battenhouse, *A Companion to the Study of St. Augustine* (New York: Oxford University Press, 1955), 257–86. I find the story of Israel among the nations as the equivalent, unifying and integrating conception of history in the doctrine(s) of history in the Yerushalmi and Leviticus Rabbah; this then means Israel forms the counterpart to the city of God, and I think that is the beginning of all systemic comparison in this context (and, I should suspect, in all others).

8. P. 303.

9. But the two parties have in common the simple fact that the representation of their respective systems is the accomplishment of others later on, indeed, in the case of sages, much later on. Note the judgment of Deane, Augustine "was not a system builder. . . . Virtually everything that Augustine wrote . . . was an occasional piece" (Herbert A. Deane, *The Political and Social Ideas of St. Augustine* (New York and London: Columbia University Press, 1963), viii. Sages' documents, it is quite obvious, do not utilize the categories for the description of the social order that I have imposed: ethos, ethics, ethnos; worldview, way of life, doctrine of the social entity. But systemic description in its nature imputes and of necessity imposes system, and that is so, whether the system is deemed social or theological in its fundamental character. I have no difficulty in defending the proposition that sages' system was in its very essence a system of society, that is, of the holy people, Israel, and the union of social and theological thought in Augustine is signaled by the very metaphors he selected for his work, in his appeal to "the city."

10. So Teselle, 270.

11. Pp. 303–4. Cf. also Burleigh, 166 ff., on Augustine's attitude toward "the concrete political structures of history."

12. P. 309.

13. Ibid.

14. P. 310.

15. Pp. 311–12.

16. P. 317.

17. P. 319. See Burleigh, 185ff., "A philosophy of history." He cites the following: "St. Augustine's De Civitate Dei . . . may be regarded as the first attempt to frame a complete philosophy of history. . . . It was . . . a singularly unsuccessful attempt; for it contained neither philosophy nor his-

tory, but merely theology and fiction." Whether or not so of Augustine, that statement seems to me an apt description of the form of history as invented in the pages of the Talmud of the Land of Israel. Burleigh describes the dominant philosophy of the age, characteristic of Augustine as well, as antihistorical. But Augustine's "Platonic Biblicism in effect brings them [history and philosophy] into the closest relation. Biblical History is Platonic idealism in time." That statement seems to me to run parallel to the characterization of the Rabbinic uses of history in the form of persons and events as exemplary and cyclical, rather than unique and linear.

18. P. 320.

19. Ibid.

20. P. 322.

21. Ibid.

22. Ibid.

23. P. 323.

24. P. 328.

25. Ibid.

26. Note Burleigh, 218: "The Fifth Century . . . was a period of radical historical change." But just as Augustine expressed no sense of "the end of an era," so in the pages of the documents surveyed here I find no world-historical foreboding, only an optimistic and unshakeable conviction that Israel governed by its own deeds and attitudes makes its own destiny every day. That seems to me the opposite of a sense that all things are changing beyond repair. I can find no more ample representation of the historical convictions of our sages of blessed memory than Burleigh's representation of Augustine's: "Rome might pass away. The protecting fostering power of her emperors might be withdrawn. But God endured. His purpose of gathering citizens into His Eternal City was not frustrated by transient circumstances. St. Augustine had no anxiety for the empire or for civilization, even 'Christian' civilization, because he found a better security in God." It is interesting to note that Burleigh gave his lectures in 1944, responding it seems to me to the impending dissolution of the British Empire in his rereading of Augustine—and dismissing an interest in the fate of empires as essentially beside the point for Augustine. So I think it was for our sages.

27. Burleigh characterizes matters in this way: "He seems to have been satisfied to show . . . that the exposition and defence of the Christian faith necessitates a survey of all History, which is in its essence God's providential government of the human race" (p. 202).

28. The basic motif of alienation—personal, cosmic, political, theological, as much as affective—characterizes the two systems because it defines the condition that provokes for each system the generative question, and because it is in the mode of reintegration that each system finds its persistent statement. True, alienation defines a purely contemporary category and forms a judgment made by us upon the circumstance or attitude of ancients. But the category does serve to specify, for our own understanding, what is at stake.

29. But while I think they are primary, as the formation of Genesis Rabbah at this time indicates, they are not alone; Israel at Sinai, David on the throne, and other historical moments serve as well. It is a mere impression, not a demonstrable fact, that the patriarchs and matriarchs provide the primary paradigm.

30. See his *Islands of History* (Chicago: University of Chicago Press, 1985).